JESUS IN
CONTEMPORARY
SCHOLARSHIP

JESUS IN
CONTEMPORARY
SCHOLARSHIP

Marcus J. Borg

TRINITY PRESS INTERNATIONAL
VALLEY FORGE, PENNSYLVANIA

Trinity Press International, P.O. Box 851, Valley Forge, PA 19482–0851

Library of Congress Cataloging-in-Publication Data

Borg, Marcus J.
    Jesus in contemporary scholarship / Marcus J. Borg.
        p.   cm.
    Includes bibliographical references and index.
    ISBN 1-56338-094-3 :
    1. Jesus Christ—Historicity—Study and teaching. 2. Jesus
Christ—History of doctrines—20th century.   I. Title.
BT303.2.B586   1994
232'.09'048—dc20   94-18255
                                                                      CIP

Printed in the United States of America

94   95   96   97   98   99   10   9   8   7   6   5   4   3   2   1

To Al Hundere

Inventor
Entrepreneur
Adventurer
Benefactor

With admiration
and gratitude

Contents

Preface

The historical Jesus is "in the news," both in the scholarly world and in the much broader world of the public. The last fifteen years have seen a revitalization of the academic discipline of Jesus scholarship, especially in North America. A third quest of the historical Jesus is underway, replacing the old quest of the nineteenth century and the short-lived "new quest" of the late 1950s and early 1960s.[1]

The resurgence of scholarly activity has been accompanied by widespread public interest. Serious books of historical scholarship on Jesus become best-sellers.[2] The scholarly study of Jesus is featured in cover stories in major news magazines and in television programs. With the 2000th anniversary of the birth of Jesus approaching in the year 1996, public interest is likely to increase even more.

It is thus an exciting time in Jesus scholarship, and I am grateful to be part of it. The essays in this volume reflect that excitement and speak of central directions, results, and questions within the discipline. In them, I report much of what has been happening in Jesus scholarship since 1980 and engage in a dialogue with it. In some essays, the emphasis is more on reporting, though an interpretive element is inevitably always present. In others, I generate my own constructions of how I see things as a result of my interaction with contemporary scholarship.

The essays reflect two facts about Jesus. He is the subject of research by scholars working within the framework of the secular academy. He is also the central figure in a living religion. In various ways and to varying degrees, Jesus matters to Christians.

Though it is impossible completely to divorce any of the essays from this second fact, it is nevertheless true that some of them reflect the first fact more than the second. In particular, the first six essays concentrate on historical Jesus research in the secular academy: what we can "see" about Jesus, without Christian presuppositions and quite apart from what significance the historical study of Jesus might have for Christians. The final three essays explicitly address the second fact: how and why historical scholarship about Jesus might be significant for Christians.

The essays are arranged thematically. Part 1, consisting of the first two chapters, provides an overview of what has been happening in Jesus scholarship since 1980. Chapter 1 describes the contemporary renaissance: sometime around 1980, a discipline that had been relatively quiet throughout much of this century crossed a threshold, and evidence of its rebirth became obvious. The 1980s saw the development of new interdisciplinary methods, the formation of new professional organizations, and a burst of publishing. Chapter 2 describes six portraits, or sketches, of Jesus that emerged in North American scholarship during the same period. Together, the construals of Jesus by E. P. Sanders, Burton Mack, Elisabeth Schüssler Fiorenza, Richard Horsley, John Dominic Crossan, and myself indicate a range of options being considered within the discipline.

Part 2 (chapters 3 through 6) explores major issues in contemporary Jesus research. Chapters 3 and 4 treat Jesus and eschatology. They report and analyze what may be a paradigm shift in our understanding of Jesus and Christian origins. Namely, the paradigm of imminent eschatology (the notion that Jesus proclaimed the coming of the messianic age or "kingdom of God" in the immediate future, which dominated much of this century's scholarship) has seriously eroded, and a new paradigm has become at least equally strong within the discipline: Jesus as a wisdom figure and social prophet. Just as the twentieth century began with a major paradigm shift in the work of Johannes Weiss and Albert Schweitzer, the century seems to be ending with another paradigm shift of equal magnitude, affecting both methodology and results.

Chapter 5 focuses on Jesus and politics. It treats the way new interdisciplinary methods illuminate and to some extent transform our understanding of Jesus in the setting of his social world. It reports how the insights generated by interdisciplinary analyses of the social dynamics of first-century Palestine enable us to see that Jesus was a political figure in the sense of being a radical social critic and an advocate of an alternative social vision.

Chapter 6 addresses an issue that is often unaddressed in modern Jesus (and biblical) scholarship: the way in which the world-view operative in the psyches of scholars affects the way we see texts, especially texts that report paranormal experiences or happenings. I argue that the "root image" of reality that has been dominant in the modern academy since the Enlightenment has led to an ignoring of the sacred and spiritual in the traditions about Jesus. This is an important and difficult issue in Jesus scholarship: to what extent are the judgments of scholars about what is real and what is possible shaped by the world-view of our particular time in history? To what extent has the Enlightenment world-view of the academy, which functions as both an image of reality and as a lens through which we see, led to reductionistic images of

Jesus? What would happen to our understanding of Jesus if we took seriously an alternative world-view or "root image" of reality, consonant with the texts themselves and with "the virtual human unanimity" prior to the Enlightenment?[3]

The third and final part (chapters 7 through 9) relates the historical study of Jesus to the life of the church. Chapter 7 explores the significance of new understandings of Jesus for Christian understandings of evangelism. What does evangelism mean in an age in which global religious pluralism is taken seriously and in which the historically widespread Christian claim to be the exclusively true religion is rapidly being abandoned by mainline Christians? If evangelism is not about converting people to believe in Jesus for the sake of eternal salvation, what is it about? What can we learn about evangelism from what we can see about Jesus?

Chapter 8 treats the potential significance and usefulness of the Jesus Seminar's color-coded *The Five Gospels* for Christians and churches. I provide an overview of the work of the Jesus Seminar and the volume itself and then make some suggestions about how *The Five Gospels* can be used in the context of the church's educational activity.

In chapter 9, I conclude the book by treating the simple but in fact difficult question: does the historical study of Jesus matter? That is, does it or should it matter for Christians? I describe some of the ways the question has been answered in the last two hundred years as well as in contemporary scholarship and then suggest my own way of thinking about it. Our image of Jesus, I argue, does in fact affect our image of the Christian life.

About half of the essays have been published before. I am grateful to the people who suggested to me that it would be useful to have them published together and to the publishers who gave permission for their re-publication. I decided not to revise them in any way, except for minor changes in format, thinking it better to leave them in their original form. My decision is perhaps in part due to sloth, but also avoids having two versions of the same essay in print. The one exception is chapter 2, which has a clearly identified addendum. Otherwise, the essays and bibliographical references are as I wrote them at the time.[4]

The book treats primarily North American scholarship and from a North American perspective. To some extent, this is because the renaissance in Jesus research has been centered in North America. It was not very many decades ago that new directions in Jesus and biblical research came primarily from Germany, but that seems to have changed.

For much of the period covered by this book, I was privileged to have an insider's view of the North American discussion. In 1987, I became chair of the Historical Jesus Section of the Society of Biblical Literature, a position I held through 1992. A few years before that, I accepted an invitation from Robert Funk to become a Fellow of the Jesus Seminar. I have learned greatly from my involvement with scholars in both groups.

Thus my vantage point is North American. Over the course of my career, there have been influences from elsewhere as well: my two main scholarly mentors were British, I studied in England for four years, and I initially fell in love with historical Jesus research through German scholarship. Nevertheless, I am aware that I see the discipline through a North American lens.

Finally, the major professional event in my life during the years this book was being written was the creation of an endowed chair for me at Oregon State University in December of 1993. My benefactor is Al Hundere of San Antonio, Texas.

Hundere is a gifted man whose life combines an American success story with an adventuresome life-embracing spirit. Raised by a single Norwegian immigrant mother after his father was killed by a falling tree limb along a river in the coastal range of Oregon when Hundere was four years old, Hundere went to Oregon State during the Depression and graduated with an engineering degree in 1938. He combined his talent in engineering with his passion for flying and became an inventor and successful entrepreneur manufacturing his own inventions.

Though not a religious man himself, Hundere nevertheless recognizes the importance of religion in shaping people's attitudes, especially toward society and the environment, and believes that an enlightened approach to religion is important for the future of the world. To Al Hundere this volume is dedicated, with admiration for what he has done with his life and grateful appreciation for the honor of being the first holder of the chair that bears his name.

Notes

1. In addition to the first two essays in this volume, see my newly published "Reflections on a Discipline: A North American Perspective," in Bruce Chilton and Craig Evans, eds., *Studying the Historical Jesus: Evaluations of the State of Current Research* (Leiden: E. J. Brill, 1994), 9–31. In the same volume, see William R. Telford, "Major Trends and Interpretive Issues in the Study of Jesus," with an impressively comprehensive bibliography. See also John K. Riches, *A Century of New Testament Study* (Valley Forge, Pa.: Trinity Press International, 1993), 89–124.

2. Two examples will do. Within three months of publication, John Dominic Crossan's *The Historical Jesus: The Life of a Mediterranean Jewish Peasant* (Harper: San Francisco, 1991) moved to the top of the *Publishers Weekly* list of best-selling books in religion, despite the fact that it was relatively expensive ($30), about five hundred pages long, and not easy to read. Two years later the Jesus Seminar's *The Five Gospels: The Search for the Au-*

thentic Words of Jesus (New York: Macmillan, 1993) sold out its first printing in a few weeks, surprising even the publisher.

3. The phrase "the virtual human unanimity" comes from Huston Smith, some of whose work I report in chapter 6. For references, see that chapter.

4. Thus I have not updated the notes to include works published after the time I completed each essay. The decision not to revise the essays leads to occasional inaccuracies in the titles of forthcoming books. In particular, the Jesus Seminar's *The Five Gospels* underwent more than one title change in the years between its conception and publication.

Part One

Jesus Scholarship in the 1980s

Chapter One

A Renaissance in Jesus Studies

A major renaissance is occurring in North American Jesus studies. The relative disinterest in the historical Jesus that characterized much of this century's scholarship has come to an end. The signs of the rebirth are manifold: new professional organizations, new questions and methods, the collapse of old consensus elements and the emergence of new ones, accompanied by a surge of publishing. The major shift from the fifty years just past indicates a lessening interest in eschatology and apocalyptic with an increasing awareness of the significance of the social-political world in which Jesus lived. An exciting development in scholarship, the renaissance also has potential relevance for the life of the church.

I

The quest for the historical Jesus went into eclipse soon after the beginning of this century. The "old quest," which flourished through much of the nineteenth century, was replaced by a period known as the time of "no quest" in the history of Jesus scholarship.[1] Throughout this period, three central convictions operated strongly in the collective consciousness of New Testament scholars and those they taught, including most mainline clergy and professors of religious studies in colleges and universities.

First, there was a strong sense of the theological irrelevance of historical Jesus research. To a large extent, this was the aftermath of Albert Schweitzer's brilliant and provocative portrait of Jesus as a mistaken apocalypticist in *The Quest of the Historical Jesus* (1906). According to Schweitzer, Jesus both proclaimed the imminent end of the world and deliberately sought to bring it about by undergoing the suffering of the

---

This essay was first published in *Theology Today* 45, no. 3 (October 1988): 280–92.

end-time in his own person. Schweitzer's work had the effect of bringing the "old quest" to an end. The Jesus he found was indeed "a stranger to our time," and Schweitzer's statement about the theological irrelevance of the historical Jesus was both powerful and persuasive.

Second, there was a strong conviction that little could be known about the historical Jesus. The foundation of this thoroughgoing historical skepticism was prepared by nineteenth-century scholarship with its emphasis upon Jesus as a teacher. It had hoped, by stripping away the supernatural and doctrinal elements in the gospels, to uncover what was most central: Jesus' message, his preaching and teaching. Jesus' *words,* detached from any picture of his person, activity, or intentionality, became the bedrock for constructing an image of him.

In the twentieth century, the bedrock seemed to turn into shifting sand. Fifteen years after Schweitzer's book, Rudolf Bultmann, this century's single most influential New Testament scholar, published *The History of the Synoptic Tradition* (1921). His study of how the traditions about Jesus developed during the oral period suggested that very little of the preaching and teaching of Jesus as reported in the gospels can be traced back to Jesus himself. The historical skepticism engendered by Bultmann's form-critical work was reinforced after World War II by redaction criticism, the meticulous study of how the evangelists modified and shaped the traditions they received to adapt them to their own times and convictions. It became very clear that everything in the gospels — not just the doctrinal and supernatural elements, but also Jesus' teaching — was thoroughly shaped by the experiences, situations, and theological beliefs of the early Christian communities, both during the oral period and in the redactional activity of the gospel authors themselves. Recovering the "message of Jesus" behind the documents seemed increasingly problematic.

A third conviction also dominated the period of "no quest." The minimalist picture of Jesus' message that could be recovered was eschatological: Jesus expected and proclaimed the imminent end of the world. The eschatological core of his message was then made relevant by filtering it through an existentialist hermeneutic. Here again, Bultmann was very influential. In a number of works, he argued that the historically authentic preaching of Jesus — a small collection of largely eschatological sayings — needed to be "demythologized" by means of existentialist interpretation.

The period of Jesus scholarship known as "the new quest" did not really change this state of affairs. Inaugurated by Ernst Käsemann in a lecture presented in 1953, the "new quest" quickly produced two book-length studies: Günther Bornkamm's *Jesus of Nazareth* (1956) and James Robinson's *A New Quest of the Historical Jesus* (1959).[2] Important as the new quest was, it continued to share the central characteristics of the "no quest" period: a minimalist portrait of the message of Jesus conceived in eschatological terms, coupled with existentialist interpretation. Its methods and results remained largely the same. What made it "new" was a theological concern: the question of the degree of continuity between the message of Jesus and the preaching of the early church. Yet, even this question was pursued within an existentialist framework which made it seem quite esoteric: whether the understanding of existence mediated by the message of Jesus was the same as the understanding of existence mediated by the kerygma. This, it was affirmed, was the proper subject matter of the quest for the historical Jesus.

The central convictions of the "no quest" period converged in an overarching conclusion that historical Jesus scholarship was an area of study that did not matter very much. Its fruits were meager and largely inedible. Not much could be known about Jesus, and what little could be seemed unrelated to theology and the practical needs of Christian preaching and teaching. The figure of Jesus seemed both remote and irrelevant.

II

Against this background, the resurgence in contemporary Jesus scholarship is remarkable. Dating the beginning of a renaissance is difficult, for a renaissance is never *ex nihilo;* it always has antecedent causes. But developments in the past decade clearly indicate that one is underway.

There has been a burst of publishing. Some of this, dating back to the 1970s, provides a more richly detailed picture of the background for understanding the ministry of Jesus.[3] New translations of primary texts have appeared.[4] A bibliography of recent scholarly books about Jesus lists over fifty titles, forty-two since 1980.[5] In the past three years alone, five major works centering on the historical Jesus have been published: E. P. Sanders's *Jesus and Judaism* (Philadelphia: Fortress, 1985), Donald Goergen's *The Mission and Ministry of Jesus* (Wilmington: Michael Glazier, 1986), Richard Horsley's *Jesus and the Spiral of Violence* (San Francisco: Harper & Row, 1987), Burton Mack's *A Myth of Innocence: Mark and Christian Origins* (Philadelphia: Fortress, 1988), and my own *Jesus: A New Vision* (San Francisco: Harper & Row, 1987). Two more by major Jesus scholars are known to be underway.[6]

Yet another sign of the renaissance is the creation of two new professional organizations. For the first time in the history of the Society of Biblical Literature, a sub-group devoted to historical Jesus research came into existence. Beginning as an experimental "consultation" in 1981 and becoming a permanent group in 1983, the Historical Jesus Section of SBL now attracts over one hundred participants to its meetings.[7]

In 1985, a second scholarly organization was born, the "Jesus Seminar." Founded by Robert Funk, its 125 Fellows have undertaken a five-year project of discussing and voting upon the historical authenticity of all of the sayings attributed to Jesus in the gospels and other early Christian sources. Not only are its results interesting, but its twice-a-year multi-day meetings provide an extraordinary stimulus to scholarship. Though best known for its controversial procedure of voting on the sayings of Jesus and for its plans to publish the results of the voting in *The New Red Letter Edition of the Five Gospels,* the Seminar's primary significance lies elsewhere. It is the first *collaborative systematic* examination of the entire Jesus tradition ever undertaken, unprecedented in the history of scholarship.[8]

A third sign of the renaissance is the emergence of distinctively new questions and methods. For much of its history, the agenda of Jesus scholarship has been set, consciously or unconsciously, by theological questions. This is not surprising, given that Christianity was until recently the dominant cultural consciousness of the West. Thus, the questions brought to the texts, whether for the sake of undermining or supporting Christian convictions, have commonly had those convictions in mind. What is the relationship between Christian doctrines and what can be known historically? Can any of the christological "titles" of Jesus be traced back to Jesus? Even the central focus of the "new quest" was set by a manifestly theological concern: the question of continuity or discontinuity between the historical Jesus and the preaching of the early church.

In the recent past, the framework for formulating the questions brought to the texts has become less specifically Christian. Changes in cultural consciousness and in the institutional settings where Jesus scholarship is done are largely responsible. Though important work continues in seminary and divinity school settings, a large majority of biblical scholars now teach in public universities or secularized private colleges. Not only would an explicitly Christian agenda be inappropriate in such settings, but, for the most part, our students no longer bring specifically Christian concerns to the texts. Instead, the questions have become more "global," that is, related to the broad sweep of human history and experience. How is the figure of Jesus similar or dissimilar to religious figures in other traditions? How is his teaching like or unlike the teaching of other great sages such as Lao Tzu or the Buddha? How is the Jesus movement similar or dissimilar to other sectarian or revitalization movements? How do studies of pre-industrial societies illuminate the world of Jesus? What understandings of reality and what kinds of religious consciousness are reflected in the texts?

The new questions have been accompanied by new methods. For most of its history, the primary methods used by New Testament scholarship have been literary and historical, with the latter understood in a fairly narrow sense. Lately, largely in the last ten years, Jesus scholars (and biblical scholars generally) have begun systematically to use insights and models gleaned from the history of religions, cultural anthropology, and the social sciences. These not only provide comparative material and theoretical understandings, but also models constructed from either empirical or historical data which can then be used to illuminate historical periods for which we have only fairly scanty data. The new questions and new methods have produced new ways of seeing familiar material: we are able to re-view the data with new lenses.

This use of new "disciplinary allies" is one of the most striking features of the renaissance. It has produced a massive amount of publishing. A recent bibliography on the use of the social sciences in New Testament studies lists over 250 items, most published since 1980.[9] It has also generated two new organizations: the Social Science and New Testament Interpretation section in the Society of Biblical Literature, and the Social Facets Seminar, which came into existence alongside the Jesus Seminar. As one scholar put it in 1984, "the historical quest for the historical Jesus has ended; the interdisciplinary quest for the historical Jesus has just begun."[10]

III

The renaissance is marked not only by new methods, but also by new results. Like all scholarly results, they are tentative and not final, the product of a particular intellectual history, radically conditioned in the way that all human knowledge is. Nevertheless, they sharply transform the image of Jesus which has dominated much of this century's scholarship. Three emergent trends might fairly be considered as elements of a new consensus.

First, the old consensus that Jesus was an eschatological prophet who proclaimed the imminent end of the world has disappeared. Though some still affirm it, the central conviction that marked the "no quest" and "new quest" periods is no longer held by the majority of North American scholars actively engaged in Jesus research. Its disappearance *as a consensus* is indicated by polls taken of two major groups of historical Jesus scholars: three-fifths to three-fourths of them no longer accept it.[11]

The erosion of the dominant consensus was gradual, even though the realization that it had happened seemed quite sudden. The old consensus was based on four main elements: the atmosphere of crisis in the gospels; the sayings which spoke of the imminent coming of the Son of Man; the kingdom of God sayings; and the fact that some within the early church expected the final eschatological events (second coming, end of the world, last judgment) in their lifetimes.

Of these elements, the "coming Son of Man" sayings were most foundational. Some of them explicitly spoke of the end of the world and the last judgment coming upon the generation then alive: "This generation will not pass away before all these things take place."[12] The imminent coming of the Son of Man was then connected to the coming of the kingdom of God, and both were used to account for the element of urgency and crisis in the gospels: there is no time to waste, for the end is at hand. Finally, the eschatological expectation of the early church was explained as a continuation of the eschatological message of Jesus. The whole was an impressively coherent picture; indeed, the image of Jesus as an eschatological prophet was persuasive to a large extent because of its great explanatory power.

But its foundation was weak. By the late 1960s, the texts that had served as its basis were being undermined. It became increasingly accepted that the coming Son of Man sayings were not authentic, but were created by Jesus' followers in the decades after Easter as "second coming" texts, expressing the early church's conviction that the crucified and exalted one would return as vindicator and judge.[13] But if these texts are seen as inauthentic, then the central reason for thinking that Jesus expected the imminent end of the world vanishes.

In the same period, a number of scholars argued that Jesus' "eschatology" was not to be understood in a chronological temporal sense, that is, not as referring to an end of actual time.[14] More recently, the centrality given to the kingdom of God as the primary motif of Jesus' message has been persuasively challenged. Though Jesus certainly did speak of the kingdom of God, our impression that it was the central element in his message is clearly due to Marcan redaction.[15] Moreover, without the coming Son of Man sayings, there is no good reason to identify the coming of the kingdom of God with the end of the world. Finally, it is now commonplace to locate the origin of the church's eschatological expectation in the Easter event. It was the conviction that Jesus had been raised from the dead (for resurrection was an event associated with the end of time) that led some in the early church to believe that they were living in the "end times."[16]

Combined, these factors have produced a growing conviction: the mission and message of Jesus were "non-eschatological."[17] That is perhaps too simple a way to put it, given the long history of the words "eschatology" and "apocalyptic" in biblical scholarship and theology. Both were initially used in Jesus studies to refer to the end of the world of ordinary history. But subsequent scholarship in this century has given the terms many different senses. "Eschatological" can be used metaphorically in a non-end-of-the-world sense: as a nuanced synonym for "decisive," or as "world-shattering," or to point to the *telos* of history entering history but not in such a way as to end history. Even "apocalyptic," we are discovering, need not refer to the end of the world; some apocalyptic literature describes experiences of another world (visions or other-worldly journeys) and does not refer to the imminent end of the world of ordinary history.[18]

Thus, there is considerable terminological confusion in the discipline. For example, I have heard one scholar argue that Jesus' message was eschatological but not apocalyptic, that is, concerned with a decisive change in history, but not with the end of the world. I have heard another scholar argue that Jesus' message was apocalyptic but not eschatological; that is, grounded in the experience of another world, but not concerned with the end of this world. Despite the directly contrasting language, at a fundamental level both scholars meant the same thing: Jesus did not proclaim the imminent end of the world of ordinary history. It is best, therefore, to specify what is meant by the phrase "non-eschatological Jesus." The contrast is specifically to the image of Jesus as one who proclaimed the imminent coming of the kingdom of God and the Son of Man, understood as involving the last judgment and the end of human history as we know it. That, according to the emergent consensus, was neither Jesus' expectation nor message.

The collapse of the old consensus creates exciting questions for reviewing the gospel texts. If the proclamation of the imminent coming of the kingdom of God was not the heart of Jesus' message, what was? Moreover, if the crisis permeating his message and ministry was not the imminent arrival of the last hour, what was it? Was it simply the crisis of individual decision or response? Or is it to be understood in another way?

A second consensus element of the renaissance is a new understanding of Jesus as teacher, especially as *a teacher of subversive wisdom*. There is a near chorus within the discipline about this, flowing out of recent studies of the forms of Jesus' teaching, especially the wisdom forms of proverb, parable, aphorism, and nature saying.[19]

Jesus' teaching as involving a "subversion of world" is seen most easily in contrast to the notion of conventional wisdom. Every culture has its conventional wisdom. It is the dominant consciousness of a culture, "what everybody knows," the taken-for-granted assumptions that comprise the "world" within which people live. Composed of two elements, world-view and ethos, an understanding of reality and a way of life, it constitutes the heart of culture.

Though the specific content of conventional wisdom is particular to each culture, it has a number of common characteristics across cultures. Seeking to be practical, it provides concrete guidance about how to live, ranging from matters of etiquette to overarching values. It orders life on the basis of rewards and punishments, whether expressed in religious notions about karma or a last judgment, or in more secularized form like success as the reward for hard work. It is thus not only practical but prudent: "Follow this way and all will go well" and "You reap what you sow" are its common themes. It also confers identity and creates hierarchies. The canons of conventional wisdom teach a person who one is. In traditional societies, such as first-century Palestine, some of these identities and the status accorded to them are, in a sense, "given": man/woman, oldest son/younger son, Jew/Gentile, aristocrat/peasant, rich/poor. Some are contingent upon measuring up to the standards of conventional wisdom: righteous/sinner, success/failure. Conventional wisdom thus creates a "world" in which one lives, providing guidance, sanctions, identity, and status.

It is this world of conventional wisdom that Jesus subverts in his teaching. His proverbs and aphorisms are crystallizations of insight which, either radical in themselves or radical in their application, frequently embody the theme of world-reversal. So also with the parables and nature sayings; they are invitations to see differently, bringing about a shattering of world. Consistently, Jesus undermined the world of conventional wisdom with its safe and prudent ethos, its notion of reality organized on the basis of rewards and punishments, its oppressive hierarchies, its categories of righteous and sinners. As a teacher, Jesus was a subversive sage, not only subverting conventional wisdom, but inviting his hearers to ground their lives in the Spirit of God rather than in the securities and identities offered by culture.

Finally, a *third* feature marking the renaissance is not so much a consensus result as a consensus focus: studies of the *social world* of Jesus have become central. To some extent, this emphasis is the result of new information. Archaeological excavations continue, highly specialized studies of extant materials proliferate, and ongoing analyses of recently discovered documents such as the Dead Sea Scrolls and the Nag Hammadi texts add to our understanding. We simply know more about the world of first-century Palestine than earlier generations of scholars did.

But the surge of interest in Jesus' social world is not due primarily to the accumulation of additional information. Rather, it flows from new ways of *construing* that information, made possible by the interdisciplinary borrowings described earlier. Central among these is the notion of "social world" itself, which entered New Testament scholarship only recently. It refers to the total social environment of a people, including especially the socially constructed reality of a people, that non-material "canopy" of shared ideas that makes each culture what it is.[20] Though it includes conventional wisdom, it is even more comprehensive, consisting of the beliefs, values, laws, customs, institutions, rituals, and so forth, by which the group orders and maintains its world.

Fundamental to the emphasis upon social world is the recognition of how radically different the social world of first-century Palestinian Judaism was from our own.[21] Because meanings are embedded in a social world, understanding the shape of a particular social world enables us to construe the meaning of things said and done in that social world. Words and actions that seem trivial or inconsequential in one culture can be of the greatest import in another. But they need to be *located* in the social world within which they occur.

For example, the attention given to purity issues in many gospel texts seems puzzling to modern ears. What could it matter whether one ate with unclean hands or with impure people? To us, it seems the preoccupation of a righteous piety tilted toward excessive scrupulosity. Moreover, the gathering of more information — of more texts showing the concern with purity — does not really enhance understanding. It is one thing to see *that* Jesus' contemporaries were concerned about issues of purity; it is another thing to see *why* purity was such an issue.

The notion of social world enables us to see why. The polarity of pure and impure, clean and unclean, was a fundamental political structure of the first-century Jewish social world. Moreover, it was correlated with a number of other polarities, all of which established boundaries: righteous and sinner, Jew and Gentile, to some extent even male and female, rich and poor. These boundaries were part of a politics of purity, which dominated the ethos of that social world, its way of life as well as the cultural dynamic shaping its historical development. Thus, disputes about clean and unclean were not trivial, but concerned the fundamental question of how society was to be structured. Disagreements about purity were potentially world-shattering and world-transforming.

The interpretive power of the notion of social world is further illustrated by a number of studies of particular features of the social world of Jesus. It was a social world in crisis, and a number of revitalization or renewal movements operated, each with its own program or set of strategies for creating a transformed social world. Within this framework, the group that formed around Jesus can be seen clearly as such a movement, competing with other Jewish renewal movements in the social world of first-century Palestine.[22] Studies of the dynamics of peasant societies provide a clearer basis for understanding popular and anti-establishment movements in the time of Jesus.[23] Studies of the cos-

mology and social dynamics of witchcraft societies illuminate the rivalry
between Jesus and his opponents.[24] An understanding of the pivotal role
played by issues of honor and shame in that social world enables us to
understand much that would otherwise be obscure.[25]

Because of the great cultural distance separating us from the social
world of Jesus, reconstructing and entering it requires a disciplined act
of historical imagination. Such reconstruction, aided by the study of
the dynamics of social worlds very different from our own, enables us
more and more to see the *rootedness* of Jesus' mission and message.
The almost discarnate picture of the teaching of Jesus, floating above
the particularities of his time and place, which dominated much of the
quest for the historical Jesus in all of its periods, is being replaced by
one that locates his words and deeds rigorously within the social world
of his time.

IV

Now I wish to move beyond reporting consensus elements of the renaissance to sharing some concluding perceptions flowing from my own
work.

One of these is a methodological observation. There remains a widespread sentiment among many colleagues in New Testament studies and
in the broader field of religious studies that it is extremely difficult to
know anything about Jesus with any degree of probability. As noted
earlier, this sentiment was one of the central tenets of the "no quest"
and "new quest" periods, and is the direct consequence of the scholarly
preoccupation with the *words* of Jesus. If one begins with the words
of Jesus, and develops one's methodology primarily by working with
his words, radical historical skepticism is the inevitable result. Seldom if
ever do we have direct quotation; the transmission of tradition did not
work that way.

But there is another starting place for the study of Jesus. Familiar-
ity with a typology of religious figures (derived from the history of
religions, anthropology, and the psychology of religion) provides an illuminating vantage point. Four types of religious personalities, known
cross-culturally as well as in the Jewish tradition, are particularly relevant: the charismatic "holy man" (a person vividly in touch with
another reality who typically functions as a healer), the sage (teacher
of wisdom), the prophet (in the sense of the classical prophets of Israel),
and the revitalization movement founder.

When the texts of the gospels are approached from this perspective,
broad strokes of a credible historical portrait emerge. It is another instance of re-viewing the gospel data with fresh lenses. That Jesus was

each of these is attested by recurring motifs and themes that permeate the gospel narratives, found in multiple sources and forms. That is to say, the model is established by a cross-cultural typology; it is then validated by what we find in the gospel texts themselves. This framework then provides a *Gestalt* for locating and understanding the traditions ascribed to Jesus; or, to change the metaphor, it provides a skeleton which can then be enfleshed.

This approach in no way denies that the traditions about Jesus developed. It accepts that in all likelihood we never have direct quotation. It acknowledges that specifically Christian affirmations cannot be attributed to Jesus. The latter include, but are not restricted to, christological affirmations, texts speaking about the social formation of the early church (including applications of Jesus' teaching as "church rules"), reflections about the meaning of Jesus' death, and, in my judgment, texts that refer to a second coming. This approach seems to me to provide a promising means for breaking the methodological impasse that has marked much of Jesus scholarship. We may be more historically certain of the larger picture than we are of the historical exactness of any particular tradition.[26]

Secondly, the increasingly clear picture we have of Jesus' social world and his relationship to it, along with the collapse of the eschatological Jesus, seem to me to suggest that his mission was much more concerned with that social world than this century's scholarship has typically affirmed. The element of crisis then appears in a new light. Rather than being the expected imminent end of the world or the crisis of individual decision, it was a crisis in the social world itself that called for a radical change. In short, the more clearly we are able to imagine the dynamics of Jesus' social world, the more obvious it seems that his mission and message were intensely and intimately involved with changing it. As a charismatic who was also a subversive sage, prophet, and renewal movement founder, Jesus sought a transformation in the historical shape and direction of his social world.[27]

Finally, it seems to me that much of the scholarly renaissance has important relevance for the life of the church. Ironically, in a time when specifically Christian questions are no longer the starting point for approaching the texts, what emerges seems more rather than less relevant. Perhaps this is not so surprising; the earlier approach to the texts, with the conscious or unconscious agenda of confirming or disconfirming continuity with Christian teachings, tended to focus the questions on the most problematic areas. Did Jesus think of himself as the Messiah? Did he think of his own death as salvific? Did he "institute" the Lord's Supper, or intend to found a "church"? To these questions, uncertain answers at best could be given. Moreover, such questions tended to give the quest an anxious flavor, an exercise in debunking or defending. No wonder the quest for the historical Jesus seemed to flounder in a sea of uncertainty.

The asking of non-Christian questions seems to be producing results that are both more certain and more interesting. In my own work, the picture of Jesus as a charismatic or "holy man" vividly in touch with what the texts call "Spirit" radically challenges the flattened sense of reality pervading the modern world-view and much of the mainline church, and suggests that reality might indeed be far more mysterious than we suppose. It invites us to consider seriously the central claim of the Jewish-Christian tradition (and most religious traditions): that we are surrounded by an actual, even though non-material, reality charged with energy and power with which it is possible to be in relationship. Similarly, the picture of Jesus as a subversive sage undermining his culture's conventional assumptions, as a prophet calling it to change its historical direction, and as a revitalization movement founder seeking to create an alternative culture, all point to a deep involvement in the life of history. The historical Jesus may well have been more historical than we supposed.

The image of Jesus as a person of Spirit whose mission focused on the transformation of his social world can provide significant content for the meaning of discipleship. Discipleship means "to follow after." "Following after" Jesus means to take seriously what he took seriously: life in the Spirit, and life in history.[28]

Notes

1. For a compact and convenient schematization of the periods of Jesus research, see W. Barnes Tatum, *In Quest of Jesus* (Atlanta: John Knox, 1982), 66–79.

2. Published as "The Problem of the Historical Jesus," Käsemann's lecture is available in his *Essays on New Testament Themes* (London: SCM, 1964), 15–47.

3. Individual studies are too numerous to mention. Multivolume reference works include the revision of Emil Schürer's *The History of the Jewish People in the Age of Jesus Christ,* ed. Geza Vermes et al. (Edinburgh: Clark, 1973 and continuing); S. Safrai and M. Stern, eds., *The Jewish People in the First Century: Compendia Rerum Iudaicarum ad Novum Testamentum* (Philadelphia: Fortress, 1974, 1976); J. Neusner, ed., *Christianity, Judaism, and Other Greco-Roman Cults* (Leiden: Brill, 1975).

4. James Robinson, *The Nag Hammadi Library in English* (San Francisco: Harper & Row, 1977); James H. Charlesworth, *The Old Testament Pseudepigrapha* (Garden City, N.Y.: Doubleday, 1983, 1985).

5. James H. Charlesworth "From Barren Mazes to Gentle Rappings: The Emergence of Jesus Research," *Princeton Seminary Bulletin* 7 (1986): 221–30.

At the beginning of his essay, Charlesworth states, "Jesus research commenced around 1980." The statement is *literally* wrong (even outrageously so), of course; but it dramatically makes the point that something new is happening.

6. James H. Charlesworth's *Jesus within Judaism,* forthcoming from Doubleday; John Dominic Crossan is writing a major treatment of Jesus that builds on his previous books on more specialized topics (especially parables and aphorism).

7. It was organized by Paul Hollenbach of Iowa State University and John Miller of Waterloo University, who continued as co-chairs through 1987.

8. For more information about the Jesus Seminar, see its journal, *Foundations and Facets Forum;* or write to the Westar Institute, Box 1526, Sonoma, CA 95476. *The New Red-Letter Edition of the Five Gospels,* scheduled for publication in 1990, will print the words of Jesus in four colors, corresponding to the votes of the Seminar: red, pink, gray, and black. The colors represent a descending degree of historical authenticity: red means in the judgment of the Seminar, "Jesus almost certainly said this"; black, "Jesus almost certainly did not"; pink and gray are intermediate judgments. Voting, of course, cannot settle questions of historical fact, but it does disclose present scholarly opinion.

9. Daniel Harrington "Second Testament Exegesis and the Social Sciences: A Bibliography," *Biblical Theology Bulletin* 18 (April 1988): 77–85. For another useful bibliography, see John Elliott, *Semeia* 35, 27–33.

10. A remark made by Bernard Brandon Scott at the annual meeting of the Historical Jesus Section of the Society of Biblical Literature in Chicago in December 1984.

11. In the spring of 1986, I conducted a mail poll of the thirty charter fellows of the Jesus Seminar and forty-two participants of the Historical Jesus Section of SBL. Combining the two groups, 59 percent said they did not think that Jesus expected the imminent end of the world in his generation. The poll was repeated at the Notre Dame meeting of the Jesus Seminar in the fall of 1986. Of the thirty-nine fellows in attendance, thirty (77 percent) said they did not think so.

12. Mark 13:30, part of Mark's "little apocalypse," and clearly referring back to the darkening of the sun and moon, the falling of the stars, the coming of the Son of Man, and the gathering of the elect described in 13:24–27.

13. See especially Norman Perrin's influential *Rediscovering the Teaching of Jesus* (New York: Harper & Row, 1967), 164–206. This view of the coming Son of Man sayings is a near consensus within the Jesus Seminar. At its spring 1988 meeting in Sonoma, California, the coming Son of Man sayings consistently received 80 percent gray or black (that is, negative) votes. Recent redactional work on Q also supports this claim. According to John Kloppenborg, *The Formation of Q Trajectories in Ancient Wisdom Collections* (Philadelphia: Fortress, 1987), the earliest stratum of Q is non-apocalyptic, with apocalyptic elements appearing only in the latest stratum, suggesting that the teaching of Jesus was "apocalypticized" by some in the early church.

14. See, for example, John Dominic Crossan, *In Parables: The Challenge of the Historical Jesus* (San Francisco: Harper & Row, 1973). Perrin also drew this conclusion in his *Rediscovering the Teaching of Jesus.*

15. It is Mark 1:15 that presents the kingdom of God as the central element of Jesus' message. Yet, scholars have regularly recognized this as Marcan redaction without raising the further question whether it is an apt condensation of Jesus' preaching. See especially Burton Mack; "The Kingdom Sayings in Mark," *Foundations and Facets Forum* 3, no. 1 (1987): 3–47.

16. See, for example, Edward Schillebeeckx, *Jesus: An Experiment in Christology* (New York: Crossroad, 1979; published in Dutch in 1974), 152, 401–23; and John Collins, *The Apocalyptic Imagination* (New York: Crossroad, 1984), 210.

17. For more complete treatment of this section, see my "An Orthodoxy Reconsidered: The 'End-of-the-World' Jesus," in *The Glory of Christ in the New Testament,* ed. L. D. Hurst and N. T. Wright (Oxford: Clarendon Press, 1987), 207–17; and "A Temperate Case for a Non-Eschatological Jesus," *Society of Biblical Literature: 1986 Seminar Papers* (Atlanta: Scholars Press, 1986): 521–35 [also published in *Foundations and Facets Forum,* 2, no. 3 (1986): 81–102, and as chapter 3 in this volume].

18. See Collins, *The Apocalyptic Imagination,* 5–8, where he distinguishes between the two main types, "historical" and "other-worldly journey" apocalypses; the latter slightly outnumber the former.

19. Especially important illustrative studies include John Dominic Crossan, *In Parables,* and *In Fragments: The Aphorisms of Jesus* (San Francisco: Harper & Row, 1983); Bernard Brandon Scott, *Jesus: Symbol-Maker for the Kingdom* (Philadelphia: Fortress, 1981), and *Hear Then the Parable* (Philadelphia: Fortress, 1988). See also earlier works by Robert Tannehill, *The Sword of His Mouth* (Philadelphia: Fortress, 1975); and by Robert Funk: *Language, Hermeneutic and Word of God* (New York: Harper & Row, 1966), 133–62; *Jesus as Precursor* (Philadelphia: Fortress, 1975); and *Parables and Presence* (Philadelphia: Fortress, 1982).

20. The use of the word "canopy" alludes to Peter Berger's important study of the relationship between religion and culture, *The Sacred Canopy* (Garden City, N.Y.: Doubleday, 1967). Each particular culture constitutes a "social world," an invisible canopy under which its members live. Other foundational studies which have been important in New Testament circles include Clifford Geertz, *The Interpretation of Cultures* (New York: Basic Books, 1973), and Hans Mol, *Identity and the Sacred* (New York: Free Press, 1976).

21. Bruce Malina's work makes this point with particular emphasis and effectiveness. See especially his *The New Testament World: Insights from Cultural Anthropology* (Atlanta: John Knox, 1981).

22. See especially Gerd Theissen, *The Sociology of Early Palestinian Christianity* (Philadelphia: Fortress, 1978). For a critical and yet appreciative analysis of Theissen's work, see John Elliott, "Social-Scientific Criticism of the New Testament and Its Social World: More on Methods and Models," *Semeia* 35 (1986): 1–33.

23. See Richard Horsley and John Hanson, *Bandits, Prophets, and Messiahs: Popular Movements in the Time of Jesus* (Minneapolis: Winston, 1985).

24. See, for example, Bruce Malina and Jerome Neyrey, *Calling Jesus' Names* (Sonoma, Calif.: Polebridge Press, forthcoming), esp. chapter 1.

25. See especially Malina, *The New Testament World: Insights from Cultural Anthropology.*

26. For this approach, see my *Jesus: A New Vision,* and the concluding chapter of my *Conflict, Holiness and Politics in the Teaching of Jesus* (New York: Edwin Mellen, 1984).

27. Jesus' concern with the transformation of his social world in a time of historical crisis is developed in both of my books referred to in the previous footnote.

28. For the development of these themes, see my *Jesus: A New Vision,* the subtitle of which is *Spirit, Culture and the Life of Discipleship,* especially the concluding chapter.

Chapter Two

Portraits of Jesus in Contemporary North American Scholarship (with Addendum)

Five portraits of Jesus by North American scholars published in the 1980s demonstrate the strength of the current resurgence in Jesus scholarship and disclose the central questions dominating the current discussion.[1] These portraits (by E. P. Sanders, Burton Mack, Elisabeth Schüssler Fiorenza, the present writer, and Richard Horsley) demonstrate that, after decades of relative disinterest, a "third quest" for the historical Jesus is under way.[2] Each portrait or *Gestalt* is interesting in its own right as a construal of the traditions about Jesus and as an exercise in historical reconstruction. Taken together, they illustrate the range of options in contemporary Jesus scholarship and point to the likely focal points of Jesus research in the 1990s.

The Context: The Renaissance in Jesus Research

It is illuminating to set these five construals of Jesus in the context of the current renaissance in Jesus research.[3] Two traits of the renaissance are particularly important.

First, the question of Jesus and eschatology has again risen in North American scholarship. In the 1980s, it became clear that the eschatological consensus that had dominated much of this century's Jesus research, beginning with Johannes Weiss and Albert Schweitzer and continuing through Rudolf Bultmann into the mainstream of scholarship, had seriously eroded. The former consensus saw Jesus as an eschatological

This essay, except for the addendum, was first published in the *Harvard Theological Review* 84, no. 1 (1991): 1–22. Copyright 1994 by the President and Fellows of Harvard College. Reprinted by permission.

prophet and sought to understand his mission and message within the framework of imminent eschatology. Though it affirmed both a present and future dimension to Jesus' proclamation of the kingdom, it typically subordinated the present to the coming kingdom, understood as a dramatic transcendent intervention in the imminent future. Moreover, this expectation was seen as the heart of Jesus' message and the conviction animating his mission.

More than half of the scholars polled in two North American samples no longer think that Jesus expected the imminent end of the world in his generation.[4] James M. Robinson described this development as "the fading of apocalyptic" and as a "paradigm shift" and "Copernican revolution" in the discipline.[5] Though the old consensus has not yet been replaced by a new one, non-eschatological understandings of Jesus are emerging, as are nonobjective and this-worldly understandings of eschatology.

Second, the 1980s produced a great increase in our understanding of the social world of first-century Palestine. To some extent this was due to discovery, publication, and analysis of new archaeological and manuscript material. To an even greater extent, it was due to the accelerating use of methods and models from other disciplines, especially the social sciences, cultural anthropology, and the history of religions.[6] These models and methods enable us to see existing material in new (and typically more interrelated) ways. We thus not only know more "facts" about first-century Palestine, but we also understand the dynamics of that social world better.

These two characteristics of the renaissance provide the framework for describing the five portraits that follow. In each case, the portrait is sketched and then related to the two questions of eschatology and Jesus' relationship to his social world. First, what role does eschatology play in each image or construal of Jesus? Is it central, denied, or integrated into another overarching image of Jesus? Second, how is Jesus seen in relationship to his social world? Is his social world of little or no consequence to him, or is it central to understanding his activity, message, and aim?

The Five Portraits

E. P. Sanders

E. P. Sanders's *Jesus and Judaism* is probably the best known of the five sketches.[7] According to Sanders, Jesus was an eschatological prophet standing in the tradition of Jewish restoration theology. Jesus believed that the promises to Israel would soon be fulfilled: the eschatological restoration of Israel was at hand. Its completion in the near future would be brought about by a dramatic intervention by God, involving the destruction of the Jerusalem temple and the coming of a new (or renewed) temple.

The method by which Sanders arrives at this conclusion is important. He correctly notes that most scholars begin their investigation of Jesus with the sayings traditions, which typically leads into a historical quagmire. Sanders argues that a different starting point is desirable: a set of indisputable or nearly indisputable "facts" about Jesus. He believes that it is possible to establish such a set.

One of these facts (Sanders lists eight) is "controversy about the temple."[8] Using as his point of departure the dramatic episode in which Jesus turned over the tables of the moneychangers and the sellers of sacrificial doves, Sanders locates the action within the framework of Jewish restoration eschatology.[9] Taken together with the tradition that Jesus spoke of destroying the temple and building a new one, Jesus' action in the temple was a symbolic destruction of the temple in anticipation of a new (or renewed) temple to be built by God as the center of a restored Israel.[10]

Jesus' action in the temple thus becomes the cornerstone of Sanders's construction of a thoroughly eschatological Jesus. In accord with the restoration theology he embraced, Jesus not only expected the destruction and divine rebuilding of the temple, but also a messianic age on earth, centered in Jerusalem, including a new social order that would be ruled over by Jesus and the Twelve.[11] Moreover, Jesus expected all of this soon. Thus, for Sanders, imminent eschatology is central to Jesus' own self-understanding and mission.[12]

Sanders's picture of Jesus' relationship to his social world is shaped by another theme of his work. Building on his detailed understanding of Jewish law and its function in first-century Palestine, Sanders is critical of how much modern scholarship portrays Jesus' relationship to Judaism.[13] He argues that many scholars have operated with a caricature of Jewish law, seeing it as a burdensome and often trivial legalistic system devoid of grace.

To some extent this misunderstanding is based on an inadequate knowledge of Jewish sources. To a greater extent, it is the result of seeing the issue of law through the lens of the Lutheran contrast between law and grace.[14] Jesus is understood as one who affirmed grace and love in contrast to a system saturated by judgment and law. Modern scholarship has thus often spoken of Jesus *against* Judaism rather than Jesus *within* Judaism.

Sanders protests against this. His main concern is to emphasize the Jewishness of Jesus. However, his insistence on Jesus' congruity with Judaism affects his view of Jesus' relationship to his social world. With Jesus set firmly within the framework of Jewish restoration eschatology and in close proximity to the Jewish law, there is little that puts Jesus in conflict with his Jewish contemporaries. Sanders grants that Jesus' self-claim and his proclamation that "the wicked" would be admitted to the coming kingdom without going through the procedure of repentance might have been offensive to some and that Jesus' threat against the temple would have been offensive to many. Moreover, the fact that Jesus spoke of a kingdom and had followers might have made the ruling elite nervous. But there were no other significant points of tension between Jesus and his Jewish contemporaries.[15]

Thus, although Sanders seeks to place Jesus firmly within a Jewish social world, Jesus ends up having very little to do with it. Jesus' relationship to it remains abstract, almost ideological. Sanders relates him to the world of ideas: the ideas of Jewish restoration theology and the Jewish law understood as "covenant nomism." Within both of these, according to Sanders, Jesus fits nicely. But precisely because Jesus differs so little from his social world, he seems remarkably unconcerned with it. He is not very interested in the historical direction of his people or about the shape of Jewish life. Rather, it is Jesus' ideas about eschatology and his acting out his convictions about a new temple that get him in trouble. Indeed, Jesus is so unconcerned about his social world that he is curiously other-worldly, or perhaps better, next-worldly.

As with all the works we shall survey, this brief summary does not do justice to the intricate argument and exegetical insight of Sanders's book. It is also the most academically traditional of the five portraits of Jesus and stands unambiguously within the formerly dominant eschatological consensus. Moreover, his construal exhibits striking resemblances to Albert Schweitzer's.[16] Like many of this century's scholars, Sanders finds Jesus to be essentially apolitical, that is, not concerned with the shape and shaping of his social world.

Burton Mack

Burton Mack sketches a very different image of Jesus in his book *A Myth of Innocence: Mark and Christian Origins*.[17] Mack's book is a provocative study of Christian origins up to the time of Mark's gospel. It includes a history of Jesus movements and "Christ cults" in the first century as well as a detailed study of the primary forms in which the synoptic tradition took shape, all in the context of illuminating the gospel of Mark. Thus most of the book is not about Jesus, and Mack does not regard himself primarily as a Jesus scholar. Nevertheless, what Mack calls a "softly focused characterization of Jesus" emerges.[18] It is an image of Jesus as a "Cynic sage" or "Cynic teacher," more Hellenistic than Jewish, in a thoroughly Hellenized Galilee.[19]

Mack's construal of Jesus is the polar opposite of Sanders's: Jesus is neither eschatological nor very Jewish. How Mack arrives at these judgments is as important as the judgments themselves. First, he argues that the oldest layer of the Jesus tradition is sapiential, consisting of aphorisms, parables, and a few *chreiai* embedded in pronouncement stories.[20] This judgment is based to a large extent on Mack's understanding of the relationship between texts (both form and content) and social groups. He argues that the multiplicity of forms in the gospels suggests a multiplicity of early Jesus groups. Each group formed its own distinctive memory of Jesus.

Because these "several traditions of memory cannot be merged into a single, coherent picture,"[21] they cannot all be viewed as equally early. Earliest is a characterization of Jesus as a clever teacher of a world-mocking wisdom. His teaching was marked by "aphoristic speech, a touch of humor, a critical stance over against social pretensions and cultural conventions, and a dare to be different, if not outrageous."[22] Because of the parallels to Hellenistic Cynic material, this earliest layer suggests that Jesus is best seen as a wandering Cynic sage.

Second, Mack argues that apocalyptic (understood as end-of-the-world expectation) does not belong to the earliest layers of the Jesus tradition. Rather, the earliest layers were buoyant and optimistic; only as the Jesus groups went "through a period of tussle and setback" and "a later period of polemic and compensatory reaction" did themes of judgment and apocalyptic enter the tradition.[23] Indeed, it is primarily Mark who introduces an apocalyptic framework into the story of Jesus.[24]

Third, Mack distances Jesus not only from apocalypticism but also from Judaism. In his work, he employs what might be called the criterion of social formation: if a text reflects a concern with one group defining itself over against another group, the text belongs to the stage of social formation that Mack sees as occurring only after Jesus' death and resurrection.[25] Therefore, texts that reflect any significant engagement with Judaism or Jewish groups tell us about the various Jesus groups as they developed their own self-understandings and ideologies in the decades after Jesus' life. They do not tell us about Jesus.

Thus, though Jewish by birth and upbringing, Mack's Jesus is not involved in the issues of the Jewish social world.[26] Though Jesus' Cynic-style teaching contained a social critique, it was a general, clever, and often playful ridiculing of the preoccupations that animate and imprison people. There was no engagement with specifically Jewish concerns or institutions. Jesus had no mission vis-à-vis Judaism; he neither criticized nor sought to reform or renew it. He did not call people into community; his message was for individuals. The kingdom of which Jesus spoke was more likely the "Cynic's 'kingdom'" than any specifically Jewish notion of "kingdom of God."[27]

Thus Mack's Jesus was a striking teacher, a gadfly or mocker, who dined in private homes with small groups of people. His clever teaching caught the imagination of some, enough so that they continued the practice of eating together after his death; from this emerged the various Jesus groups. Jesus himself had no sense of mission or purpose; in an important sense, he was aimless.[28] Only a core of wisdom teaching, stripped of any world-ending or world-building elements, is authentic to Jesus.

Much of Mack's portrait of Jesus is consistent with the image of Jesus that has emerged from the massive scholarship on the parables and aphorisms of Jesus in the last two decades: Jesus as a teacher of subversive wisdom who undermined his world's assumptions. Moreover, like Mack, many of these scholars have stressed a non-eschatological understanding of Jesus.[29] Mack differs in that he separates Jesus from his Jewish world. The thoroughgoing skepticism created by his perception of the relationship between texts and social history is also unique. His method creates a minimalist portrait.[30] Indeed, his construal is the most historically skeptical of these five.

Thus Sanders and Mack represent opposite poles in the current discussion of Jesus. Far from standing in a stream of Jewish restoration eschatology, Mack's Jesus stands on the very margin of Judaism. Yet the two portraits share an important feature. In neither case is Jesus' involvement with his social world significant. For Sanders, Jesus' social world provided him with the ideology of restoration theology; for Mack, Jesus' social world was thoroughly Hellenized. Neither sees Jesus in significant conflict with his social world or passionately concerned for it. For Sanders, Jesus is so much within Judaism that there is no significant conflict with it; for Mack, Jesus is too much outside of Judaism for there to be such a conflict.

In each of the next three portraits, however, Jesus' relationship to his social world is central. Like Sanders, all agree that Jesus is deeply Jewish. Unlike Sanders, they see Jesus in considerable conflict with the dominant ethos and institutions of his social world and as the originator of an intra-Jewish renewal movement with an alternative vision of Jewish life and community. Though they are conflictual portraits, they are not pictures of Jesus against Judaism. Jesus was not against Judaism any more than were Jeremiah and the other prophets. Moreover all three see the alternative that Jesus affirmed as grounded in the Jewish tradition. Thus, though they affirm that Jesus advocated a transformation that engaged the social structures of his day, they see Jesus as a definitely Jewish voice within Judaism.

Elisabeth Schüssler Fiorenza

Though feminist scholarship in North America has not yet produced a book-length study of the historical Jesus, Elisabeth Schüssler Fiorenza's *In Memory of Her* (1983) contains a comprehensive sketch.[31] Schüssler

Fiorenza presents a picture of Jesus as a wisdom prophet and founder of a Jewish renewal movement with a socially radical vision and praxis. Jesus and his movement were intrinsically sociopolitical, challenging both the ideology and praxis of the dominant ethos of the Jewish social world.

Schüssler Fiorenza's work reflects the changes occurring within the discipline in three ways. She notes with approval the shift from a theological paradigm to a more historical one, from "almost sixty years of focusing predominantly on theological-kerygmatic issues" to the historical task of searching for "the social context and matrix of early Christian literature."[32] She uses an interdisciplinary approach, especially "new integrative heuristic models" drawn from the sociology of religious movements.[33] Finally, her angle of vision is feminist; she brings to her reading of New Testament texts the awareness that these texts are both androcentric and patriarchal.[34] These texts not only "see" from a male perspective, but to varying degrees reflect the patriarchal social world out of which they come. A critical feminist reading therefore does not see the texts themselves as normative (theologically or historically), but seeks to reconstruct the social reality behind the texts.

In her portrait of Jesus, Schüssler Fiorenza defines that social reality as the movement around Jesus.[35] Using sociological models as a way of ordering data from the earliest traditions, she sees the group around Jesus as "an inner-Jewish renewal movement." As "an alternative prophetic renewal movement within Israel"[36] and intrinsically sociopolitical, it articulated an alternative ethos and followed an alternative social praxis.

The sociopolitical characteristics of Jesus' vision and movement are most clearly seen in a dialectic with the dominant ethos of the Jewish social world. That ethos was expressed in the image of Israel as a "kingdom of priests and holy nation," and its central symbols were temple and Torah.[37] In the social system purity and holiness became correlated with the hierarchical structure of a patriarchal society.[38]

Jesus and his movement challenged the purity system, offered an alternative interpretation of Torah and temple, and practiced inclusive wholeness in "a discipleship of equals," one of her most frequent epithets for the movement. Its praxis was marked by festive table-sharing. As a social movement, it specifically included the impoverished and destitute, the sick and crippled, tax collectors, outcasts, and prostitutes. This egalitarian praxis was intended as an alternative ethos for Israel, subverting and intruding upon the dominant ethos. It was an alternative life-style not simply for individuals, but for a community.[39]

Schüssler Fiorenza's feminist perspective enables her to see the movement's challenge to patriarchy. Given that our texts are androcentric, the traces of women's stories found in them indicate that women played a much larger role in the movement than has typically been recognized. She argues convincingly that women were prominent among the first followers of Jesus in the "discipleship of equals," and that they were the central figures in the early Christian missionary movement.

She finds an antipatriarchal thrust to the antifamily texts and to the text prohibiting calling anybody on earth "father." They call one away from the patriarchal family (and patriarchy itself) as the center of identity and security.[40] She finds Jesus' use of the image of God as father to be iconoclastic: to say that God is father means that there are no other fathers, just as the confession of God's lordship means there are no other lords.[41] She correlates Jesus' frequent use of the wisdom form "parable," in which he speaks of the "gracious goodness of God," with texts in which Jesus speaks of the wisdom of God as "Sophia,"[42] and argues that Jesus perceived God "in a woman's *Gestalt* as divine *Sophia.*"[43] She concludes that the earliest movement understood Jesus "as Sophia's messenger and later as Sophia herself" and that Jesus probably understood himself "as the prophet and child of Sophia."[44]

This provocative suggestion about Jesus' own self-consciousness as the prophet and child of Sophia should not obscure the more basic outline of her construal of Jesus. Unlike Sanders and Mack, she sketches a portrait of Jesus as deeply engaged with his social world. It was not just the background for his activity (whether as restoration prophet or as Cynic), but his central concern.

For Schüssler Fiorenza, Jesus was a "wisdom prophet" in two senses. First, he was a prophet of wisdom in that he was a spokesperson for Sophia. Second, Jesus was a social prophet who subverted the dominant structures of the time with a different vision of reality and human community.[45] His proclamation of the gracious goodness of God called into existence "a discipleship of equals" based upon "a vision of inclusive wholeness." His purpose was the creation of such a community within Israel for the sake of the renewal of Israel.

Imminent eschatology plays little role in Schüssler Fiorenza's construal. Rather, she integrates eschatology into her image of Jesus as a socially radical wisdom prophet and movement founder. Though affirming a form of the formerly dominant eschatological consensus, she emphasizes the presentness of the kingdom. In Jesus' ministry, "eschatological salvation and wholeness" were "already experientially available."[46] The coming of the kingdom already had social impact: Jesus' *"praxis* and *vision* of the *basileia* is the mediation of God's future into the structures and experiences of his own time and people."[47]

Though she acknowledges that Jesus' *basileia* language also refers to a future in which death and suffering will be no more, this expectation plays no significant role in her image of Jesus and his movement. It was not an "end-of-the-world" movement; rather, Jesus was concerned with a this-worldly transformation of Jewish life. It was not about a future reversal soon to come, but about a reversal that was already happening. Her eschatology is thus this-worldly or transformist.

Marcus J. Borg

My own portrait of Jesus is developed in two books, *Conflict, Holiness and Politics in the Teachings of Jesus* (1984), and *Jesus: A New Vision* (1987).[48] In these two books, a sketch of Jesus with four main strokes emerges: he was a charismatic healer or "holy person," a subversive sage who undermined conventional wisdom and taught an alternative wisdom, a social prophet, and an initiator of a movement the purpose of which was the revitalization of Israel.

The last two are the subject of my 1984 book. It contains two major arguments, the first of which is suggested by the title. The book is a study of the conflict traditions in the synoptic gospels, in the context of a Jewish social world the dominant ethos of which was holiness. The result is a picture of Jesus as more political than we are accustomed to. Jesus was political in the sense of being concerned with the shape and direction of the historical community of Israel.[49]

Central to this portrait of Jesus is an understanding of the cultural dynamics of his social world. I argue that the dominant ethos of the Jewish social world in first-century Roman Palestine, its cultural paradigm or core value, was holiness, understood as purity.[50] Holiness generated a social world ordered as a purity system, with sharp boundaries not only between places, things, and times, but also between persons and social groups. The ethos of holiness had become embodied in a politics of holiness. Within this context, conflicts about holiness and purity were political: the historical shape and direction of Israel were at stake.

I then examine the synoptic traditions' reports of conflict over holiness issues: table fellowship, sabbath conflicts, purity texts, and temple controversy. Two claims emerge: Jesus radically criticized holiness as the paradigm structuring his social world; and he advocated compassion as the alternative paradigm for the transformation of Israel's life. Jesus replaced "Be holy as God is holy" with "Be compassionate as God is compassionate."[51]

Compassion, like holiness, was firmly grounded in the Jewish tradition. The conflict between Jesus and his Jewish opponents was thus an intra-Jewish conflict (with the elite who represented the dominant ethos) about how to interpret the tradition. It was a hermeneutical struggle with sociopolitical consequences. Thus, like Schüssler Fiorenza but without specifically feminist elements, I portray Jesus as deeply engaged in his social world, relating to it as prophet and revitalization movement founder.[52]

The second argument in my 1984 book is a case for a non-eschatological understanding of Jesus. I argue that imminent eschatology (understood as involving the traditional eschatological events of divine intervention, judgment, resurrection, and beginning of a new world or age, all occurring in a publicly visible or objective way) was not part of the message of Jesus.

This case rests on three supporting points. First, with the erosion of the "coming Son of man" sayings as authentic Jesus sayings, there is very little exegetical basis for affirming that Jesus had an imminent eschatology.[53] Second, the element of crisis in the synoptics is more plausibly understood in historical terms. To some extent, this argument is a corollary of seeing Jesus' deep involvement with his social world, which draws him away from other-worldly eschatology. Third, belief in the imminent end of the world among the followers of Jesus arose with belief in the second coming, which clearly developed after Jesus' death. I conclude that the image of Jesus as eschatological prophet is mistaken and misleading. As a prophet, Jesus was much more concerned about Israel's historical direction and shape than about a kingdom beyond the eschaton.

In my 1987 book, a more comprehensive, general treatment, I add two further strokes to this portrait of Jesus. In addition to being a social prophet and movement founder, he was also a "holy person" and sage or wisdom teacher.

This book uses a cross-cultural and interdisciplinary typology of religious personality types that help order the traditions about Jesus. The understanding of holy person is derived from the history of religions, cultural anthropology, and psychology of religion.[54] It designates a person experientially in touch with the holy who also becomes a mediator of the holy.[55] There are many ways of describing this religious personality: mediator of the numinous, technician of the sacred, charismatic healer, delegate of the tribe to the other world, spirit warrior, or person of power. All share a vivid sense of another reality and the ability to mediate that reality.

When "holy person" is seen as a phenomenological category, it is clear that such figures were central in the Jewish tradition, from Moses and Elijah through the prophets to charismatic healers near the time of Jesus such as Hanina ben Dosa and Honi the Circle-Drawer.[56] Jesus clearly belongs among them.[57] He had an experiential relationship to the spirit (as numinous, a phenomenological rather than doctrinal or trinitarian category), and this realization is central to his historical identity: a charismatic healer with a vivid sense of the reality of God. Indeed, it is tempting to see him as a Jewish mystic.[58]

Second, I argue that he was also a sage, a teacher of wisdom. Here I accept the image of Jesus as a teacher of a world-subverting wisdom that has emerged in the parables and aphorisms scholarship of the last twenty years. Setting that work in the context of a cross-cultural understanding of conventional wisdom, I argue that Jesus' wisdom both subverted conventional wisdom (the broad way) and invited his hearers to an alternative path (the narrow way). Thus Jesus' message contains both subversive and alternative wisdom, namely, a vision of life centered in spirit.

With the images of holy person and sage added to prophet and movement founder, a fairly full portrait of Jesus results, an image that integrates much of the Jesus tradition. He was a charismatic healer who also felt called to a public mission that included radical criticism of the dominant ethos of his social world and affirmation of another way. He spoke as both a subversive sage and a prophet and initiated a movement whose purpose was the revitalization of Israel.[59] In short, Jesus was a charismatic wisdom prophet and movement initiator.

Richard Horsley

More emphatically than any other North American scholar, Richard Horsley has made Jesus' engagement with his social world central to his portrait of Jesus. The most prolific contemporary Jesus scholar, Horsley has published four books since 1985. Two are studies of the first-century Jewish social world: *Bandits, Prophets, and Messiahs* (1985) and *The Liberation of Christmas: The Infancy Narratives in Social Context* (1989). Two concern Jesus and the Jesus movement directly: *Jesus and the Spiral of Violence* (1987) and *Sociology and the Jesus Movement* (1989).[60] In these works, Horsley portrays Jesus as a social prophet standing in the radical prophetic tradition of Israel.

Like Sanders, Horsley stresses the necessity of locating Jesus firmly within the context of first-century Jewish Palestine. However, Horsley understands that context in materialist rather than idealist terms. That is, the context is not a set of ideas (about the Messiah, the temple, restoration eschatology, the law, etc.), but the concrete social situation.

His perception of the social situation is provided by studies of preindustrial peasant societies and the social dynamics operating between rural peasants and urban, ruling elites. When applied to our ancient data, these studies suggest a more concrete picture of first-century Jewish Palestine. It was a colonial situation of class struggle and conflict between economically oppressive urban, ruling elites and economically oppressed rural peasants (perhaps 90 percent of the population).[61] The social situation generated a variety of social bandits and popular prophets, and the spiral of violence (which moves from institutional violence to protest to counter-repression to revolt) was under way.

This situation of colonial oppression existing between the Jewish, Herodian, and Roman ruling groups and the bulk of the people becomes the context for the Jesus traditions. What emerges is a picture of

Jesus as a social revolutionary involved with the peasant population of Palestine. Standing in the covenantal-prophetic tradition of Israel, Jesus took the side of the poor and indicted the ruling elites. He threatened the temple, the symbolic as well as economic center of the Jewish social world, and criticized the high-priestly establishment who had made it "an instrument of imperial legitimation and control of a subjected people."[62]

Although Jesus was opposed to domination by Rome and to the priestly aristocracy's collaboration with Rome, he did not organize a political revolution, but a social revolution. Horsley stresses the importance of this distinction: a political revolution is "top down," involving a change of leadership; a social revolution is a change in society from the "bottom up."[63] For Jesus, the social revolution and restoration of Israel were to begin through the reorganization and renewal of village society in accord with the egalitarian covenantal tradition of Israel.

Horsley's thorough social contextualization of the Jesus tradition is evident in his treatment of the "radical" sayings of Jesus. The sayings about forgiveness of debts, lending without regard to repayment, and giving up possessions were not intended for itinerant Cynics or for an elite group of wandering charismatics.[64] Neither are they to be understood in a framework of eschatological renunciation. Rather, they were intended as guidelines for ordinary people in local communities. They were part of the program of socioeconomic cooperation that Jesus envisioned as he sought to reorganize village society into relatively autonomous communities of solidarity.[65] Similarly, in Jesus' context the traditions about "loving one's enemy" refer to relationships of solidarity within the community.[66] Moreover, these local communities were to be egalitarian; hierarchical and patriarchal relationships were abolished.[67]

Finally, Horsley also gives a social reading to the difficult saying about the disciples sitting on twelve thrones judging the twelve tribes. He argues that "judging" is better translated as "liberating/redeeming/establishing justice for" and refers the saying to the twelve administering justice in the restored Israel.[68]

Horsley subsumes eschatology into his portrait of Jesus as a social revolutionary in two ways. First, he sees apocalyptic texts as having a historical orientation and gives them a sociopolitical reading. Arising out of conditions of oppression, such texts have three functions: remembering past deliverances, creatively envisioning a radically different and better life, and critically demystifying the established order by stripping the ruling class of divine authority and exposing its demonic character.[69] Apocalyptic texts express "in ordinary contemporary language eager hopes for an anti-imperial revolution" to be brought about by God.[70] They do not have an other-worldly orientation, but express the hope for a this-worldly transformation.

Second, Horsley argues for a primarily this-worldly understanding of the kingdom of God. He speaks of it as a political metaphor that refers to a historical transformation already under way, a society or people already coming into existence.[71] The kingdom meant wholeness of life in a community marked by "a new spirit of cooperation and mutual assistance."[72]

At only one point does a vestige of imminent eschatology remain, and Horsley integrates it by returning to his distinction between social and political revolution. Horsley argues that Jesus expected God to complete the social revolution Jesus had begun by bringing about the "top down" political revolution: "God would soon judge the oppressive imperial regimes."[73] Imminent end-of-the-world language thus refers to a coming dramatic change in political control, to be accomplished by God. Yet it seems that it would be easy for Horsley to eliminate imminent eschatology. It plays no fundamental role in his construal of Jesus; it is neither the foundation of Jesus' self-understanding, nor the motivation behind his mission, nor the primary content of his message. Rather, it is assimilated to a picture of Jesus as a social prophet passionately engaged in shaping his social world.[74] Like Schüssler Fiorenza, Horsley's understanding of eschatology is thus this-worldly and transformist.

Conclusions and Prospects

These five portraits disclose the vitality of contemporary mainstream Jesus scholarship in North America as well as its range and diversity. With regard to the two questions central to the renaissance in Jesus research — Jesus and eschatology, and Jesus' relationship to his social world — the five portraits diverge considerably. One is boldly cast in the mold of imminent eschatology (Sanders). Two explicitly deny imminent eschatology (Mack and Borg), with one of them denying eschatology to Jesus altogether (Mack).[75] Two (Schüssler Fiorenza and Horsley) articulate a this-worldly and transformist eschatology by integrating eschatology into a sociopolitical reading of the Jesus traditions. Regarding Jesus' relationship to his social world, two deny any sociopolitical purpose to Jesus' activity (Sanders and Mack); the other three argue that such engagement was crucial for the historical Jesus, indeed at the center of his activity and purpose. These agreements and disagreements point to what are likely to be focal points of Jesus research in the 1990s.

First, the eschatological debate will continue. Indeed, it is perhaps only beginning to be engaged. The news that the eschatological consensus has collapsed is bringing scholarly discussion of the relationship between Jesus and eschatology into the foreground again.

Central to this discussion will be a clarification of what is meant when one uses the term "eschatology." Does it intrinsically have to do with the end of the world, as its traditional association with "the last things" would suggest? What is meant by "end of the world"? Is it to be defined as involving the end of the earth, the physical universe, entailing a meltdown of the elements, what might be called a molecular or nuclear eschatology? If so, there is very little end-of-the-world eschatology in either the Hebrew Bible or the New Testament.[76] But surely that restricts the meaning of "end of the world" too much. Can it legitimately be used of any major world-changing event, so that the tearing down of the Berlin wall can be referred to as an eschatological event? That seems too broad. Or is it legitimate to use it to refer to an internal event in the life of an individual, so that end of the world is both internalized and individualized, and to claim that this is what it means to say that the message of Jesus was eschatological? Is any position that affirms an afterlife to be labeled eschatological? Or is it legitimate to use "end" in a teleological sense, so that any position that affirms an ultimate purpose, hope, or ideal vision is eschatological?

This range of meanings of eschatology and end of the world has produced serious confusion in the discussion. Twenty years ago, the French scholar J. Carmignac lamented that eschatology had lost all precise exegetical meaning and suggested that it be dropped from our vocabulary.[77] That is probably unrealistic; we seem stuck with the term. We can insist, however, that one specify the sense in which one is using these terms.[78] What is being affirmed or denied when one does or does not ascribe an imminent eschatology to Jesus?[79]

A related question concerns how we are to understand "kingdom of God" in Jesus' message. When the eschatological consensus was intact, the phrase had a clear meaning: it referred to the coming messianic kingdom, and/or to the power (reign) of God by which that kingdom would be established. With the collapse of the imminent eschatological consensus, there is no longer a clear framework for locating the meaning of kingdom of God. If Jesus' use of kingdom language did not pertain to the imminent end of the world, how are we to understand it?

Necessary for this clarification is a fresh and thorough investigation of the varieties of eschatology and kingdom language in ancient Judaism at the time of Jesus. For example, how often are the eschatologies of noncanonical apocalypses associated with the imminent end of the world?[80] Scholarship may have been misled by the imminent end-of-the-world emphasis of Daniel and Revelation, as if they were typical of the apocalyptic genre and consciousness. And what is the range of uses of kingdom language in first-century Judaism?[81]

Second, the question of Jesus' relationship to his social world is likely to become more central. More remarkable than the disagreement among the five portraits about this question is the agreement among three of them (Schüssler Fiorenza, Borg, and Horsley) that Jesus' ministry had a strong sociopolitical dimension. The three see Jesus' teaching and activity as both a protest against the dominant ethos of the Jewish social world and as an affirmation of an alternative vision.

This emphasis upon the sociopolitical is fresh in Jesus scholarship. Few mainstream portraits of Jesus have stressed a radical sociopolitical edge to his mission; rather, most scholars of the history of Jesus have tended to deny that Jesus had any significant involvement in sociopolitical questions. To a large extent, this was because they saw only two alternative models: Jesus was either an anti-Roman revolutionary (the Zealot hypothesis) or an apolitical nonrevolutionary. Scholars have generally denied the first and affirmed the second.[82] A third alternative has now become prominently visible: Jesus as deeply sociopolitical, though not as an advocate of armed revolt against Rome.[83]

The contrast between this sociopolitical understanding of Jesus and individualistic and/or imminent eschatological understandings of Jesus is considerable. It generates a number of research questions that are likely to receive increased attention. Do we think Jesus was concerned with community, or was his vision of human existence radically individualistic? Was there conflict between Jesus and some of his Jewish contemporaries, and if so, what was it about? What was his relationship to the temple? Did he seek the revitalization of Israel? Or do we think all of these were nonissues for him? Are conflict elements in the synoptic tradition all products of conflict between the Jesus movement and Jewish groups in the second half of the first century?[84]

Finally, the two questions of eschatology and social world are related. The kind of eschatology ascribed to Jesus affects how one sees his relationship to his social world. Sanders's eschatology of imminent radical divine intervention, like Schweitzer's, distances Jesus from anything political.[85] So also do most versions of existentialist eschatology, with their thorough internalization and individualization of the end of the world. Consistently in Jesus scholarship an emphasis on imminent eschatology has led to a deemphasis on human community and history. Thus two of the questions central to the renaissance in Jesus research — Jesus' eschatology and his relationship to his social world — are intertwined.

*   *   *

John Dominic Crossan

Since I finished this essay in 1991, another book of major significance has been published by a North American scholar: John Dominic Crossan's *The Historical Jesus: The Life of a Mediterranean Jewish*

Peasant.[86] It could be the most important book on the historical Jesus since Albert Schweitzer's *Quest of the Historical* Jesus at the beginning of this century, both because of its brilliance, elegance, and freshness, and because of its likely effect on the discipline. Crossan has also written a more popular version, which he affectionately refers to as his "baby Jesus" book, to be published in late 1993 as *Jesus: A Revolutionary Biography.*[87] With these two books, Crossan has established himself as the premier Jesus scholar in North America. In the following remarks, I will focus on two matters of equal importance: method and results.

Crossan's Method

Crossan begins his 1991 book by commenting that historical Jesus research has become "something of a scholarly bad joke." To counteract this, he pays very careful attention to method, one of the most remarkable features of his book. His method is essentially twofold: the first for assessing what may be attributed to Jesus, and the second for interpreting what that material means.

His method for deciding what goes back to Jesus seeks to be as objective and quantitative as possible. He uses an explicitly archaeological model, involving two steps. The first step involves "layering," or establishing a stratigraphy of the Jesus tradition. He layers the written traditions about Jesus into four strata:

Layer One: 30 to 60 C.E.

Layer Two: 60 to 80 C.E.

Layer Three: 80 to 120 C.E.

Layer Four: 120 to 150 C.E.

Into the earliest layer, he puts Q, early Thomas, the genuine letters of Paul (without 2 Corinthians, Philemon, and Philippians), a miracles collection, and a few minor and perhaps questionable sources. In passing, it is noteworthy that the gospel of Mark drops out of layer one.

The second step in his archaeological model involves quantification, or counting the number of independent attestations of material attributed to Jesus in each layer. He does this by arranging the traditions about Jesus into "complexes." A complex, for example, is all sayings referring to "kingdom and children," and he asks "How many times is each complex independently attested?" He then assigns to each complex two numbers, separated by a slash mark: the number to the left is the stratum or layer in which the complex is first found, and the number to the right is the number of independent attestations. Thus, for example, the complex "kingdom and children" is 1/4, which means "first stratum, four independent attestations." The general rule that emerges from this:

the lower the number to the left and the higher the number to the right, the greater claim a saying has to be something like something Jesus said.

This part of Crossan's method is essentially a tightened and refined version of a method that has long been used by Jesus scholars: the "criterion of multiple attestation." This does not minimize Crossan's achievement, but shows his continuity with earlier Jesus scholarship. It is interesting that his primary criterion is not the "criterion of dissimilarity" (one can accept as authentic to Jesus only that which is dissimilar from both Judaism and early Christianity) that dominated much of Jesus research immediately prior to the current renaissance.

The second part of Crossan's method focuses on the interpretation of material found in the earliest layer. Here Crossan sets what we can know about Jesus and the environment of first-century Jewish Palestine within a multi-disciplinary and cross-cultural context. Models and insights drawn from cultural and social anthropology, medical anthropology, the sociology of colonial protest movements, the dynamics and structure of pre-industrial peasant societies, honor-shame societies, patron-client societies, and so forth, dominate the pages of his book. The breadth of Crossan's reading outside the traditional boundaries of Jesus scholarship and the intelligent and illuminating use to which he puts it are most impressive.

This makes his book a goldmine of information about interdisciplinary models and insights, quite apart from how Crossan himself uses them (though I happen to think he uses them quite well). Moreover, in addition to containing all these models, Crossan's use of them will, I think, become a model. Indeed, I think he has significantly changed the discipline with this book — a simply "historical" quest for the historical Jesus will no longer do. Thus, in this part of his method, we see the most comprehensive use yet of the multi-disciplinary approach that is characteristic of the present renaissance in Jesus scholarship.

Results: Crossan's Construal of Jesus

What picture of Jesus emerges in Crossan's book? I will put it in a sentence and then unpack it: Jesus was a Jewish Cynic peasant with an alternative social vision.

First, Jesus was a *peasant* whose primary audience was peasants. To some extent simply an identification of social class, this emphasis also has two immediate implications for Crossan. It means that Jesus was not of the scribal class and therefore did not have scribal skills or scribal awareness. In all likelihood, Jesus did not know Scripture *as texts,* neither reading nor quoting Scripture. Moreover, his message and activity had to make sense to peasants. It could not have been too "heady" or theoretical, but must have been much more concrete. To use a phrase from Crossan's forthcoming popular book on Jesus, Jesus' message must not have been as "talky, preachy, speechy" as much of scholarship has presented it.

Second, Jesus was a *Jewish Cynic,* with adjective and noun equally important. He was both like and unlike Hellenistic Cynic teachers. To paraphrase Crossan closely, both Jesus and the Hellenistic Cynics taught and enacted a shattering of convention: both involved practice, not just theory; both involved a way of looking and dressing, eating, living, and relating. The primary difference between Hellenistic Cynic sages and Jesus is that they were urban, active in the marketplace, and individualistic; Jesus spoke to rural peasants and had a social vision.

Third, that *social vision* was embodied in the two most characteristic activities of Jesus: "magic and meal," "free healing" and "open commensality." Together, they disclose what Crossan calls Jesus' "corporate plan" and alternative "social vision."

Magic. Jesus was a healer. Crossan's preferred term is "magician," which, he emphasizes, he uses in a neutrally descriptive and non-pejorative sense. He uses "magician" in part because it is provocative, but also because it fits: a magician is "somebody else's" healer. That is, a magician is a healer operating outside of recognized religious authority, and therefore outside of the system. Once again to paraphrase Crossan closely, magic is "religious banditry": magic is to religion as social banditry is to politics. Social banditry challenges the ultimacy and legitimacy of political power, and magic challenges the ultimacy of established religious power. Magic is subversive, unofficial, unapproved, and often lower-class religion.

One comment before I turn to Crossan's treatment of meal: it is striking how much importance Crossan assigns to Jesus as healer. No recent scholar, at least not in North America, has made Jesus' healing activity so centrally important.[88]

Meal. Here Crossan emphasizes the "open commensality" of Jesus, often called by other scholars the "table fellowship" of Jesus. It is directly connected to Crossan's emphasis upon magic or healing: in exchange for free healing, Jesus and his followers would be given a meal by peasants. It was not *payment* for healing (though it tended to become that as the tradition developed, when local hospitality came to be understood as the "wages" of the wandering charismatics). Rather, for Jesus and his earliest followers, open commensality embodied an alternative social vision. To eat with others without regard for social boundaries, Crossan argues, subverted the deepest boundaries society draws: between honor and shame, patron and client, female and male, slave and free, rich and poor, pure and impure. Thus, for Crossan, magic and meal together, free healing and common eating, "embodied a religious and economic egalitarianism that negated the hierarchical and patronal normalcies of Jewish religion and Roman power."[89]

Finally, Crossan's construal of Jesus is non-eschatological. To be more precise, Crossan denies an apocalyptic eschatology to Jesus. The "coming Son of man sayings" are rejected. Though John the Baptizer was apocalyptic, Jesus was not. Jesus did not understand the kingdom of God as an apocalyptic event in the near future, but as a mode of life in the immediate present. The kingdom of which Jesus spoke was a sapiential kingdom, not an apocalyptic kingdom.

Thus, though with differences of nuance, Crossan's sketch of Jesus belongs to the same family of portraits as those sketched by Horsley, Schüssler Fiorenza, and myself. It departs from the previously dominant eschatological consensus, and affirms a social vision that shattered the taken-for-granted conventions of his day.[90]

Notes

1. A version of this article was presented at the International Meeting of the SBL in Vienna in August 1990.
2. N. Thomas Wright has described the 1980s as bringing forth a "third quest" of the historical Jesus, succeeding the "first quest" of the nineteenth century and the "second quest" (or "new quest") of the 1950s and 60s. See Wright and Stephen Neill, *The Interpretation of the New Testament 1861–1986* (New York: Oxford University Press, 1988), 379–403.
3. See my essay, "A Renaissance in Jesus Studies," *Theology Today* 45 (1988): 280–92 [chapter 1 in the present volume]. See also James Charlesworth, *Jesus within Judaism* (New York: Doubleday, 1988), 9–29, 187–207, 223–43.
4. See my "A Temperate Case for a Non-Eschatological Jesus," *Foundations and Facets Forum* 2, no. 3 (1986): 98–99 [and in the present volume pp. 59–60].
5. In a paper presented at the International Meeting of the SBL in Vienna in August 1990, Robinson further described the imminent eschatological understanding of Jesus as an "old model which is frayed and blemished, with broken parts, a Procrustean bed in which the discipline squirms," and proposed instead a sapiential model.
6. So fruitful is this development that it marks a new era in Jesus scholarship. As Bernard Brandon Scott remarked at the meeting of the SBL in Chicago in December 1984: "The historical quest of the historical Jesus has ended; the interdisciplinary quest has just begun." For a bibliography of over 250 works that use interdisciplinary approaches, see Daniel Harrington, "Second Testament Exegesis and the Social Sciences: A Bibliography," *Biblical Theology Bulletin* 18 (1988): 77–85.
7. E. P. Sanders, *Jesus and Judaism* (Philadelphia: Fortress, 1985).
8. Ibid., 11. The other seven are: (1) Jesus was baptized by John the Baptist; (2) Jesus was a Galilean who preached and healed; (3) Jesus called disciples and spoke of there being twelve; (4) Jesus confined his activity to Israel; (5) and he was crucified by Roman authorities. After his death, (6) his followers continued

as an identifiable movement, and (7) at least some Jews persecuted some parts of the new movement.

9. Mark 11:15–17. Sanders rightly notes that it is often erroneously called the "cleansing" of the temple, as if the issue were purification or reform. Such a reading domesticates the act: Jesus becomes a defender of "pure religion" against the corruption of business practices.

10. Sanders, *Jesus and Judaism,* esp. 61–76.

11. Ibid., 146–48. See Matt. 19:28, with a near parallel in Luke 22:28–29. One of the virtues of Sanders's construal of Jesus is that it can make sense of this difficult verse. For a quite different understanding of it, see the treatment by Horsley later in this article.

12. Imminent eschatology is even central for Jesus' self-claim. Though Sanders agrees with most scholars that the traditions that report Jesus affirming himself to be Messiah and Son of God must be viewed as the creation of the church, he argues that many traditions point to a strong implicit self-claim: Jesus may have thought of himself as king, or as soon-to-be king of the coming kingdom ("a strong inference," ibid., 307, 321–22, 324), and as "God's last messenger" (318).

13. Sanders, *Jesus and Judaism,* esp. 24–51. See also his *Paul and Palestinian Judaism: A Comparison of Patterns of Religion* (Philadelphia: Fortress, 1977).

14. Given that this understanding has come largely from German scholarship, Jesus' relationship to Judaism has perhaps unconsciously been seen as a version of Luther's relationship to late medieval Catholicism.

15. Sanders, *Jesus and Judaism,* esp. 270–93; see also 294–318. For Jesus' "self-claim," see n. 12 above.

16. Sanders's construal resembles Schweitzer's in three important respects. First, as with Schweitzer, Sanders holds that Jesus expected the coming of the kingdom of God as a decisive event to be brought about by God in the immediate future; imminent eschatology remains (see ibid., 142–48, 152–54, 318, 327). Second, Jesus' purpose in going to Jerusalem was to accomplish the decisive deed that would bring about dramatic divine intervention (for Schweitzer, Jesus' own death; for Sanders, the symbolic destruction of the temple). Third, it follows that Jesus was deeply mistaken about the central expectation that drove his ministry. What Jesus expected to happen did not happen: his belief in restoration eschatology was a mistake (ibid., 327). Sanders seeks to differentiate his position from Schweitzer, chiefly by claiming stronger evidence for his portrait; see ibid., 327–30.

17. Burton L. Mack, A *Myth of Innocence: Mark and Christian Origins* (Philadelphia: Fortress, 1988).

18. Mack, *Myth of Innocence,* 56. Professor Mack has kindly sent me two as yet unpublished essays that treat the theme of Jesus as Cynic: "Cultural Critique in Antiquity: Diogenes the Cynic and Jesus," and "The Lord of the Logia: Savior or Sage?" Also relevant are his "The Kingdom Sayings in Mark," *Foundations and Facets Forum* 3 (1987): 3–47, and "The Kingdom That Didn't Come," in David J. Lull, ed., *SBL 1988 Seminar Papers* (Atlanta: Scholars Press, 1988), 608–35.

19. "Jesus as Cynic" was the topic of a major session at the Annual Meeting

of the SBL in November 1990. With some differences, the Cynic image has been developed in England by F. G. Downing, *Jesus and the Threat of Freedom* (London: SCM, 1987), and idem, *The Christ and the Cynics* (Sheffield: Sheffield Academic Press, 1988).

20. A *chreia* is a common Cynic form. An anecdote about a teacher, it typically consists of an objection and response.

21. Mack, *Myth of Innocence*, 54.

22. Mack, "Cultural Critique in Antiquity," 9.

23. Mack, *Myth of Innocence*, 125.

24. See also Mack, "Kingdom Sayings in Mark." Mack's argument that Mark 1:15 is responsible for the impression that kingdom of God was the *central message* of Jesus needs to be taken seriously. Though scholars have long recognized that Mark 1:15 is redactional, many yet continue to treat it as an accurate summary of Jesus' message. Without Mark 1:15, would we see kingdom of God as the central message of Jesus or simply as a major theme or metaphor?

25. Mack applies this criterion rigorously. He sees social formation not only in texts that reflect institutionalization (e.g., Matt. 16:16–20 and 18:18), but in all texts reporting conflict with groups: they involve boundary definition.

26. Mack also locates Jesus in a very Hellenized Jewish social world, emphasizing the Hellenization of Galilee and that Cynics and Cynic traditions were known there.

27. Mack, *Myth of Innocence*, 73.

28. There is a friendly joke circulating among Jesus scholars: Burton Mack's Jesus was killed in a car accident on a freeway in Los Angeles. The point: for Mack, there is no significant connection between what Jesus was like and the fact that he was executed. His death was, in an important sense, accidental.

29. For example, in the work of Robert Funk, John Dominic Crossan, and Bernard Brandon Scott.

30. His foundational presupposition that the different forms of the tradition could not all be remembered in the same community seems doubtful to me. In the only way I have been able to understand it, it seems obviously false. In talking with members of new religious movements with a living master, I have found that the same people tell different kinds (forms) of stories about the master. Sometimes they quote a short saying of the master, sometimes they tell a story about the master, and sometimes they tell a story that the master told. Without Mack's foundational presupposition, his minimalist portrait of Jesus begins to collapse (or, to change the metaphor, begins to burst because of expansion).

31. Elisabeth Schüssler Fiorenza, *In Memory of Her: A Feminist Theological Reconstruction of Christian Origins* (New York: Crossroad, 1983). Her construal of Jesus (like Mack's) is part of a larger work treating the origins of Christianity; most relevant to her sketch of Jesus and the earliest Jesus movement are pp. 72–159.

32. Ibid., 70–71.

33. Ibid., 71; pp. 72–84 provide a useful summary and critical evaluation of

the use of such heuristic models by Robin Scroggs, John Gager, Gerd Theissen, Wayne Meeks, etc.

34. Androcentrism refers to a perspective, patriarchy to a social system. See ibid., 29: "While androcentrism characterizes a mindset, patriarchy represents a social-cultural system in which a few men have power over other men, women, children, slaves and colonialized people."

35. She stresses that we know Jesus only through the community around him and repudiates any attempt "to distill the historical Jesus from the remembering interpretations of his first followers." Thus she does not pursue a historical Jesus separate from his followers, but Jesus "as his life and ministry is available to historical-critical reading of the earliest interpretations of the first Christians" (ibid., 103; see also 121). Yet it seems clear that she thinks we do learn about Jesus (and not just about his followers) from the texts, for Jesus and the community around him are normative for her historical and theological reconstruction of Christian origins.

36. Ibid., 102, 100.

37. Ibid., 110–15. In this she largely follows her own earlier work and the work of Jacob Neusner. For her use of Neusner's description of woman as "the other" in the Mishnaic world-view, see pp. 56–60.

38. Schüssler Fiorenza repeatedly warns against simply identifying first-century Judaism with patriarchy. First, ancient Judaism was not monolithic in this respect; there is an alternative voice, a "feminist impulse," within Judaism (ibid., 107; see especially her striking treatment of Judith, 115–18). Second, patriarchy was of course found outside of Judaism as well, enabling her to emphasize that the problem was patriarchy, not Judaism.

39. Ibid., 118–30, 135.

40. Ibid., 140–54.

41. Ibid., 149–51.

42. "Sophia" is Greek for "wisdom"; in both Hebrew and Greek, "wisdom" is feminine.

43. Schüssler Fiorenza, *In Memory of Her,* 132. Given that she also recognizes that Jesus spoke of God in a man's *Gestalt* as "father," her point is not that Jesus used a woman's *Gestalt* to speak of God instead of a man's *Gestalt;* rather, he used both.

44. Ibid., 134–35.

45. Ibid., 142: Jesus' message subverts the structures of oppression by envisioning a different future.

46. Ibid., 119–20. See also 111–12, 121.

47. Ibid., 121.

48. Marcus J. Borg, *Conflict, Holiness and Politics in the Teachings of Jesus* (New York/Toronto: Edwin Mellen, 1984); idem, *Jesus: A New Vision* (San Francisco: Harper & Row, 1987).

49. I define politics in a broad and nonexclusionary sense, based upon its derivation from the Greek word for city (*polis*): politics is concern with the shape and shaping of the city and, by extension, of any human community. By nonexclusionary, I simply mean that to say Jesus was political does not exclude

anything else; it does not mean political and (therefore) not religious. To see the political dimension of Jesus' activity does not exclude seeing other dimensions.

50. Borg, *Conflict, Holiness and Politics,* 27–72. "Paradigm" is the term I most often use for the central value or cultural dynamic that structures a social world; for the same notion as "core value" and a lucid, compact analysis of first-century Jewish Palestine as a purity system, see Jerome Neyrey, "A Symbolic Approach to Mark 7," *Foundations and Facets Forum* 4, no. 3 (1988): 63–91, and idem, "The Idea of Purity in Mark's Gospel," *Semeia* 35 (1986): 91–128.

51. Lev. 19:2 contrasted to Luke 6:36. Given that "compassion" is etymologically linked to "womb" in Hebrew, it is tempting to translate Luke 6:36 as, "Be like a womb, as God is like a womb."

52. Her book was published while my *Conflict, Holiness and Politics* was in press. I would now incorporate most of her feminist insights.

53. Beginning with Norman Perrin's *Rediscovering the Teaching of Jesus* (New York: Harper & Row, 1967), esp. 164–206, these sayings have increasingly been seen as inauthentic in North American scholarship. The voting of the Jesus Seminar indicates how far the erosion of the "coming Son of man" sayings has gone: about 80 percent have consistently voted against their authenticity. The remaining threat and judgment texts in the synoptics do not point to the imminent end of the world, but are about evenly divided between threats of historical disaster and threats of unidentifiable or unspecified consequences. Though a few make use of eschatological motifs, they do not contain the element of imminence. See Borg, *Conflict, Holiness and Politics,* 203–21, esp. 210–12.

54. "Holy person" is the gender-inclusive version of the semitechnical term "holy man," a person who was a mediator of "the holy," that is, of the *numinous,* the uncanny *numina* that lie beneath phenomena and that are "known" in extraordinary moments.

55. Such persons, known throughout the history of cultures, have vivid experiences of the holy as another dimension or layer of reality, a sense of encountering or being touched by it, or entering or seeing into it. They then become mediators or agents of the holy, often as healers, but also as prophets, lawgivers, clairvoyants, diviners, oracles, rainmakers, and gamefinders.

56. Geza Vermes is primarily responsible for introducing this element into the current discussion; see especially his *Jesus the Jew* (New York: Macmillan, 1973), 65–78, 206–13. See also James G. Dunn, *Jesus and the Spirit* (Philadelphia: Westminster, 1975).

57. The tradition that Jesus was a healer and exorcist is very strong, as are traditions that suggest an unusual experiential intimacy with God and a sense of authority not grounded in institution or tradition. Moreover, the synoptic picture of him as a practitioner of prayer and fasting who sometimes experienced visions is plausible in this context. See Borg, *Jesus: A New Vision,* 39–75.

58. For an account of what we can surmise about first-century Jewish mysticism, see Alan Segal, *Paul the Convert: The Apostolate and Apostasy of Saul the Pharisee* (New Haven: Yale University Press, 1990), 34–71.

59. I argue that there are two focal points to this fourfold portrait: spirit

and social world. Jesus' relationship to the spirit was not only the source of his healing powers, but also the source of his sense of mission and of the perspective from which he spoke as a sage and prophet. His social world, rather than being the background of his activity as eschatological prophet or Cynic sage, was the center of his concern.

60. Richard Horsley and John S. Hanson, *Bandits, Prophets, and Messiahs: Popular Movements at the Time of Jesus* (Minneapolis: Winston, 1985); Richard Horsley, *Jesus and the Spiral of Violence* (San Francisco: Harper & Row, 1987); idem, *The Liberation of Christmas: The Infancy Narratives in Social Context* (New York: Crossroad, 1989); idem, *Sociology and the Jesus Movement* (New York: Crossroad, 1989).

61. The urban elites as landowners extracted money from peasants in the form of rent and taxes. Horsley points out that in Galilee there were three layers of taxation: the tithes mandated by the Torah, Herodian taxes, and finally those collected by the Romans.

62. Horsley, *Spiral of Violence,* 287; see also 285–306.

63. Ibid., 324.

64. Mack argues for the former, Gerd Theissen for the latter. Theissen (*Sociology of Early Palestinian Christianity* [Philadelphia: Fortress, 1978]) argues that the Jesus movement in Palestine consisted of two groups: itinerant charismatics (who were the authority figures) and communities of local sympathizers. The radical commands of the synoptic tradition were intended for the former. Much of Horsley's *Sociology and the Jesus Movement* is a critique of Theissen's approach. For Horsley's critique of the Cynic hypothesis in the same volume, see 116–19.

65. Horsley, *Spiral of Violence,* 246–55.

66. Ibid., 255–73.

67. Ibid., 231–45.

68. Ibid., 199–206.

69. Ibid., 143–44. See also 129–45.

70. Ibid., 160.

71. Ibid., 170–72, 190–92, 207. On p. 207, he writes: "God was imminently and presently effecting a historical transformation." Horsley's orientation toward a present understanding of the kingdom is signified by a wordplay: Jesus' words about the kingdom are not to be understood in the sense of last or final things, but in the sense of "Finally, at last!" (168).

72. Ibid., 324–25.

73. Ibid., 322.

74. It is interesting to note how the ghost of Schweitzer still walks. Despite the fact that Horsley provides a thoroughly historical way of reading both apocalyptic and the mission of Jesus, he seems to take for granted an imminent eschatology that requires assimilation.

75. In my own case, though I deny imminent eschatology, I do not exclude eschatology altogether from Jesus' message. In addition to speaking of the kingdom of God as a present power, Jesus apparently used kingdom language to refer to the eschatological banquet with Abraham, Isaac, and Jacob (Matt. 8:11–12; cf. Luke 13:28–29) and seems to have affirmed a life beyond death in

response to a question about resurrection (Mark 12:18–27). He seems to have spoken of a last judgment (e.g., the Q passages Luke 10:12–15, 11:31–32). However, these "events" were not said to be imminent; rather, in the judgment when it comes, the "men of this generation" will fare worse than Gentiles from the past. It is not said that the judgment is imminent. Instead, the function of these sayings seems to be to subvert or reverse popular eschatological expectations: the last judgment and the kingdom, when they come, will be very different from what is expected.

76. Most of the texts in both the Hebrew Bible and the New Testament that refer to a new world beyond the eschaton envision a continuing earth, for example, in Revelation: the New Jerusalem descends to a new or renewed earth. For one passage that envisions the meltdown and disappearance of the elements, see 2 Peter 3:10–12.

77. J. Carmignac, "Les dangers de l'eschatologie," *New Testament Studies* 7 (1970–71): 365–90, esp. 388–90.

78. For example, George Caird, *The Language and Imagery of the Bible* (London: Duckworth, 1980), 243–71, specifies seven different senses in which eschatology is used.

79. My own understanding of end-of-the-world eschatology (see above pp. 26, 70–71) need not involve the end of the earth; in the messianic age, the world of Jerusalem, banquets, and vineyards may remain. But it is an objective change of affairs that results in "everything being different," in such a way that even outsiders or non-believers will have to say, "Yes, you were right, the end was coming." (I owe this way of describing "objective" eschatology to a conversation with John Dominic Crossan.) Thus, when I deny imminent eschatology to Jesus, I am denying that he expected this kind of divine intervention in the near future.

80. Some of this work has already been done. See the report of the work on apocalyptic literature done within the SBL in the 1970s in John Collins, ed., *Apocalypse: The Morphology of a Genre, Semeia* 14 (1979), and idem, *The Apocalyptic Imagination* (New York: Crossroad, 1984).

81. See, for example, Bruce Chilton's work on kingdom language in the Targums in *God in Strength* (Linz: Plöchl, 1979). Also, Brian Rice McCarthy ("Jesus, The Kingdom, and Theopolitics," *SBL 1990 Seminar Papers* [Atlanta: Scholars Press, 1990], 311–21) suggests that the term would have had an intrinsically political meaning to the occasional hearers who were Jesus' audience.

82. There have been exceptions, of course, but they have not played much part in the scholarly discussion. For a review of scholarship's tendency to see Jesus' social stance within these two polarities, see my *Conflict, Holiness and Politics,* 4–17. Horsley also stresses this point in *Jesus and the Spiral of Violence.*

83. See also the insightful essay by Walter Wink, "Neither Passivity nor Violence: Jesus' Third Way," in David J. Lull, ed., *SBL 1988 Seminar Papers* (Atlanta: Scholars Press, 1988), 210–24; and idem, "Jesus and the Domination System," in David J. Lull, ed., *SBL 1991 Seminar Papers.*

84. Central to addressing these questions is a clearer understanding of Jesus'

social world, identified earlier in this essay as one of the central emphases of contemporary scholarship.

85. The connection between imminent eschatology and the denial of anything political to Jesus can also be seen in John P. Meier's recent essay, "Reflections on Jesus-of-History Research Today," in James H. Charlesworth, ed., *Jesus' Jewishness* (New York: Crossroad, 1991), 92: "Jesus seems to have had no interest in the great political and social questions of his day. He was not interested in the reform of the world because he was prophesying its end."

86. Published by Harper (San Francisco) in 1991. Early sales have been impressive. In the first eighteen months after publication in November 1991, it sold 55,000 copies, 33,000 in hardbound and 22,000 in paperback. This is remarkable for a scholarly book of some five hundred pages, which, moreover, is not easy to read. Crossan has been well-known in historical Jesus scholarship for the past twenty years, especially for his work on parables and aphorisms. See *In Parables: The Challenge of the Historical Jesus* (New York: Harper & Row, 1973); and *In Fragments: The Aphorisms of Jesus* (San Francisco: Harper & Row, 1983).

87. Also published by Harper San Francisco.

88. There is an ambiguity in his treatment, hinging on the distinction some medical anthropologists make between disease and illness. "Disease" is the physical condition, "illness" consists of the social meanings attributed to the physical condition. Did Jesus treat both? Did he cure disease as well as heal illness? Crossan clearly speaks of the latter, but not so clearly of the former. But can "healing illness" without "curing disease" make much sense in a peasant society? Are peasants (or anybody else, for that matter) likely to be impressed with the statement "your illness is healed" while the physical condition of disease remains?

89. Crossan, *The Historical Jesus,* 422.

90. Not included in this survey of North American portraits is volume one of John P. Meier's *A Marginal Jew: Rethinking the Historical Jesus* (New York: Doubleday, 1991). Volume 1 treats preliminary matters (sources, background, birth stories, etc.) and takes the reader only up to the beginning of Jesus' ministry; it does not contain Meier's sketch of the adult Jesus. Meier projects two more volumes, neither of which were yet published when this addendum was written.

Part Two

Issues in Contemporary Jesus Research

Chapter Three

A Temperate Case
for a Non-Eschatological Jesus

This paper virtually takes the form of a letter to my associates in the academy — most directly to my colleagues in Jesus studies, but also to colleagues in the disciplines of New Testament, introduction to religion, history of Christianity, theology, and the history of religions. In short, it is addressed to anybody who teaches (or preaches) about Jesus at all, even if only briefly for a period or less in an introductory religion course. It treats one of the "big" questions about Jesus and calls for a reexamination of the image of the historical Jesus which has dominated Jesus scholarship in this century. This image has been widely shared not only by those of us in New Testament studies but also by scholars in other disciplines who to a large extent depend upon us for their understanding of Jesus and early Christianity — just as we depend, for example, upon Buddhist specialists for our understanding of Buddhism.

Specifically the essay challenges the basic image of the historical Jesus as "the eschatological Jesus." Because I will use this phrase frequently, I want to define it both precisely and compactly at the outset. By it I mean an image or *Gestalt* of the historical Jesus which sees his mission and message within the framework of his expectation of the end of the world in his generation, understood in an objective and not purely subjective sense.[1] The purpose of the historical Jesus, according to this image, was to call his hearers to repent before it was too late, to ground themselves in God because the world was soon to pass away, indeed in that generation.

In my argument for a non-eschatological Jesus, I point to recent developments within our discipline which decisively undermine the foundation of the eschatological Jesus. This involves me in a treatment

This essay was first published in *Foundations & Facets Forum* 2, no. 3 (September 1986): 81–102.

of the themes of the "coming Son of man"[2] and the kingdom of God in the synoptic gospels. In a concluding section, I report the results of a poll which indicate that there is no longer a consensus among us regarding the eschatological Jesus and suggest some of the implications for us. But before describing the reasons for replacing the eschatological Jesus with a non-eschatological Jesus, I want to begin by speaking of the dominant position occupied by the former in our discipline.

1. The Dominance of the Eschatological Jesus

The eschatological Jesus entered the mainstream of biblical studies through the work of Johannes Weiss and Albert Schweitzer around the turn of this century. Many of the highly specific details of Schweitzer's reconstruction of the mission of Jesus have not been accepted by subsequent scholarship. For example, few scholars have agreed with Schweitzer's claim that Jesus initially expected the end of the world in the middle of his ministry and then, because it did not come, went to Jerusalem deliberately to provoke the authorities to kill him so that God would intervene and transform him into the eschatological Son of man. But Schweitzer's basic claim — that Jesus' ministry is to be understood within an eschatological framework — has become one of the paradigmatic convictions of New Testament scholarship.

Its dominance is particularly evident in German scholarship. In the work of Rudolf Bultmann and his "school," it constituted the core element of the portrait of Jesus and of Bultmann's demythologizing hermeneutic: Jesus was the proclaimer who proclaimed the imminent coming of the kingdom of God; and Jesus' proclamation of the imminent end points to the understanding of existence which Bultmann found to be central to Jesus' message. The eschatological Jesus is portrayed in Günther Bornkamm's *Jesus of Nazareth*, probably the most widely read scholarly book on Jesus in the thirty years since its publication. It continues to dominate German New Testament scholarship, including the work of "new generation" scholars such as Gerd Theissen.[3]

Especially indicative of the consensus in German scholarship is the treatment of the historical Jesus by Hans Küng. At the heart of his weighty and yet best-selling *On Being a Christian* is a lengthy section on the historical Jesus.[4] His account is brilliant, thick with incisive insights and quotable phrases which catch some of the passion of the gospels themselves. Yet running throughout is a picture of Jesus as one who expected the end of the world in his generation.[5] What makes Küng's work so illustrative of the consensus is that he is not a New Testament scholar but a systematic theologian. His treatment of Jesus is grounded in what he perceives the consensus of New Testament scholarship to be; it provides the historical data with which he works theologically.[6]

The consensus extends beyond Germany, of course. Two works on the kingdom of God published in 1963 — one by the Swedish scholar Gösta Lundström and the other by Norman Perrin, an Englishman trained in Germany who spent much of his teaching and publishing career in the United States — both made the eschatological understanding of the kingdom central to their exposition and evaluation of previous research.[7] Whether or not scholars recognized that Jesus used the phrase "kingdom of God" in an *eschatological* sense was one of the primary criteria for assessing their scholarly contribution. The eschatological understanding of the kingdom (and Jesus) had become one of the "results" of scholarship in light of which the history of scholarship could now be seen.

The extent to which the eschatological Jesus has become one of the paradigmatic convictions within New Testament studies can be seen in the many guises in which he appears. For Bultmann and many in both Germany and elsewhere who were affected by the German tradition, Jesus was the proclaimer of the end who called his hearers to an existential decision for God. For more recent scholars in this tradition, his message (including its forms, especially parables and aphorisms) brought "end-of-world" to those who responded to it. Even scholars who have emphasized a political dimension to Jesus' message often work within the eschatological paradigm. S. G. F. Brandon, for example, in his trilogy which argued that Jesus was a Zealot sympathizer, saw the cleansing of the temple as Jesus' purification of the temple for the coming kingdom of God, understood as an imminent supernatural event.[8] More recently, William Herzog has sought to align Jesus' apocalyptic message with liberation theology.[9]

Thus the normative pattern for speaking about Jesus both within the guild of Jesus scholars and in disciplines which make use of our work is to speak of him and his message as eschatological. However, the consensus is not unanimous, and indeed there are signs that it no longer is one, as I shall report later. But before turning to the reasons for calling it into question, it may be relevant to tell my own story of how I moved from an initial acceptance of the eschatological Jesus to my present understanding.

My own impression of the dominance of the eschatological Jesus as the "orthodox" image of Jesus in our discipline began with my first year in divinity school (Union Theological Seminary, New York, in 1964). Like many of us, I went to graduate school without really knowing that there was a question here. I had heard of Albert Schweitzer, but mostly as a medical missionary and modern saint whose "reverence for life" perhaps extended even into the insect and micro-organic kingdoms. I did not know what he had said about the kingdom of God. My professor at Union was W. D. Davies, a Welshman trained in England with intellectual kinship to C. H. Dodd, the "dean" of British New Testament studies and famous for his rejection of Schweitzer's position with his own case for "realized eschatology." I cannot recall if Davies took sides on this issue; but the reading which we were assigned certainly did. Much of it was German.

There was (and is) something impressive about German scholarship. The great names of our discipline are disproportionately German, a tribute to the study of theology in German universities. I read Schweitzer and Bultmann and Bornkamm and Conzelmann, impressive writers all. The "hot" book in synoptic studies was Tödt's *The Son of Man in the Synoptic Tradition;* there I learned that the only significant remaining question about the "coming Son of man" sayings was whether Jesus was referring to his own coming as the "Son of man" or whether he was referring to a future figure other than himself.[10]

And so, despite the fact that my mentor was British, I came to believe that Jesus expected the end of the world in his own generation. The picture painted by German scholarship was consistent with what I was learning about the early church as well; it was an eschatological community, and many early Christians, including Paul, expected the world to end soon. Dodd and other scholars influenced by the "British school" seemed to me to be fighting a rearguard action, sniping at the main column as it marched by. Besides, there was something unconvincing about "realized eschatology." Though I could understand the argument for saying that the kingdom of God was proclaimed by Jesus as a *present* reality, as soon as I tried to *think* of it as present, it vanished. I could not figure out what was present that could legitimately be called the kingdom of God. The inability to see may have been in me rather than in Dodd's exposition; I am not sure.

Then I went off to Oxford for a year and studied with George Caird. In his lectures and tutorials, Caird frequently took potshots at German scholarship, especially calling into question the eschatological Jesus. I found his thrusts and parries provocative and enjoyed them immensely, but finally did not find them persuasive. I listened to other students talking about Caird "defending the walls of Oxford against the German invasion"; and, horror of horrors, the walls had already been breached in the figure of Dennis Nineham, rumored to be a "Bultmannian."[11]

Though I still thought the British were probably wrong on this issue, I returned to Oxford three years later for the doctorate with Caird as my thesis supervisor. During those years, I came to believe that a respectable case could be made for a non-eschatological Jesus, and it was one of the themes of my thesis.[12] At the time I considered my position one that could reasonably be defended, but perhaps not convincing outside a circle of scholarship already favorably disposed to it.

Over the years, however, in part because of my own continuing study and even more so because of the work of others, I have become convinced that the evidence really does lie in favor of a non-eschatological Jesus.[13] I do not know finally what to make of this emerging conviction; it is possible that it is the product of a way of seeing that has now become habituated. We never know, as one of my colleagues put it, when what we think is the philosopher's stone might turn out to be our pet rock.[14] I want to be corrected if I am off target, confirmed if I am headed in the right direction, encouraged if this seems important but unresolved.

In any case, my own turn-about from affirming an eschatological Jesus to seeing Jesus in non-eschatological terms has been the product of three factors: (1) the realization that the primary foundation of the eschatological Jesus is the "coming Son of man" sayings, and that these are now commonly viewed by scholars as inauthentic — not part of the words of Jesus; (2) a second realization, namely, that the understanding of the kingdom of God as the imminent end of the world is without basis in the kingdom texts themselves; imminence has to be imported from the coming Son of man texts; (3) a rethinking of the kingdom of God that seeks to place it in a framework other than the temporal paradigm of present/future which has dominated much of twentieth-century scholarship.

2. The "Coming Son of Man" Sayings

A number of sayings in the gospels speak of a future coming of the "Son of man," portrayed as a figure of the end-time who will play a critical role in the final judgment, as either advocate or judge. His coming is often associated with angels or the clouds of heaven. Judgment, coming, and angels are all found in one of the classic texts:

> For whoever is ashamed of me and of my words in this adulterous and sinful generation, of him will the *Son of man* also be ashamed, when he comes in the glory of his Father with the holy angels.[15]

Not all of the coming Son of man sayings speak of the coming as imminent, but some do. Mark 13:24–30 speaks of the heavenly bodies being darkened and falling, the coming of the Son of man in clouds with the angels, and then affirms, "This generation will not pass away before all these things take place."

These sayings have been the foundation for the eschatological Jesus from the beginning. They were central for Schweitzer, for whom Jesus was essentially one who believed that he himself was the "coming Son of man" who would soon judge the world and rule over the new world. The element of imminence came especially (though not exclusively) from Matt. 10:23, in which Jesus said to the disciples as he sent them out on a missionary journey in the midst of the ministry, "Truly, I say to you, you will not have gone through all the towns of Israel before the Son of man comes." Though much of subsequent scholarship has rejected the authenticity of this passage in particular,[16] the conviction that Jesus proclaimed the imminent coming of the Son of man (whether himself or another) has continued in the works of Bultmann, Kümmel, Tödt, Jeremias, and others. All of them accepted the authenticity of some (at least) of the coming Son of man sayings, and in one way or another made them central to their understanding of Jesus' message and mission.

It is important to realize how central the coming Son of man sayings are for this position. Without them, there is very little in the gospels which would lead us to think that Jesus expected the end of the world soon. The notion that Jesus did proclaim the end flows from the connection made in the texts between the "coming Son of man" and "supernatural" end-time phenomena such as the last judgment, the sending of the angels, the clouds of heaven, the darkening of the sun and moon, and the falling of the stars. If one did not think these sayings were authentic, most of the exegetical foundation for the eschatological Jesus would disappear.

Yet exactly this has happened in much of New Testament scholarship over the past two decades. The undermining of these sayings has occurred through the convergence of three lines of argument, any one of which alone would be enough. First, an increasing number of scholars no longer think any of the "coming Son of man" sayings is authentic. This movement was perhaps signaled by Norman Perrin in his *Rediscovering the Teaching of Jesus*, published in 1967. There Perrin argued that these sayings were the product of Christian scribal interpretation of Dan. 7:13–14 in the decades following Easter.[17] After a lengthy treatment, he concluded: "the apocalyptic Son of man tradition has itself developed from an early Christian interpretation of the resurrection and early Christian passion apologetic."[18] His conclusion has been increasingly accepted, recently by Barnabas Lindars in his 1983 book.[19]

Second, there is increasing agreement that "Son of man" was not a designation in early first-century Judaism for a supernatural or end-of-the-world figure. The assumption that it was such a designation reached both its zenith and nadir in Colpe's essay on the "Son of man" published in one of the widely used dictionaries in our field. Colpe granted that no existing Jewish source provides any evidence for a "supernatural" Son of man associated with the end of the world; and then he argued that we must posit a missing source to account for it.[20] His argument thus shows how deeply ingrained the assumption has been. The fact that there is no evidence that the phrase had any special meaning in Jewish literature of the time has led other scholars to draw the more obvious conclusion, and it is now routine to say that "Son of man" was not an apocalyptic title in Judaism.[21] Thus Jesus could not have used this phrase as a "shorthand" way of referring to a figure of the end-time, whether to himself in a transformed state or to somebody other than himself.

Third, Geza Vermes has argued convincingly on linguistic grounds that the phrase "Son of man" in Aramaic not only had no pre-Christian titular usage, but was such a common idiom that it could not have been heard by the hearers of Jesus as having special or titular significance.[22] The upshot of these last two lines of argument is that language about a "coming Son of man" (whether referring to Jesus or a figure other than himself) would not have been intelligible to Jesus' audience. However, it would have been intelligible in the early church after Easter as a way of speaking of their belief in the second coming of Jesus, a point we shall return to in the fourth section of this essay.

With the disappearance of the coming Son of man sayings as authentic words of Jesus, the primary exegetical reason for thinking that Jesus expected the imminent end of the world disappears. Yet this implication is often not seen, perhaps because it is often thought that it is Jesus' proclamation of the kingdom of God that is the main exegetical basis for the eschatological Jesus. But, as we shall see, there is very little in Jesus' kingdom proclamation that refers to an imminent end.

3. The Kingdom of God

As virtually every scholar affirms, the kingdom of God is the central focal point of Jesus' proclamation, of both his mission and message. The coming of the kingdom is the core of Mark's advance summary of the gospel: "Repent, for the kingdom of God is at hand."[23] It is widespread throughout the synoptic tradition in diverse forms: parables, proverbs, beatitudes, controversy stories. But how is it to be understood?

From the time of Schweitzer, it has largely been understood to refer to "the end of the world," i.e., eschatologically. Having made the coming Son of man sayings central to understanding the mission of Jesus, Schweitzer attached the imminence associated with them to the notion of the kingdom of God, and both "imminence" and "end of the world" have remained connected to the kingdom ever since. To be sure, in part because of C. H. Dodd's emphasis on "realized eschatology," scholarship by mid-century had begun to speak of the kingdom as *both* present and future; this was the great synthesis noted by both Perrin and Lundström in their histories of research. But even within this synthesis, it seemed that the future kingdom received greater emphasis.[24] That was what was near, the imminent arrival of the kingdom-as-end and, it would be added, the powers of that coming kingdom were already in some sense present in the ministry. The future dimension provided the essential definition or the clearest conception. *It* was the main thing, and because it was coming it could be "proleptically realized" in Jesus.

Yet the association of imminence, end of the world, and kingdom is not justified by the kingdom texts themselves. It is very striking that "kingdom of God" and "the coming Son of man" are not found in the same texts; they seem to represent two quite distinct traditions.[25] Thus it is illegitimate uncritically to transfer the imminence associated with the coming Son of man to the kingdom of God sayings.

Moreover, the kingdom of God sayings by themselves do not have the element of imminence in them. The sayings do use the language of time to speak of the kingdom (as near, as present, and as future), but what is lacking is a clear link between the coming of the kingdom and the end of the world temporally tied to that generation. The one apparent exception to this statement is Mark 9:1: "Truly, I say to you, there are some standing here who will not taste death before they see the kingdom of God come with power." The verse is not without its problems. It is not clear that the coming of the kingdom in power refers to the end of the world; the verse permits a number of interpretations[26] and is sometimes viewed as inauthentic.[27] In any case, one verse is a slender thread upon which to hang such a weighty case.

To repeat, without the coming Son of man sayings, there is no reason to think of the kingdom of God as the imminent end of the world. "End of the world" imagery and imminence are connected together only in the coming Son of man sayings. They are not found together in the kingdom of God sayings. The texts do associate "end of the world" imagery with the kingdom (e.g., in the parables of judgment and the image of the messianic banquet); but it is not said that this is imminent. So also in other texts in the gospels which speak of "end-time" events; the element of imminence is missing. Especially illuminating are a number of last judgment sayings, in which Jesus warned his hearers that Gentiles from the past (the men of Nineveh, the queen of Sheba) would arise at the judgment and testify against the "men of this generation"; but it is not said that "this generation" will live until then.[28] Indeed, the most natural way to read the texts is to suppose that both "this generation" and the Gentiles from the past will need to be raised at the judgment. Jesus, like many of his Jewish contemporaries, apparently believed that history had a final judgment at its boundary, but neither this nor the "final" kingdom of God is said to be imminent.

The notion that the kingdom of God is the imminent eschatological kingdom is thus without foundation in the kingdom texts. The element of imminence has to be imported from the coming Son of man sayings. Yet modern scholarship has found the coming Son of man sayings to be inauthentic without substantially calling into question the picture of an imminent kingdom (and an eschatological Jesus).[29] The lesson to be learned is clear: when one discards something as major as the coming Son of man sayings, one had best take another look at one's data base.

This completes the case for saying that there is no convincing exegetical basis for understanding Jesus' proclamation of the kingdom of God as involving the imminent end of the world. Yet, in part because it seems slightly unsatisfactory to conclude on a negative note without at least suggesting the presence of a satisfactory alternative, and in part because I find it interesting, I wish to sketch an alternative briefly. It is only a sketch; to provide anything like a full treatment would go far beyond the scope of this essay. Moreover, as a sketch it is more like an alternative framework within which many different and more precise elaborations could be spun.

The way toward a compelling alternative is pointed to by Norman Perrin's final work, published ten years ago in the year of his death.[30] There he argued that the phrase "kingdom of God" was a *symbol*, whose purpose was to evoke a myth. It has been a persistent mistake of Jesus scholarship, he argues, to think of the term "kingdom" as pointing to a *concept* (e.g., as the end of the world, or the rule of God in the human heart, or the "brotherhood of man"). Instead, it was a symbol which evoked Israel's myth (or story) of God's kingship over Israel and the world. That story contained several elements. As king, God created the universe and the earth, and then created Israel in the exodus event. As king, God continued to rule in the present, even though the divine rule often seemed puzzlingly obscured or eclipsed. As king, God both invited and commanded the Jewish people to put themselves under the divine kingship (to take upon themselves the "yoke" of the kingdom). Finally, as king God would one day establish the everlasting kingdom of compassion and justice, which would involve the judgment of both Israel and the nations. In short, the phrase "kingdom of God" evoked the whole story of God's relationship to Israel and humankind. We can also see why Perrin stresses that kingdom is a *tensive* symbol, i.e., one with a number of nuances of meaning. It does not have a singular meaning, but resonates with the various meanings which Israel's story of God's kingship combined.

Fruitful as Perrin's work is, it needs to be taken one step further. In order to understand this myth, it is helpful to see it as one form of an even more basic way of understanding reality, namely, as a particular cultural form of what Huston Smith has called the "primordial tradition."[31] The "primordial tradition" (a root metaphor?) is a way of "imaging" reality that appears in a multiplicity of cultural forms (indeed, in virtually as many cultural forms as there are cultures; Smith refers to it as almost a cultural universal, the "human unanimity" prior to the modern period).[32] Essential to it are two central claims. First, in addition to the visible material world disclosed to us by ordinary sense perception (and modern science), there is another dimension or level or layer of reality. It is the image of reality as having, minimally, two levels, "this world" and a "world of Spirit."[33] Moreover, the "other world" — the world of Spirit — is seen as "more" real than "this world." Indeed, the "other reality" is the source or ground of "this world." Second, and very importantly, the "other world" is not simply an article of belief, but an element of experience. That is, the notion of another reality does not have its origin in pre-modern speculation (or anxiety), but it is grounded in the religious experience of humankind.[34] It is not merely "believed in," but known.

Most basically, myths are stories which seek to speak about the other world and its relationship to this one.[35] Israel spoke about the relationship between the two worlds with its story of the kingship of God. That story affirmed that "this world" had its origin in the power and sovereignty of God. God's kingship continued into the present; even now the world was ruled by God. Moreover, Israel affirmed that the "other world" and "this world" were connected, intersecting at a number of points: historically, especially in the exodus and the return from exile, though also in other central events of Israel's history; personally, in Spirit-filled mediators such as Moses and the prophets, as well as in the devotional and non-ordinary experience (visions and hierophanies) of less prominent figures; cultically, in the temple of Jerusalem, the *axis mundi* or navel of the earth connecting this world to the other world which was its source. Israel also affirmed that one day "this world" and the "other world" would be visibly reunited, i.e., that the kingdom of God would come in some final sense. "End of the world" is thus one nuance of meaning, but only one. In Israel's story of God's kingship, the two worlds are related to each other at the beginning (creation), in the present (the "other world" can be known and experienced), and at the end (consummation).

The primordial tradition is not completely palatable to modern tastes. Indeed, in many ways it was the understanding of reality which needed to be overthrown in order for the modern age to begin. The Western Enlightenment increasingly saw reality as basically one-dimensional, and we in the academy are to a large extent the product of the Enlightenment. It is interesting that it is precisely the primordial tradition which Bultmann thought needed demythologizing. The "three story" model of the universe found in the imagery of the New Testament is a form of the primordial tradition, one which used spatial and vertical imagery. Bultmann objected quite properly that it cannot be taken "literally" (almost geographically). But he failed to see that it was meant ontologically — i.e., as an affirmation of the reality of another world, a world of "Spirit."[36] Perhaps our difficulty in comprehending Jesus' proclamation of the kingdom has flowed from the modern antipathy toward taking seriously the reality of a world of "Spirit." But if one does, then Jesus' proclamation of the kingdom forms a coherent whole.

Put most simply, within the framework of the primordial tradition, "kingdom of God" was for Jesus a symbol pointing to the kingship of God — the divine power and sovereignty, compassion and justice. The reality of God as king could be known, and the power of the Spirit (God acting as king) could flow into this world. Kingdom could also refer to the way of being engendered by that reality — joy, compassion, purity of heart. Moreover, the image of kingdom suggests that that way of being was communal and not simply individual. Finally, kingdom was also a symbol for the final state, "paradise restored." The most satisfactory understanding of the kingdom of God is one in which "end of the world" becomes one nuance among many, rather than being the defining nuance. The final kingdom is part of Israel's story about the kingship of God, but kingdom-as-end was not the central element in Jesus's message. Nor did he say that kingdom-as-end was imminent. Jesus did not emphasize a future act of God (the end of the world), but emphasized the present kingly power of God and invited his hearers to "enter" it and have their lives shaped by it.[37] The story of God's kingship, understood as Israel's version of the primordial tradition, thus provides a "home" within which Jesus' language about the kingdom can be understood. It refers to the kingship of God at the beginning of time, in the present, and at the end of time; and to life in that kingdom, i.e., to a way of being created by the kingship of God.

Whatever is thought about this alternative framework for understanding Jesus' use of the symbol "kingdom," I do not wish it to detract from the main thread of this argument. That thread is the claim that there is no significant exegetical basis for the eschatological Jesus. To that main thread we now return.

4. Some Clarifying Remarks

There are two further elements in the New Testament which have sometimes been thought to point to an eschatological Jesus. One of these is the church's expectation of the end of the world in that generation; the second is the element of crisis in the synoptic tradition.

The argument that Jesus proclaimed neither the imminent coming of the Son of man nor the imminent final kingdom may be thought to leave unexplained the church's expectation of the end. Some (at least) expected the "end of the world" in their generation, including the resurrection of the dead, the last judgment, and the "new heavens and new earth." Where did this expectation come from? It is tempting — and even "natural" — to think of it as a continuation of Jesus' proclamation of the imminent end. Thus the expectation of the early church is often seen as evidence for what Jesus himself expected.

But the expectation of the early church does not need to be grounded in Jesus' own expectation. Indeed, another ground seems more likely. The church's expectation of the "last things" is more plausibly understood as a post-Easter development, a deduction based upon the Easter event itself. As is well-known, "resurrection" (as distinct from resuscitation) in Judaism was an event expected at the end of time. To some within the church, the fact that a resurrection had occurred was an indicator that the general resurrection must be near; Christ was the "first fruits" of those to be raised from the dead.

Moreover, the church did not talk about the imminent coming of the kingdom; neither did it speak simply about the end of the world in a general way. Rather, it spoke of the imminent end of the world only in connection with the return of Jesus. The belief in the imminent end of the world appears in the context of the belief in the second coming; it does not appear independently. Rather than supposing that the expectation of the imminent end of the world originated with Jesus, it is more plausible to affirm that it originated with the expectation of his return.

Furthermore, as already noted, language about a "coming Son of man" who would function as advocate or judge at the last judgment is not intelligible in the pre-Easter setting of the ministry. But it is intelligible in the post-Easter setting of the early church, by which time the church spoke of the second coming of Jesus using the language and imagery of Daniel 7. The one who had been victimized and judged had now been vindicated and would return for judgment. The "coming Son of man" sayings express the church's expectation of Jesus' return, of his "second coming." The expectation of the imminent end of the world thus originates with the church's expectation of Jesus' return as Son of man. The belief in the imminent end of the world is best understood as a post-Easter development.

Finally, it is important not to exaggerate the extent to which the early church was an "end-time" community. Despite the explicit statements affirming an imminent end, it is not clear that this was very central (except, perhaps, in the book of Revelation). The letters of Paul and the gospel of John, for example, both contain such explicit statements, but clearly the emphasis of both authors is on the present as a time when the reality of God can be known, and not upon the future.[38] The image of the church as an intense eschatological community struggling with the delay of the parousia goes beyond our sources. Thus I do not deny that some in the church thought the end was at hand; but I do not think their conviction originated with Jesus.

Nor do I deny the element of crisis running through the synoptics. But the crisis is not the imminent end of the world; it becomes that only if one reads the crisis sayings in light of the coming Son of man sayings. Rather, the crisis is the end of the world of conventional wisdom as a basis for existence, as well as the threatened end of the "social world" of Judaism (including the threat of war and the destruction of Jerusalem and the temple).[39] The crisis of the ministry flowed out of the radicality of Jesus' teaching in a time when the sociopolitical stakes were high. There is a sense in which the mission of Jesus does bring about the end of a world, both in a "world-deconstructing" way and in the sense of the birth of a new age or new way of being. But there is no reason to think that he also proclaimed the imminent end of the world of history.

5. The Consensus in Collapse?

Throughout this essay I have spoken as if there were a virtual unanimity within scholarship regarding the eschatological Jesus. That is not quite the case, as I shall soon mention. But it was (and to a large extent, still is) the German consensus when most of us (and our colleagues in other religious disciplines) received our formative scholarly education. We (or at least I) received the consensus as one of the "results" of research, one of those foundation stones that did not need to be quarried again.

There have consistently been exceptions to the eschatological Jesus from his conception onwards. There were Dodd and Caird in the British school, for example, as well as other scholars.[40] There are also signs that it is weakening or dying the death of a thousand qualifications. The later Perrin (as well as others) made the future dimension much less specific and definite, almost to the point of denying "temporality" to it.[41] In other works, "eschatology" is understood in other than an end of the world and judgment sense. Two recent Roman Catholic works sharply call it into question. Edward Schillebeeckx in his recent massive book on the historical Jesus denies that Jesus had in mind the approaching end of the world: "No historically firm evidence allows us to argue this with any degree of cogency." He adds, "It nowhere appears from the texts that Jesus identifies this coming (of the kingdom of God), this drawing near, with the end of the world."[42] G. S. Sloyan reaches the same conclusion in his more introductory work.[43]

A poll of scholars in our own discipline also suggests that the consensus is weakening. Indeed, it discloses that there is no consensus, but a relatively even division that actually tilts toward a negative verdict. In preparation for the writing of this paper, I decided to take a simple poll of two groups of Jesus scholars, the thirty "charter fellows" of the Jesus Seminar and forty-two participants in the Historical Jesus Section of the Society of Biblical Literature.[44] I asked a single question, with four options for response:[45]

> Do you think Jesus expected the end of the world *in his generation,* i.e., in the lifetime of at least some of his contemporaries?[46]
>
> Strongly think so ____
>
> Inclined to think so ____
>
> Inclined to think not ____
>
> Strongly do not think so ____

The division within the Jesus Seminar was almost exact. Of the twenty-one who responded (out of a total of thirty), ten thought so (strongly or inclined to), and eleven did not. The eighteen who responded (out of forty-two) from the Historical Jesus Section were less evenly divided: only six thought so, whereas twelve did not. Combining the two groups, sixteen thought so, twenty-three did not.[47] I am fully aware, of course, that historical issues cannot be settled by taking a vote; but such a poll does show what we think.

Thus no consensus exists, despite the appearance of one in much of our work. This has interesting implications for us, it seems to me. If no consensus exists, if this question is clearly up for grabs, we need to be clear about that, both for the sake of our own discipline and for the sake of scholars in other disciplines who depend upon our work.[48] Quite frankly, I was surprised by the results of the poll. More than half of us share a fundamental perception that Jesus probably did not expect the imminent end of the world. I would not have guessed that from my reading of the literature, and have sometimes felt like a maverick because of suggesting a non-eschatological framework for understanding the ministry of Jesus. It is good to know that I am not alone. In addition to being clear that no consensus exists, there is, of course, the need to look at this whole question very closely in order to discern which image is more historically compelling.

Beyond that, the disappearance of the consensus creates exciting possibilities for us. There is the opportunity to construct a variety of images of a non-eschatological Jesus. Just as the eschatological Jesus has appeared in many guises, so the task of historical clarification and il-lumination will require a variety of portraits of a non-eschatological Jesus. There is the excitement of looking at texts in new ways and of doing our more detailed studies without presuming the validity of the eschatological framework as a paradigmatic conviction.[49]

As we engage in these tasks, I think it is likely that the question of Jesus' relationship to culture — both to culture understood as "conventional wisdom" and culture understood as "social world" — will become more prominent in our work. To a considerable extent, we have not dealt much with that question in this century, at least partly because the eschatological Jesus obscured that question. We have tended to assume that, because Jesus proclaimed the end of the world, he was therefore not interested in questions pertaining to a continuing social and historical order. But if we see Jesus non-eschatologically, then those questions return as significant questions. The movement which Jesus began will be seen not as an end-of-the-world movement unconcerned with culture, but as a "contrast-society" or "alternative community,"[50] a community seeking to live in history under the kingship of God.

Notes

1. There is a need to define the phrase precisely because of the wide range of meanings that the word "eschatology" has come to have. As a number of scholars have noted, "eschatology" is one of those words that have lost all precise exegetical meaning; see, e.g., J. C. Beker, "Biblical Theology Today," *New Theology Number Six,* ed. M. Marty and D. G. Peerman (New York: Macmillan, 1969), 27; J. Carmignac, "Les dangers de l'eschatologie," *New Testament Studies* 17 (1970/71), *passim,* but especially 388–90. I am defining it to include as an indispensable element the notion that the world itself will come to an end, including the traditional expectation of last judgment, resurrection, and dawn of the new age. *The eschatological Jesus is one who thought this was imminent.* Thus, with the term "eschatological," I do not mean "end" in more metaphorical senses, either in the sense of a dramatic change in Israel's history, or in the sense of a radical change in the individual's subjectivity which one might describe by speaking of the (old) world coming to an end for that individual. When these meanings are meant, I think other adjectives are more apt than "eschatological." See also my *Conflict, Holiness and Politics in the Teaching of Jesus* (New York: Edwin Mellen Press, 1984), 10–13.

2. For those readers to whom the technical phrase the "coming Son of man" may be unfamiliar, a number of sayings attributed to Jesus speak about a "Son of man" coming in the future, often explicitly associated with end-of-the-world phenomena. The meaning will be elaborated further in section 2 of this paper. Classic texts are Mark 8:38, Luke 12:8–9, Mark 13:24–27, Mark 14:62, Matt. 10:23.

3. See especially Gerd Theissen, *Sociology of Early Palestinian Christianity* (Philadelphia: Fortress Press, 1978). Theissen's book is the finest introduction to the Jesus movement in its Palestinian setting known to me.

4. Hans Küng, *On Being a Christian* (Garden City, N.Y.: Doubleday & Co., 1984). About half of the six hundred pages of text is devoted to Jesus.

5. *On Being a Christian*, esp. 216–20, where he stresses the element of immediacy: " . . . whether Jesus expected the advent of God's kingdom at his death or immediately after it" is unclear, but it is " . . . clear that he expected [it] in the immediate future" (216).

6. For Küng, that consensus is based almost exclusively on German scholarship. But the consensus would not have been much different if he had also taken into account North American scholarship.

7. Gösta Lundström, *The Kingdom of God in the Teaching of Jesus* (Edinburgh: Oliver and Boyd, 1963); Norman Perrin, *The Kingdom of God in the Teaching of Jesus* (Philadelphia: Westminster Press, 1963). For a similar comment on the significance of these two books, see Bruce Chilton's excellent introduction to the fine anthology which he recently edited, *The Kingdom of God in the Teaching of Jesus* (Philadelphia: Fortress Press, 1984), 16. Chilton also speaks of a "post-war consensus" on this issue (15).

8. See especially S. G. F. Brandon, *Jesus and the Zealots* (Manchester: University Press, 1967), 336–38. The other two books in his trilogy are *The Trial of Jesus* and *The Fall of Jerusalem and the Christian Church*.

9. William R. Herzog, "The Quest for the Historical Jesus and the Discovery of the Apocalyptic Jesus," *Pacific Theological Review* 19 (1985): 25–39. Herzog actually takes his essay in a direction very compatible with the thesis of this paper: he argues that Jesus' apocalyptic proclamation (which he does not deny) is not to be referred to the "natural" or "physical" world, but to the "social world" (see especially p. 32). I agree, but wonder if "apocalyptic" is a helpful way of designating such an expectation, for it requires using "apocalyptic" in a sense very different from its most common use.

10. H. E. Tödt, *The Son of Man in the Synoptic Tradition* (Philadelphia: Westminster Press, 1965). Tödt was not the first to treat this particular question, but I first encountered it in his book.

11. And now the walls have not only been breached, but Caird's own chair has been occupied. Caird's successor as Dean Ireland Professor at Oxford is E. P. Sanders, whose recent impressive book, *Jesus and Judaism* (Philadelphia: Fortress Press, 1985), unequivocally affirms a Jesus who expected the imminent restoration of Judaism in a full-blown eschatological sense. In his book which was the product of the Bampton Lectures given in Oxford in 1980, A. E. Harvey also affirms that Jesus spoke of the end of the world in his own time; see Harvey, *Jesus and the Constraints of History* (Philadelphia: Westminster Press, 1982), 86–90.

12. Borg, "Conflict as a Context for Interpreting the Teaching of Jesus," Ph.D. diss., Oxford University, 1972. The basic line of argument, thoroughly revised and expanded, is central to my 1984 book (see n. 1 above).

13. In addition to the 1984 book, see "The Historical Jesus and Christian Preaching," the *Christian Century* 102 (1985): 764–67; "An Orthodoxy Reconsidered: The 'End-of-the-World Jesus,' " in a memorial volume for George Caird (Oxford: Oxford University Press, forthcoming in 1986); and *Jesus: A New Vision* (San Francisco: Harper & Row, forthcoming), a book on the historical Jesus.

14. Nicholas Yonker, chair of Religious Studies at Oregon State University,

and author of an interesting book which falls into the category of "global theology" or "theology of religions": *God, Man, and the Planetary Age* (Corvallis: Oregon State University Press, 1978).

15. Mark 8:38; see Matt. 16:27 and Luke 12:8–9.

16. See my *Conflict, Holiness and Politics*, 366 n. 38, where I report the negative verdicts of Bultmann, Perrin, Bammel, Tödt, Higgins, Hahn, Fuller, Manson, and Kilpatrick.

17. Norman Perrin, *Rediscovering the Teaching of Jesus* (New York: Harper & Row, 1967), 164–206.

18. Ibid., 203; see also 198: "all [of the apocalyptic Son of man sayings] reveal themselves to be products of the early Church."

19. B. Lindars, *Jesus Son of Man* (Grand Rapids: Wm. B. Eerdmans, 1984). Lindars's argument differs from Perrin's in many ways; for example, he finds a number of the Son of man sayings which speak of the Son of man as *present* to be authentic; however, he agrees that the *coming* Son of man sayings are inauthentic. This represents a reversal of an earlier position he took in "Re-Enter the Apocalyptic Son of Man," *New Testament Studies* 22 (1976): 52–72. N. Thomas Wright takes the argument in a different direction. He argues that some of the coming Son of man sayings are authentic, but that they refer to a historical judgment upon Israel. Thus he denies them an "end-of-the-world" meaning. The details differ, but the result is the same; see his "Jesus, Israel and the Cross," *Society of Biblical Literature Papers* (Atlanta: Scholars Press, 1985).

20. Colpe, "ὁ υἱὸς τοῦ ἀνθρώπου" in *Theological Dictionary of the New Testament,* ed. Gerhard Friedrich and Gerhard Kittel (Grand Rapids: Wm. B. Eerdmans, 1972), 8:400–477. Apparently a draft was already complete by 1965 (Perrin, *Rediscovering the Teaching of Jesus,* 260).

21. R. Leivestad made this argument in 1967 in his provocatively entitled essay, "Der apokalyptische Menschensohn: ein theologisches Phantom," *Annual of the Swedish Theological Institute,* 6 (1967); he concludes that the apocalyptic Son of man is a phantom, a "theologische Erfindung der letzten hundert Jahre" (theological fabrication of the last hundred years; p. 101). See also his "Exit the Apocalyptic Son of Man," *New Testament Studies* 18 (1971/72): 243–67. Perrin also reached the same conclusion in 1967; see *Rediscovering the Teaching of Jesus,* 172–73, 260. Lindars similarly treats the "myth" of the apocalyptic Son of man on pp. 3–8 of *Jesus Son of Man.*

22. Geza Vermes, *Jesus the Jew* (New York: Macmillan, 1973), 160–91; see also pp. 89–99 of his *Jesus and the World of Judaism,* a shorter form of which appeared in *Journal of Jewish Studies* 29 (1978). Lindars, *Jesus Son of Man,* 17–28, reviews the linguistic argument and though he modifies Vermes's conclusion, he agrees that the linguistic evidence means that Jesus could not have used it in an apocalyptic titular sense.

23. Mark 1:15. Their importance for Mark can be seen in the fact that these are the first words attributed to Jesus in Mark, his "inaugural address."

24. Explicitly affirmed by Sanders, *Jesus and Judaism,* who affirms that Jesus spoke of the kingdom as both present and future and then adds, p. 154: "...if Jesus truly expected God to act decisively in the future, we must also assume that this expectation *dominated and controlled* his activity and message and

that *the future event is what primarily defines Jesus' view of 'the Kingdom'"* (italics added).

25. A quite obvious point when one examines the texts. The insight is often credited to P. Vielhauer in his essay, "Gottesreich und Menschensohn in der Verkundigung Jesus," in *Festschrift für Günther Dehn,* ed. W. Schneemelcher (Neukirchen: Verlag der Buchhandlung des Erziehungsvereins Neukirchen, 1957), 51–79. Perrin notes, however, that it appears in two English-language works published in the 1940s (*Rediscovering the Teaching of Jesus,* 187 n. 2).

26. As Chilton notes, *The Kingdom of God in the Teaching of Jesus,* 15. See also his *God in Strength: Jesus' Announcement of the Kingdom* (Linz: Plöchl, 1979), 264–66. Chilton's work on the kingdom of God is both solid and promising, suggesting a way forward that moves away from an imminent eschatological understanding.

27. See, e.g., Perrin, *Rediscovering the Teaching of Jesus,* 16–20, 199–201.

28. Luke 11:29–32=Matt. 12:38–42. See also Luke 10:13–14=Matt. 11:21–22 and Luke 10:12=Matt. 10:15. For more detailed treatment, see my *Conflict, Holiness and Politics,* 210–11.

29. Vielhauer's argument (n. 25 above) is an interesting example of this widespread tendency. Having noted that the coming Son of man and the kingdom are not linked, and having pronounced all of the coming Son of man sayings to be inauthentic, he nevertheless keeps the element of imminence in his understanding of the kingdom of God.

30. Perrin, *Jesus and the Language of the Kingdom* (Philadelphia: Fortress Press, 1976).

31. Huston Smith, *Forgotten Truth: The Primordial Tradition* (New York: Harper & Row, 1976).

32. This is an important point; the primordial tradition is not to be identified with a particular cultural expression, as often happens when it is identified with "the great chain of being." As I understand it, the "great chain of being" is one form in which the primordial tradition appears, and a highly detailed one at that. If one thinks of "primordial tradition" and "great chain of being" as synonymous, then one will not find the primordial tradition to be central to the biblical tradition. But such a highly particular identification is incorrect.

33. This basic "cut," in which reality is seen to have minimally two "divisions," can be spoken of in many ways — as the sacred and the profane, the holy (or numinous) and the mundane, spirit and matter, etc. What is most important is the notion of a "cut" rather than any particular set of terms.

34. That is, this basic distinction flows out of the experience of reality as having both ordinary and non-ordinary aspects. Thus it is important to understand terms such as "sacred" and "profane," "the holy" and "the mundane," etc., as phenomenological terms and not, e.g., simply as ingredients in an intellectual argument (whether Eliade's, Otto's, etc.).

35. So, for example, Mircea Eliade. Myths are stories about the other reality and its relationship to this one. See especially *Myth and Reality* (New York: Harper & Row, 1963). The title of the book is significant. In the modern world, we tend to contrast myth and reality; but Eliade's point is that "myth" is the way one speaks about reality, i.e., about that which is "most real," namely, the

other world. Dennis Duling briefly employs Eliade's understanding of myth in his extension of Perrin's work; see Duling, *Jesus Christ through History* (New York: Harcourt Brace, 1979), 19–20.

36. There is a significant difference between thinking of symbols and myths as ways of speaking of another reality and thinking of them as metaphorical ways of speaking about our existence — our condition and potentiality.

37. As I see it, this understanding of the kingdom is very consistent with Bruce Chilton's important recent works on the kingdom of God (see n. 26 above). Though he does not make the connection to the primordial tradition, he concludes that Jesus' public announcement of the kingdom refers primarily to "God acting in strength," i.e., to "God's disclosure of himself," and secondarily to the human response to that disclosure.

38. See, e.g., Robin Scroggs, *Paul for a New Day* (Philadelphia: Fortress Press, 1977), and Robert Kysar, *John: The Maverick Gospel* (Atlanta: John Knox Press, 1976). For both Paul and John, the emphasis was upon the "new age" which had already dawned; both spoke of the "new creation" or "eternal life" as realities which were already being experienced; i.e., their emphasis (like Jesus?) was upon the present experiential reality of the "new age."

39. I realize that I have not talked about the relationship between Jesus' mission and the "conventional wisdom" and "social world" of his day in this essay. This has been a theme of much of my published research thus far, and is also one of the two central topics in my forthcoming *Jesus: A New Vision*.

40. Without trying in any way to be comprehensive, I would add several books by T. F. Glasson (beginning in 1945) and Lloyd Gaston's *No Stone on Another* (Leiden: E. J. Brill, 1970).

41. Unless this is done carefully, a curious result occurs. It is sometimes said, for example, that Jesus put no limit on the expectation of the end, that he had no "calendar," etc. But so long as kingdom continues to retain its "end-of-the-world" connotation, the effect of the revision is to suggest that Jesus proclaimed, "The kingdom-as-end can come at any time, now, or hundreds of years from now." One might presume that Jesus had more of an insight (and message) about the kingdom than that.

42. E. Schillebeeckx, *Jesus* (New York: Vintage, 1981), 152. Like the present essay, Schillebeeckx also finds the origin of the expectation of Jesus' imminent return in the Easter experience of the church. Somewhat ironically, despite denying the element of imminent end of the world in the preaching of Jesus, Schillebeeckx continues regularly to speak of Jesus as "eschatological." Why continue to use the term if the reason for introducing it into the discussion (Schweitzer's end-of-the-world Jesus) has disappeared?

43. G. S. Sloyan, *Jesus in Focus: A Life in Its Setting* (Mystic: Twenty-Third Publications (1983), especially chapter 8.

44. There is, so far as I know, no "official" membership in the Historical Jesus Section. The list of forty-two people with some degree of participation in the section was supplied by Prof. Paul Hollenbach, co-chair of the section.

45. I also asked a second question; namely, I asked respondents to indicate their age by checking an appropriate block (sixty-five or over, fifty-five to sixty-four, forty-five to fifty-four, etc.). I was interested to see if there would be any

difference by "generation"; however, the sample proved to be too small for any significant generalization.

46. I included the following commentary as a way of clarifying the question: "I am not simply asking whether, for example, Jesus expected a drastic change in the life of Israel, or whether he was referring to a dramatic internal or subjective change that might be referred to as 'end of world' for one who experienced it. Rather, I am asking whether you think he thought *the end was near*, understood as a cataclysmic change in the 'objective' world, however we might interpret that expectation or proclamation today."

47. The exact results were as follows. Jesus Seminar: six strongly thought so, four were inclined to, five were inclined not to, and six strongly thought not. For the SBL group, the totals (in the same order) were three, three, six, and six. I do not know what to make of the higher percentage response from the Jesus Seminar; perhaps they are more accustomed to polls. I wish to thank Mrs. Pat Rogerson, secretary of Religious Studies at Oregon State University, for conducting the survey.

48. Some of us may feel a responsibility to the church as well, simply because many of us are involved in the education of future clergy, whether as seminarians or pre-seminarians. I have suggested elsewhere (in "The Historical Jesus and Christian Preaching"; see n. 13 above) that the mainstream church is rather quiet about the historical Jesus, in part because of the difficulty of adapting the eschatological Jesus to Christian preaching and teaching. Obviously, the needs or wishes of the church cannot be a factor in our historical judgments; but if a non-eschatological Jesus is judged on historical grounds to be more probable, then seminarians deserve to know that.

49. Our view on this deeply affects how we see texts. In recent decades, much work on the gospels (and the New Testament generally) has assumed that a major issue for the early church was the delay of the parousia. For example, Conzelmann's seminal work on Luke sees Luke's picture of Jesus as "the middle of time" as a substitute for a more original image of Jesus as "the end of time" The gospel is understood as an attempt to deal with the fact that the end did not come as the early Christians (and presumably Jesus) expected. Of course, some texts do deal with the delay of the parousia (though not all that many). But there are two very different ways of "seeing" what was going on. If we assume the eschatological model of Jesus, then the inference follows that the early church as a whole was saddled with the problem that the world did not come to an end as he had expected. The image is of a disappointed community, struggling to accommodate its founder's mistake. But if we assume that the belief in the return of Jesus originated after Easter, then we would understand the texts which address the delay of the parousia as indicators that there were some early Christians who took the expected return of Jesus in both an imminent and literal sense, and some who did not. That is, the different views of the end (including its timing) reflect different views held within the church, rather than the church as a whole trying to cope with the mistaken expectation of Jesus himself.

50. The phrases come from, respectively, Gerhard Lohfink, *Jesus and Com-*

munity (Philadelphia: Fortress Press, 1984), and Walter Brueggemann, *The Bible Makes Sense* (Atlanta: John Knox Press, 1978).

Works Consulted

Beker, J. C. "Biblical Theology Today." *New Theology Number Six*. Ed. M. Marty and D. G. Peerman. New York: Macmillan, 1969.

Borg, Marcus. *Jesus: A New Vision*. San Francisco: Harper & Row, forthcoming.

————. "An Orthodoxy Re-Considered: The 'End-of-the-World Jesus.' " In a memorial volume for George Caird. Oxford: Oxford University Press, forthcoming in 1986.

————. "The Historical Jesus and Christian Preaching." *Christian Century* 102 (1985): 764–67.

————. *Conflict, Holiness and Politics in the Teaching of Jesus*. New York: Edwin Mellen Press, 1984.

————. "Conflict as a Context for Interpreting the Teaching of Jesus." Ph.D. diss., Oxford University, 1972.

Brandon, S. G. F. *Jesus and the Zealots*. Manchester: University Press, 1967.

Bornkamm, Günther. *Jesus of Nazareth*. New York: Harper & Row, 1960.

Brueggemann, Walter. *The Bible Makes Sense*. Altanta: John Knox Press, 1978.

Bultmann, Rudolf. "New Testament and Mythology." Pp. 1–16 in *Kerygma and Myth*. Ed. H. W. Bartsch. New York: Harper & Row, 1961.

————. *Jesus and the Word*. New York: Charles Scribner's, 1934.

Carmignac, J. "Les dangers de l'eschatologie." *New Testament Studies* 17 (1970/71): 388–90.

Chilton, Bruce, ed. *The Kingdom of God in the Teaching of Jesus*. Philadelphia: Fortress Press, 1984.

————. *God in Strength: Jesus' Announcement of the Kingdom*. Linz: Plöchl, 1979.

Colpe, C. "ὁ υἱὸς τοῦ ἀνθρώπου." Pp. 400–477 in *Theological Dictionary of the New Testament*. Ed. Gerhard Friedrich and Gerhard Kittel. Vol. 8. Grand Rapids: Wm. B. Eerdmans, 1972.

Conzelmann, H. *The Theology of St. Luke*. New York: Harper & Row, 1960.

Dodd, C. H. *The Founder of Christianity*. London: Collins, 1971.

————. *The Parables of the Kingdom*. New York: Charles Scribner's, 1961.

Duling, Dennis. *Jesus Christ through History*. New York: Harcourt Brace, 1979.

Eliade, Mircea. *Myth and Reality*. New York: Harper & Row, 1963.

Gaston, Lloyd. *No Stone on Another*. Leiden: E. J. Brill, 1970.

Harvey, A. E. *Jesus and the Constraints of History*. Philadelphia: Westminster Press, 1982.

Herzog, William R. "The Quest for the Historical Jesus and the Discovery of the Apocalyptic Jesus." *Pacific Theological Review* 19 (1985): 25–39.

Kümmel, W. G. *Promise and Fulfilment*. London: SCM, 1957.

Küng, Hans. *On Being a Christian*. Garden City, N.Y.: Doubleday & Co. 1984.

Kysar, Robert. *John: The Maverick Gospel*. Atlanta: John Knox Press, 1976.

Leivestad, R. "Exit the Apocalyptic Son of Man." *New Testament Studies* 18 (1971/72): 243–67.

———. "Der apocalyptische Menschensohn: ein theologisches Phantom." *Annual of the Swedish Theological Institute* 6 (1967).

Lindars, B. *Jesus Son of Man*. Grand Rapids: Wm. B. Eerdmans, 1983.

———. "Re-Enter the Apocalyptic Son of Man." *New Testament Studies* 22 (1976): 52–72.

Lohfink, Gerhard. *Jesus and Community*. Philadelphia: Fortress Press, 1984.

Lundström, Gösta. *The Kingdom of God in the Teaching of Jesus*. Edinburgh: Oliver and Boyd, 1963.

Nineham, D. E. *Saint Mark*. New York: Penguin, 1969.

Perrin, Norman. *Jesus and the Language of the Kingdom*. Philadelphia, Fortress Press, 1976.

———. *Rediscovering the Teaching of Jesus*. New York: Harper & Row, 1967.

———. *The Kingdom of God in the Teaching of Jesus*. Philadelphia: Westminster Press, 1963.

Sanders, E. P. *Jesus and Judaism*. Philadelphia: Fortress Press, 1985.

Schillebeeckx, E. *Jesus*. New York: Vintage, 1981.

Schweitzer, Albert. *The Mystery of the Kingdom of God: The Secret of Jesus' Messiahship and Passion*. 1st German ed. 1901. Trans. Walter Lowrie. New York: Schocken Books, 1964.

———. *The Quest of the Historical Jesus: A Critical Study of its Progress from Reimarus to Wrede*. 1st German ed. 1906. Trans. W. Montgomery. New York: Macmillan, 1961.

Scroggs, Robin. *Paul for a New Day*. Philadelphia: Fortress Press, 1977.

Sloyan, S. *Jesus in Focus: A Life in Its Setting*. Mystic, Conn.: Twenty-Third Publications, 1983.

Smith, Huston. *Forgotten Truth: The Primordial Tradition*. New York: Harper & Row, 1976.

Theissen, Gerd. *Sociology of Early Palestinian Christianity*. Philadelphia: Fortress Press, 1978.

Tödt, H. E. *The Son of Man in the Synoptic Tradition*. Philadelphia: Westminster Press, 1965.

Vermes, Geza. *Jesus the Jew*. New York: Macmillan, 1973.

Vielhauer, P. "Gottesreich und Menschensohn in der Verkundigung Jesus." Pp. 51–79 in *Festschrift für Günther Dehn*. Ed. W. Schneemelcher. Neukirchen: Verlag der Buchhandlung des Erziehungsvereins Neukirchen, 1957.

Weiss, Johannes. *Jesus' Proclamation of the Kingdom of God*. 1st German ed. 1892. 2d German ed. 1900. Ed. and trans. R. H. Hiers and D. L. Holland. Philadelphia: Fortress Press, 1971.

Wright, N. Thomas. "Jesus, Israel and the Cross." *Society of Biblical Literature Papers*. Atlanta: Scholars Press, 1985.

Yonker, Nicholas. *God, Man, and the Planetary Age*. Corvallis: Oregon State University Press, 1978.

Chapter Four

Jesus and Eschatology: Current Reflections

In the seven years since I wrote the previous essay, I have returned to the topic of Jesus and eschatology a number of times.[1] What I advanced in 1986 as "a temperate case for a non-eschatological Jesus" can now be described as a change that has occurred in the discipline, at least in North America. As noted in the second chapter of this book, James Robinson has spoken of the movement away from an "apocalyptic Jesus" as a Copernican shift of paradigms.[2] Five of the six portraits of Jesus sketched in the same chapter see the relationship between Jesus and eschatology quite differently from the primary way in which it has been seen in much of this century's scholarship.

The movement away from an eschatological Jesus is by no means unanimous, of course. There are important scholars who still affirm some variation of the previous consensus.[3] Moreover, the claim that a change has occurred still seems to be a source of surprise (and perhaps even consternation) to colleagues in other areas of scholarship on Christian origins. Thus, though it seems clear that the old consensus *as a consensus* is gone, it would be misleading to say that it has been replaced by a new non-eschatological consensus. Rather, the discipline is divided, perhaps about evenly, though my own sense is that the division is currently tipped in favor of a non-eschatological reading of the Jesus tradition. Yet considerable uncertainty remains, both on the part of those most actively involved in the North American discussion as well as among those observing it from other sub-disciplines of New Testament studies and the broader field of religious studies. Thus it is likely (and necessary) that significant scholarly discussion and debate of this question will continue for the next several years.

In the present essay, I wish to report on and contribute to that discussion by treating four topics. I begin with a section on the clarification of terms, move to an extended set of reflections flowing out of E. P. Sanders's image of Jesus as a prophet of restoration eschatology, comment briefly on the coming Son of man and kingdom sayings, and conclude with some clarifying remarks about the role of eschatology in the Jesus traditions and in the early Christian movement.

Terminology: The Ambiguity of "Eschatology"

In my judgment, much of the uncertainty in the present discussion flows from a blurring and broadening of the meaning of the word "eschatology." The word has been used in both a narrow and broad sense in the history of scholarship. Examining its history of usage can contribute much to clarifying the current discussion.

Its narrow and more precise sense was the most common meaning until this century. So far as we know, the term "eschatology" entered theological discourse in the seventeenth century. First used by a Lutheran theologian named Abraham Calov in 1677, it was the title of the last section of his dogmatics, in which he treated death, judgment, consummation, hell, everlasting death, and life everlasting.[4] Eschatology thus meant "last things" (as the Greek roots of the word suggest) in the context of Christian theology.

Within the quite ahistorical framework of post-Reformation Christian theology, however, the term did not have much of a temporal meaning. That is, "last things" referred primarily to the ultimate post-death fate of individuals. When the term began to be used in biblical scholarship (at least by the time of Reimarus in the mid-1700s),[5] it acquired the more temporal meaning associated with Jewish (and early Christian) hopes and expectations regarding the future. It referred to a future decisive act of God that could be variously spoken of as the coming of the kingdom of God or the messianic age or the life of the age to come, or, in Christian circles, the second coming of Christ. Central to this more biblical notion of eschatology is chronological futurity and divine intervention, resulting in a state of existence radically different from life in the present, a change of such great magnitude that it can be referred to as "the end of the age."

In an important sense, Jewish eschatologies did not typically involve "the end of the world," if by that is meant the end of the space-time universe.[6] What a colleague has helpfully called "molecular eschatology" — the disappearance of the material world — is not part of the expectation.[7] Jewish (and early Christian) eschatologies most commonly envision a continuing earth; in the messianic age, the world of Jerusalem, banquets and vineyards may very well continue. But the conditions of life would be so different in a visible and tangible way, involving the kinds of changes that could not be brought about simply by human activity, that one may properly speak of the end of the present age/order/world and the coming of a new age/order/world established by God.[8]

This fairly narrow and quite precise use of "eschatology" continued to be the primary meaning of the term in biblical scholarship into the early decades of this century. The term had this meaning for Johannes Weiss and Albert Schweitzer, and for the scholars of the nineteenth century whose work Schweitzer reported. Thus, when Weiss and Schweitzer said that Jesus' message, activity, and self-understanding were dominated by imminent eschatology, they meant that Jesus expected this kind of supernatural world-changing event soon.

Since then, the word "eschatology" has come to have a much broader range of meanings. The broadening occurred in part, and in different ways, through the work of Rudolf Bultmann and C. H. Dodd, arguably the most important German and British New Testament scholars of the middle third of this century. Bultmann accepted the claim that imminent eschatology (in the sense specified above) was central to the message of Jesus; thus far there is direct continuity with Weiss and Schweitzer. Then Bultmann demythologized it by means of an existentialist hermeneutic. The result is what has been called an existentialist eschatology: an understanding of eschatological language as referring to a dramatic internal change within an individual so that one may speak of the world (as the ground of identity and security) having come to an end for that individual. Hence Bultmann could speak of "eschatological existence" as a present reality and as the heart of the Christian message. Eschatology had thus been individualized and internalized; it could be used in a sense that involved neither chronological futurity nor change in the outer world.

Dodd took a different road (though the ultimate result, oddly, was somewhat the same). Against Weiss, Schweitzer, and Bultmann, Dodd rejected the claim that imminent eschatology was central to Jesus' message and argued that Jesus spoke of the kingdom of God as present rather than as future. Then, unfortunately, he used the phrase "realized eschatology" to express the notion of a present kingdom. But to speak of a "present eschatology" (at least when the objective conditions of existence remain unchanged) is a contradiction (almost like speaking of a square circle). At best, it might be a provocative paradox; at the least, it stretches the meaning of the word "eschatology" so far as to risk making it meaningless.[9]

In contemporary usage, the broad meaning of "eschatology" has become common.[10] There is the understanding of eschatology as the shattering of the conceptual-linguistic world brought about by the subversive effect of Jesus' parables and aphorisms. It is sometimes used virtually as a synonym for "the future" or "concern with the future."

Or it can be used to refer to any world-changing event, or perhaps to any really important event, so that the tearing down of the Berlin wall has been described as an "eschatological event" by a contemporary New Testament scholar. It is therefore not surprising that George Caird, a persistent critic of the eschatological consensus in the decades when it was still dominant, was able to catalogue seven different senses in which "eschatology" is used.[11] Other scholars have noted its loss of precise exegetical meaning and suggested a moratorium on its use.[12]

The narrow and broad meanings of eschatology are well-illustrated by two recent works. David Aune in his impressive *Anchor Bible Dictionary* essay on eschatology initially defines it in what I am calling the narrow meaning: biblical eschatology "refers to a time in the future in which the course of history will be changed to such an extent that one can speak of an entirely new state of reality"; it concerns "the last things in a worldwide and historical sense, e.g, an apocalyptic, cosmic cataclysm, and a new age followed by utopian bliss."[13]

It is when Aune turns to a survey of what scholars have said about biblical eschatology that he is compelled by the discipline itself to use it in a much broader sense. Thus he speaks (as Old Testament scholars have done) of the eschatology of the pre-exilic prophets, despite the fact that the judgment of which they spoke was manifestly within history: the military conquest of their kingdoms by a foreign empire. Here "end" means "an eschaton of statehood."[14] Thus the historical event of one's nation being conquered by a foreign power is included in the subject matter of eschatology, even though it does not involve any of what are normally called "end-time" events: the coming of the messianic age, the vindication of Israel or the elect, sometimes a last judgment and resurrection of the dead, and so forth.

The broad meaning of "eschatology" reflected in Aune's survey of scholarship is in fact wide enough to include any teaching regarding the future activity of God, whether in fulfilment of promise or execution of judgment, whether through mundane historical events or dramatic divine interventions. In this broad sense, much of the Bible is eschatological. Aune's awareness of (and I think preference for) the narrower meaning of "eschatology" appears again as he begins to treat the eschatology of Enoch: "In a clear and meaningful way, one can speak here of 'eschatology' — teaching about the end."[15] Implicitly, he sees himself as not having treated eschatology "proper" up to this point.

Thus Aune's essay shows the presence of both the broad and narrow meanings of eschatology within the discipline. In a somewhat different way, so does John Dominic Crossan's recent book on Jesus. Crossan distinguishes between "apocalyptic eschatology" and "eschatology," a distinction corresponding quite closely with what I am calling the narrow and broader meanings of eschatology. Apocalyptic eschatology, he suggests, is concerned with an imminent "end of the world." For Crossan, this need not involve the end of the space-time world, but it would be "a divine intervention so transcendentally obvious that one's adversaries or enemies, oppressors or persecutors, would be forced to acknowledge it and to accept conversion or concede defeat."[16] That, Crossan argues throughout his book, was not what Jesus expected.

Yet he chooses to retain the word "eschatology" for speaking about Jesus, explaining that eschatology is: "the wider and generic term *for world-negation* extending from apocalyptic eschatology . . . through mystical or utopian modes, and on to ascetical, libertarian, or anarchistic possibilities."[17] Clearly, of course, this is what I have been calling a broadened meaning of "eschatology."[18]

Awareness of the presence of both broad and more precise meanings of "eschatology" in the discipline is thus an important ingredient in the on-going discussion. Whether or not one thinks Jesus was an eschatological figure depends to a considerable extent upon whether one defines "eschatology" broadly or more narrowly.[19] If one uses the word in its broadened sense, then it seems obvious that Jesus was eschatological. But the affirmation becomes virtually meaningless, given the wide range of meanings it encompasses. It could mean anything from "Jesus thought something really important was going to happen" to "he affirmed some form of world-negation" to "he taught that you could experience a new life now" to "he was concerned with the hope of Israel" to "he expected the resurrection of the dead and the last judgment in his own generation." When eschatology is used in this broad sense, to say "Jesus was an eschatological figure" has no meaning without further specification.

Thus, in my own work, I prefer to use "eschatology" in the more narrow and precise sense. Essential to this more narrow sense is an expectation involving the following elements: (1) chronological futurity; (2) dramatic divine intervention in a public and objectively unmistakable way, resulting in (3) a radically new state of affairs, including the vindication of God's people, whether on a renewed earth or in another world. Additional elements are sometimes part of the expectation (e.g., resurrection, last judgment), but these are the ones I think constitutive of the more precise meaning of "eschatology" in a Jewish and/or early Christian context. Throughout the rest of this essay (and this book), this is the sense in which I will use it.

Thus, when I speak of "the eschatological Jesus" or "Jesus as eschatological prophet," it is shorthand for a *Gestalt* or construal of Jesus that sees this kind of expectation as central to his mission and message. Conversely (and obviously), when I speak of a "non-eschatological Jesus," I mean an image of Jesus in which this expectation is not central. This is the image of Jesus for which I have consistently argued.[20]

The crucial question in the current discussion, however, is finally not whether we use the words "eschatological" or "apocalyptic" or "apocalyptic eschatology" in our characterization of the pre-Easter Jesus (though I think it is important to specify the sense in which we use our terms). Rather, the crucial question is the more specific one: what role (if any) did expectation of an imminent future event involving direct divine intervention in an objectively unmistakable form play in the message and activity of Jesus? (And all of the adjectives and adverbs in that sentence are important). What I have called "the eschatological consensus" saw such expectation as central. It is that consensus that now seems to have become a minority position in North American Jesus scholarship.

Reflections on Sanders's Eschatological Jesus

I move now to E. P. Sanders's understanding of Jesus. Sanders sees Jesus as an eschatological figure in the more narrow and precise sense of the word: chronological futurity and the expectation of a dramatic divine intervention that would produce a radically new state of affairs are central.

A somewhat extended set of reflections on Sanders's work is important for two reasons. First, his is the best-known voice in the current discussion arguing for a form of the previously dominant consensus, and the book in which he makes this argument — *Jesus and Judaism* — has been highly acclaimed. It was heralded at the time of its publication in 1985 as likely to be "the most significant book of the decade in its field,"[21] and, after the decade had ended, received the prestigious Grawemeyer Award as the best book in religious studies in the 1980s. It is an impressive book. A brilliantly sustained and detailed argument over four hundred pages long is advanced with extraordinary clarity (one always knows what Sanders is saying) and verve (there is an energy in his prose). Thus it is important to pay attention to Sanders's work because of its importance within the field.

It is important for a second reason as well. Because Sanders's understanding of Jesus fits within the previous eschatological consensus, analysis of his work leads to reflections on larger questions concerning that consensus. What are its foundations, and how adequate are they? What is the image of Jesus that emerges when he is seen eschatologically, and what are the effects of that image on how we "see" the traditions about Jesus? What is involved in assessing the adequacy or inadequacy of a comprehensive image of Jesus? Thus I will be using Sanders's work as a springboard for reflecting on some of the larger questions involved in historical Jesus scholarship.[22]

Sanders's Method

In a previous chapter, I provided a sketch of Sanders's understanding of Jesus.[23] In this chapter I wish to focus on the method by which he arrived at his conclusions about Jesus and eschatology. His method has two important steps. First, he generates a list of indisputable or nearly indisputable facts about Jesus (Sanders's list includes eight), and argues that these (rather than the sayings or words of Jesus, whose historical authenticity is very difficult to assess) should be the point of departure for the historical study of Jesus.[24] The second methodological step or move is to set these facts within a particular interpretive context, namely, the framework of Jewish restoration eschatology.

Both methodological steps are crucial to his argument. The way they work together can be illustrated by beginning where Sanders begins: Jesus and the temple. "Jesus engaged in a controversy about the temple" is one of Sanders's eight facts, and he highlights two things as he treats this: the temple action in which Jesus overturned tables, and the accusation that Jesus spoke of the temple being destroyed and rebuilt.[25] Sanders argues persuasively that the common view of the temple action as a "cleansing" or "purification" or "reform" is inadequate. He thus suggests another: namely, the act of overturning tables, together with the indications that Jesus probably said something about the temple being destroyed and rebuilt, can be read within the framework of Jewish restoration eschatology.[26]

The Interpretive Context: Restoration Eschatology

"Restoration eschatology" — which in various forms concerned the restoration of Israel and the coming of "the messianic age," all in fulfilment of God's promises — often included the notion of a new or renewed temple. Thus language about "a new temple" and the destruction of the old (as symbolized by overturning tables) can find an interpretive "home" within the framework of restoration eschatology. If seen within that framework, they mean that Jesus expected the destruction of the old temple and the coming of a new temple and thereby "predicted the imminent appearance of the judgment and the new age."[27]

It is important to see this methodological move (what I am calling the second step in Sanders's method) and its centrality for his argument: *if* we see these traditions about Jesus and the temple within the framework of restoration eschatology, *then* this is what they would mean. Indeed this is the "macro" methodological move underlying the book as a whole: if we set the traditions about Jesus within the framework of restoration eschatology, within this particular interpretive context, this is what they cumulatively mean. The crucial question then becomes the justification of the methodological move to this particular interpretive context. What are the warrants for seeing the traditions about Jesus through this particular lens, namely, within the framework of Jewish restoration eschatology?

Sanders cites three main categories of evidence to justify the move. These three indicators of restoration eschatology (one of which he says is most important) together generate the particular interpretive context of restoration eschatology.[28]

The first of the less important ones is evidence in Jewish sources for the linkage of *eschaton* and "new temple": restoration eschatology often included the expectation of a new temple.[29] Sanders's case is persuasive. By itself, however, evidence that eschaton and new temple are frequently linked within Judaism says nothing directly about Jesus; he may or may not have made the connection, or may have made it in a different way. The linkage is a necessary condition for interpreting Jesus' temple action as Sanders does. But it is not more than that. The fact that some (or even many) within Judaism thought that the messianic age would include a new temple does not have anything to do with whether this is what Jesus expected, or whether this is what he intended to symbolize with his act of overturning tables. If we were confident that Jesus expected a new temple that would physically replace the old one, then we could say that Jesus was operating within the framework of restoration eschatology; but, of course, this is what Sanders is seeking to demonstrate, not something already established.

The second of the less important categories of evidence pointing to restoration eschatology as the interpretive context is the claim that Jesus chose twelve disciples.[30] This, Sanders argues, symbolized the twelve tribes of Israel, and *"would necessarily mean 'restoration.'"*[31] The strength of this argument depends initially on whether the choosing of "twelve" goes back to Jesus or whether the notion is created by the early Christian movement, a question about which scholars are thoroughly divided. But even if it does go back to Jesus (which, on the whole, I am still inclined to affirm, though I recognize that it is a "weak" as opposed to a "strong" historical judgment), it need not point to the eschatological scenario that Sanders sketches. It would indicate that Jesus saw his mission as having to do with "Israel," but it need not imply the framework of imminent restoration eschatology.[32]

Thus it is the third category of evidence that provides the primary foundation of Sanders's case that imminent restoration eschatology was central to Jesus.[33] Sanders crystalizes this point with the compact formula "From John the Baptist to Paul." Expanded, the formula points to the fact that the historical Jesus is the "middle term" between John the Baptizer and the post-Easter Christian movement. For both John and the early Christian movement, Sanders affirms, imminent eschatology was central. John preached an imminent judgment, and the early church preached the imminent return of Christ at the judgment. In short, Jesus' predecessor and mentor was eschatological, the early community that followed him was eschatological, and it seems a natural and strong inference to suppose that the figure in between the two was eschatological also.

Sanders rightly identifies this as the most important warrant for interpreting the traditions about Jesus within the framework of imminent restoration eschatology. It has an immediate persuasive power. Its central ingredients are all part of the common wisdom of New Testament scholarship. Most of us take it for granted that John the Baptizer's message was eschatological, and that Paul (and others) expected the return of Christ and the last judgment in their generation. Indeed, I suspect that what Sanders calls "From John the Baptist to Paul" is the major reason that the eschatological consensus was dominant for so long, and why its announced demise is often greeted with surprise or skepticism. Because it has been part of the common wisdom of the discipline, reflecting about it at some length is worthwhile.

I begin with John the Baptizer. Two considerations are worth thinking about. First, it is possible to read the traditions about John non-eschatologically. I am not very persuaded of this myself, but John's language of an imminent coming judgment can be read historically rather than eschatologically. So George Caird argued some thirty years ago: John was warning of an impending historical judgment, much as the classic prophets of Israel did.[34] Or one could argue that John's language of judgment (along with much of apocalyptic language) can be read in a much more sociopolitical way.[35] Here the function of the language would not be to announce a coming "final" judgment, but a judgment against the ruling elites. Finally, it is worth noting that Josephus presents John non-eschatologically.[36]

Second, it is possible to read the traditions about John eschatologically, and yet to read the Jesus traditions non-eschatologically. So Crossan does in his recent study of Jesus. Crossan accepts that John was Jesus' mentor and that John had an apocalyptic eschatology, but then argues that Jesus' own message was radically different from John's.[37] Other scholars have done this too, of course; it is a commonplace to point to the contrast between John's message of judgment and the quite different texture of Jesus' message. Sanders is also aware of this, noting the strong emphasis upon an imminent judgment and the consequent need for repentance in the preaching of John and the relative absence of both in the words of Jesus.[38] He suggests that the explanation may be that Jesus felt that John had sufficiently emphasized judgment and repentance, and therefore he did not need to.[39] Thus difference is assimilated into continuity. But the common scholarly perception of significant discontinuity between the message of John and the message of

Jesus has a strong basis, and the affirmation of substantial continuity is questionable.

I move now from the first term in the formula to the end term: the eschatological orientation of the early Christian movement. I agree that many within the movement expected that Jesus would return in the near future and usher in the eschatological events of resurrection, judgment, and the everlasting kingdom. It is the most natural way to read a number of passages in Paul and the gospels, and it is the presupposition of the book of Revelation. Thus I agree that imminent eschatology was among the beliefs of early Christians. The important question, however, is whether this provides evidence that Jesus himself was eschatological in a central way. Or, to put that differently, is the eschatology of the early movement most persuasively accounted for by supposing that it is a continuation of the eschatological orientation of Jesus himself?

Two considerations are important. The first is *what* the early movement expected: they expected *the return of Jesus.* Most scholars (including those who interpret Jesus eschatologically) do not think Jesus expected this himself; that is, most of us do not think Jesus spoke of his own second coming. This is an important realization, in part because it means that the eschatological expectation of the early movement was not simply a continuation of something going back to Jesus, and in part because it points to a plausible alternative explanation of the origin of the movement's eschatology. When did expectation of *the return of Jesus* arise? Most scholars agree that this is a post-Easter development. It is very possible (and a considerable number of scholars have argued this) that it not only originated after Easter, but *because of* Easter. That is, within Jewish eschatologies of the time, "resurrection" was seen as an "end-time" event — and if a resurrection has occurred, then the eschaton may well be near. In short, I am suggesting that the *particularity* of the early movement's eschatology (namely, the expectation of the return of Jesus) raises a serious question as to whether its eschatological orientation can simply be seen as a continuation of Jesus' own understanding.

Like the first consideration, the second consideration grants that eschatological expectation is part of the early Christian movement. It is there — but it does not seem to be the dominant texture of the movement and its message. Most of us know of Christian groups today for whom the imminent expectation of the second coming and the final judgment is central. What we know about the early Christian movement, generally speaking, does not sound like what we associate with those groups. Though this is not the place to provide a sketch of the early movement, it seems by and large to have been a community with a strong experiential sense of the Spirit of God, quite egalitarian, and to a considerable degree boundary-shattering and culturally subversive.[40]

And they (or at least some of them) also believed that Jesus would return soon. But that doesn't seem to have been the center of their message or their life together. The dominant emphasis of Paul's message, for example, seems to have been the new life in Christ available in the present, not primarily (or even very much) the need to repent before the judgment. In short, the early movement does not sound like movements we know of that emphasize, "The second coming and the judgment are at hand; therefore repent!"

So the belief was there, but (excepting, once again, the book of Revelation) it does not seem to have been central. In this context, it is also worthwhile pointing out that the image of the early community facing a major crisis when the second coming did not occur goes beyond the evidence. There are a few passages that speak of its delay, but not nearly enough to justify the common scholarly notion that "the delay of the parousia" was the central theological problem of first-century Christianity.[41] Rather, it seems that its non-occurrence was not of great import. This suggests something about its relative importance. It may also suggest that there were eschatological literalists and non-literalists in the movement then, just as there are today.

To return to the broader point, it is quite possible to imagine that first-century Christians generally expected the return of Jesus soon, without supposing that their whole framework (and Jesus' whole framework) was dominated by eschatological expectation. The alternative possibilities I have mentioned do not establish the opposite case (namely, that Jesus' own orientation toward eschatology was different from the Baptizer and the early church). But they do undermine the "of course" quality of the inference drawn about Jesus from the allegedly pervasive eschatological orientation of John the Baptizer and early Christianity and call into question the "self-evidentness" of Sanders's case that the texture of his exposition sometimes suggests. They raise serious doubts about the primary warrant justifying the methodological move of reading the traditions about Jesus within the interpretive context of restoration eschatology.

Before I turn to what for me is the most important factor tipping the balance scale away from seeing Jesus within that interpretive context, I want to comment briefly about the role of Jesus' sayings in Sanders's justification of an eschatological context. Consistent with his own methodological claim that "facts" provide much firmer ground than the "quagmire" into which study of the sayings of Jesus can lead, Sanders assigns little evidential role to what have sometimes been seen as "foundational" eschatological sayings. He is not much interested in "the coming Son of man" sayings, though he does find one of them (Matt. 16:27) to be probably authentic, and another (Matt. 19:28) to be nicely explained by the eschatological context.[42] He makes some but not much evidential use of the kingdom of God sayings; much of his focus as he treats them is to undermine the case that the kingdom is primarily present, not to demonstrate that an authentic core of sayings proves its imminent futurity (for example, he does not, so far as I can find, even mention Mark 9:1). Indeed, one might argue that the only crucial saying in Sanders's foundation — in the justification given for the interpretive context of imminent eschatology — is one in which Jesus speaks of the temple being destroyed and rebuilt.[43] Thus his case for an eschatological framework rests almost exclusively on Jesus being the middle term between an eschatological Baptizer and an eschatological community, not on a collection of sayings. The sayings are not used to establish a context; rather, they are interpreted within a context largely generated by other means.

Gestalt, Lens, and Explanatory Power

This last comment illustrates the importance of Sanders's second methodological move, which I now wish to express at a a greater level of abstraction. Namely, it illustrates how a *Gestalt* or image becomes a *lens*. That is, in his case, an eschatological *Gestalt* of Jesus becomes a lens through which the traditions about Jesus are seen.

There is nothing illegitimate about this. All of us as historians are involved in this step at some stage in our work. At some point, the data begins to constellate itself into a *Gestalt,* an image of the whole, and the *Gestalt* then becomes a lens, that is, an overall hypothesis or particular interpretive context within which one attempts to see the rest of the data. This step of the historian's work — this methodological move — is like the hunching stage of the detective process, to which it has often been compared. At some point, based on clues, the detective makes a hunch about what happened (a *Gestalt,* a sense of the whole emerges) and then sees how well the rest of the evidence fits into place (and some of the evidence will perhaps be seen not to have been evidence after all; some of it may be seen to have been in the category of "false leads"). That is, a hunch (the hypothesizing of a particular interpretive context) flows out of evidence and then begins to affect how evidence is seen. *Gestalt* becomes lens.

The question then becomes, how adequate is the lens? How does the evidence look through it? How adequately does the *Gestalt*-become-lens enable us to see the evidence fitting together into a more or less coherent image of the whole? How much explanatory power does it have? What evidence does not fit, and how good are the grounds for laying it aside as not really relevant evidence after all?

This leads me into my final set of comments about Sanders's advocacy of restoration eschatology as the interpretive context for seeing the traditions about Jesus. My own strong sense is that it generates a *Gestalt* or image of Jesus that is difficult to reconcile with material in the Jesus traditions that has a strong claim to being "evidence." To put that differently, I think the lens of "Jesus as prophet of restoration eschatology" enables us to see too limited a range of data and forces us to set aside too much data. Its explanatory power is inadequate.

To explain this, I will begin by sketching the image of Jesus that results when the traditions about him are set within the framework of restoration eschatology. As Sanders does this, the following portrait of Jesus emerges. Central to Jesus' understanding was the conviction that the time of restoration eschatology was at hand and that this would involve the coming of a new (or renewed) temple. The meaning of his action in the temple (coupled with the tradition that he said something using the language of destroyed/rebuilt) may be paraphrased as *God will destroy this temple and replace (or renew) it*. Moreover, the expectation is quite literal: the new (or renewed) temple will be *in Jerusalem*. It will come from God, or be built by God (and this is not metaphorical language — God will do it in a manifestly direct way).[44] Its coming will mark the beginning of the messianic age, which Jesus thought he and the twelve would rule over from the new temple in Jerusalem. All of this will occur within the space-time world, though conditions will be quite different. It will involve a new social order in some respects radically different from the present age. Jesus expected all of this soon (and, of course, was wrong).

Sanders also suggests that the context of restoration eschatology may enable us to glimpse something about Jesus' self-understanding. Granting that we cannot say that Jesus thought of himself in terms that became important within early Christianity (as messiah or Son of God), Sanders suggests that it is nevertheless "a strong inference" that Jesus may have thought of himself as the king or soon-to-be king of the coming kingdom of God.[45]

To complete the picture briefly, Sanders also sees Jesus as a healer. He finds this to be not inconsistent with being an eschatological prophet, though it is not otherwise integrated into his portrait. He sees Jesus as basically a follower of "covenant nomism," the understanding of Judaism common to most Jews of the time. Jesus differed from it only in minor and very particular ways. For example, he promised "the wicked" a place in the coming kingdom without requiring that they go through the prescribed procedures of repentance. In short, what most distinguished Jesus from his Jewish contemporaries was the eschatological scenario that operated in his mind.

Moreover — and crucially — these beliefs about the coming eschaton and a new temple were not tangential or peripheral to Jesus, but central. This is what Jesus expected, and his intention, mission, activity, and teaching were all integrally bound up with it. In this (though the details differ), Sanders's portrait is also representative of the previous eschatological consensus: the "lens" through which Jesus is to be viewed is the interpretive context of imminent eschatology.

To turn now to reflection and evaluation: it is difficult for me to reconcile this image of Jesus with a large body of data that seems to me to have solid claim to be "real evidence," and not to be put in the category of "false leads" or seen as tangential. I am referring to wisdom material, which is broadly and strongly attested in the earliest layers of the Jesus tradition. The last twenty years have been marked by intensive study of the wisdom forms (largely parables and aphorisms) of Jesus' teaching, and by a growing consensus that there is a broad and early sapiential base to the gospel tradition.[46] That research has not only confirmed that parables and aphorisms are the bedrock of the Jesus tradition, but has also disclosed their functions as oral forms of speech. It has yielded a persuasive analysis of them (advanced by many scholars) as subversive forms of speech whose purpose was to undermine conventional ways of seeing and invite a very different way of seeing.

This is not the place to do an extensive exposition of the subversive wisdom of Jesus.[47] Rather, I restrict myself with reporting a twofold emerging consensus: (1) wisdom is central to the Jesus tradition; and (2) this material suggests that, whatever else also needs to be said about Jesus, he was a teacher of subversive wisdom. That he was a "parabler" and aphorist, a teller of subversive stories and a speaker of provocative one-liners, seems to be one of the most certain things we can know about him.[48]

Moreover, Jesus' wisdom sayings are important not just because they tell us some of the things that Jesus said, but also because they disclose a way of seeing, a perspective. As such, they disclose something of the "mentality" of the speaker. It is a mentality deeply aware of the conventions that dominate people's lives, animating, preoccupying, and ensnaring them. It is a mentality that has seen differently itself and that invites people into that way of seeing.

This large body of wisdom material — and the glimpse of Jesus I think it provides — fits poorly with the image of Jesus as an eschatological prophet. To return to Sanders's particular version of it, I find it very difficult to reconcile the mentality that we see at work in the subversive wisdom of Jesus with a mentality that could literally expect that God would miraculously (and soon) build a new temple on Mt. Zion and establish Jesus and the twelve as the rulers of the new age. They seem like two different mentalities; it is difficult to imagine them combined.

To continue the reflection: could somebody who so regularly subverted taken-for-granted notions be such a literalist about eschatology? To put the question in the form of "could" is probably the wrong way of putting it. I grant that it is not an impossible combination. Perhaps

Jesus as a teacher of subversive wisdom could hold quite literalistic beliefs about a new temple provided by God, a messianic age and kingdom geographically centered in Jerusalem, the re-gathering of Israel, and his own destiny as the ruler (with his disciples) of the new kingdom.

To expand the point beyond the particularities of Sanders's portrait to the broader *Gestalt* of Jesus as eschatological prophet, perhaps it is possible that Jesus taught a world-subverting wisdom and also proclaimed: the last judgment is literally at hand, and nothing is more important than making sure that you have a place in the elect community. To risk caricaturizing the broader image of Jesus as an eschatological prophet, I suppose one could imagine that Jesus taught a world-subverting wisdom and also said, "By the way, the last judgment is at hand, you better be ready, so repent!"[49] Though the language is colloquial, it does express a central dynamic of the eschatological image of Jesus.

So it may be a possible combination — but how likely is it? It seems improbable to me. To echo the analogy I used earlier when reflecting about the extent to which the early movement in the decades after Easter was permeated by imminent eschatology, most of us have heard street preachers (and others) whose message essentially is, "The end is at hand, repent!" In my experience, people who strongly believe "the end is near" sound very different from what I hear in the Jesus tradition considered as a whole.

Thus I consider it unlikely that "Jesus the teacher of subversive wisdom" could also have believed in a quite literal imminent eschatology.[50] They sound like two different mentalities, and I find it difficult to imagine that they were combined in Jesus. In making this judgment, I am of course making a judgment about what is a possible or probable combination in a first-century Jewish mind. We have often been rightly cautioned about presuming what it is possible or probable for a person to think in a time and place so far removed from us. But scholars who take the opposite point of view — that such a combination is possible or probable — are involved in the same kind of judgment. Such judgments seem unavoidable when one moves beyond collecting and analyzing data to imaging a sense of the whole.

Thus the difficulties I have with Sanders's portrait of Jesus and, more generally, the difficulties I have with the formerly dominant eschatological consensus, are essentially twofold. (1) Its foundation is not nearly as assured as its advocates have often affirmed. The warrant for its basic methodological move (seeing the traditions about Jesus within the interpretive context of imminent eschatology) does not have the degree of "of courseness" that it needs to have in order to be so foundational. (2) It produces a *Gestalt* of Jesus that is difficult to reconcile with much of what seems central to the traditions about Jesus. It leaves too much of the data unassimilated and unaccounted for. Not only does it give the wisdom material insufficient place, but it also leaves unintegrated the traditions that point to Jesus as a Spirit person and a social prophet.

Finally, I want to conclude this set of reflections about Sanders's work by returning to the methodological proposal with which he began his book. I agree that much is to be gained by generating a set of "facts" about Jesus rather than simply focusing on the words of Jesus, as much of this century's scholarship has tended to do. I think there are some things we can know about Jesus with considerable certainty, and these can provide a *Gestalt* within which to place his words.

To this broad agreement with and appreciation of his methodological proposal, I wish to add three remarks. First, it makes all the difference in the world what one includes in one's primary list of facts.[51] Second, the sayings cannot be as cleanly relegated to second place as Sanders suggests; the historical study of Jesus involves a complex interplay between the sayings and what else we can know with some certainty about Jesus. Third, it also makes all the difference in the world how one interprets one's list of facts. That is, what is the "macro-context" — imminent eschatology, or something else — within which to see the Jesus tradition?

"Coming Son of Man" and "Kingdom" Sayings

As noted in chapter 3, two categories of Jesus' sayings have been most important — indeed, foundational — in the history of the eschatological consensus: the coming Son of man sayings, and (some) kingdom of God sayings.[52] I also reported that both categories are now commonly understood by scholars in ways that undermine them as supports for the interpretive context of imminent eschatology. Here I wish to add a few more comments about each.

The Coming Son of Man Sayings

To begin with a reminder, in my earlier essay I stressed three things about the "coming Son of man" sayings. First, it is crucial to be aware of how important they have been for establishing the interpretive context of imminent eschatology. They were important for Weiss and Schweitzer and continued to be throughout the first two-thirds of this century for mainstream scholarship in Germany and North America, which generally accepted a core of them as authentic to Jesus.[53] Second, I reported a major change in the scholarly assessment of them, beginning in the late 1960s: the consensus about the authenticity of at least some of them has been replaced by its opposite. By the time of my earlier essay, the "weight" of scholarly opinion (which, of course, can be wrong) had shifted from seeing them as original to Jesus to seeing them *all* as belonging to the developmental stage of the early Christian tradition in the decades after Easter. Third, I drew the obvious inference: given their centrality in establishing the eschatological context, their disappearance as authentic sayings of Jesus radically calls that context into question.

The years since that essay have not rehabiliated the coming Son of man sayings. Rather, two recent studies have amplified the case against their authenticity. First, Crossan in his recent Jesus book applies his stratigraphical and quantifiable method to the coming Son of man sayings with striking results.[54] To exposit this, I must first explain the numbering system Crossan uses in his "numerical summaries" of complexes in the Jesus tradition. The first number indicates the number of complexes in which a motif appears (in our case, the "coming Son of man" motif); the second number is the number of those complexes that have plural (more than one) independent attestation; the third number is the number that have only single attestation. To illustrate, the "numerical summary" for complexes in which the apocalyptic Son of man appears is 18: 6 + 12. This means that eighteen complexes refer to it, six of these have plural attestation, and twelve have only single attestation.

Now to move beyond the illustration to the crucial numerical summary. Though "apocalyptic Son of man" *complexes* have six plural attestations, *the phrase* "Son of man" in those same complexes does not have a single plural attestation.[55] Thus the true "numerical summary" for *the phrase* "Son of man" in apocalyptic Son of man complexes is 18: 0 + 18; none have plural attestation, all have only singular attestation. The clear inference: the phrase "Son of man" in an apocalyptic context is not firmly grounded in the earliest layers of the tradition.[56] Thus Crossan's numerical analysis yields a result consistent with much of recent scholarship: language about an apocalyptic Son of man originates post-Easter.[57] The coming Son of man sayings do not go back to Jesus, but are the product of the community.

Second, Douglas Hare's recent book on the Son of man begins in a different place and has a different purpose, and yet produces a similar result.[58] Whereas Crossan focuses on what can be assigned to the early layer of the tradition, Hare concentrates on the final or redactional level of the tradition. His primary purpose is to examine the actual use of the phrase on the "surface level" of the gospel texts (like the archaeological strategy of beginning "at the top of the tell," as he puts it).[59]

His major conclusion is significant: the phrase "Son of man" does not have connotative meaning in the gospels, but only a denotative meaning. That is, the phrase is used in the gospels to *denote* Jesus, but it does not have a set of associations or allusions that are used to interpret the significance of Jesus.[60] To relate this specifically to the "coming Son of man" sayings, Hare concludes that it is not the case that Jesus spoke of the coming of the Son of man, and that the movement after his death then identified the Son of man with Jesus. Rather, it was the early Christian movement that spoke of the coming of the Son of man, and by it they meant the return of Jesus.[61] "Son of man" is hence simply a designation for Jesus; in itself, it has no apocalyptic or eschatological connotations or resonances. Thus, for Hare as for Crossan, and consistent with much of recent scholarship, the coming Son of man sayings disappear from the data base for constructing a historical image of Jesus.[62] Without these sayings, the textual basis for saying Jesus expected an imminent eschaton becomes very slender.

The Kingdom of God

The other major category of sayings commonly seen as pointing to an imminent eschaton are kingdom of God sayings. It is important to note that only a small number of them actually point to an eschatological context by speaking of an imminent coming of the kingdom.[63] Sayings about entering the kingdom, the beatitudes that speak of the kingdom as belonging to certain groups, even the prayer "Thy kingdom come," do not in themselves imply an imminent eschatological kingdom.

However, in this century's scholarship, seeing the kingdom sayings eschatologically has been dominant and has been fueled by two factors. The first factor was described in chapter 3: the role of the coming Son of man sayings in the interpretation of the kingdom sayings. Namely, the imminence associated with some of the coming Son of man sayings was imported into the kingdom sayings and created the impression that the tradition speaks widely of an imminent eschatological kingdom.[64]

The second factor is the role Mark's gospel has played in the eschatological reading of the Jesus tradition, including the kingdom sayings. It is Mark, of course, who reports the first words of Jesus' ministry to have been, "The kingdom of God is at hand! Repent (1:15)." As Jesus' "inaugural address" in Mark, it suggests two things: that the kingdom of God was the heart of Jesus' message and mission, and that Jesus spoke of it as "at hand."

A second verse in Mark has also contributed strongly to an understanding of the kingdom as imminent eschaton. This is the most plausible way of reading Mark 9:1: "Truly, I tell you, there are some standing here who will not taste death until they see the kingdom of God come in power."[65] Imminent eschaton is also pointed to by "the little apocalypse" of Mark 13, which climaxes with the darkening of the sun and the moon, "the Son of man coming in clouds with great power and glory," and the gathering of the elect, all of which was to occur in that generation (13:24–30).

The gospel of Mark has thus played a major role in generating the impression that imminent eschatology was central to Jesus. Yet the picture created by Mark has been sharply called into question in recent scholarship. We may begin with Mark 1:15. Though scholars routinely recognize Mark 1:15 is redactional, it has also been common to treat it as if it were historically on target. This is odd. Matthew and Luke, it should be noted, each report the "inaugural address" of Jesus differently. Unless we are willing to say that Mark is more historical simply because he is earlier, there is no reason to see Mark 1:15 as a historically accurate crystallization of what Jesus was most centrally about.[66] Rather, it is *Mark's* thematic summary of Jesus' message.

Indeed, Mark 1:15, 9:1, and the little apocalypse of chapter 13 seem to be "all of a piece" and reflective of Mark's theology. Taken together, they suggest that the author of Mark, writing around the year 70, thought that the eschaton was imminent. Mark 13 is especially instructive, with its clear reference to a crisis involving the temple. A "desolating sacrilege" in the temple — along with wars and rumors of wars, false prophets, and persecution — is among the events to occur shortly before the coming of the Son of man. All of this, the Jesus of Mark says, would happen before that generation passed away. But rather than representing an original eschatological orientation going back to Jesus, Mark may represent an intensification of eschatological expectation triggered by the Jewish war of rebellion against Rome in the years 66–70, and the threat (and actuality) of the temple's destruction that those years brought. Mark is "a wartime gospel," and the picture we get of the centrality and imminence of the kingdom of God may well be the product of Mark's redaction during a time of intensified eschatological expectation.[67]

Thus Mark is increasingly viewed as an "apocalyptic gospel," and Mark 1:15 is seen as Mark's announcement of his apocalyptic theme. The recognition that Mark 1:15 is redactional and thematic should give us pause. Without Mark 1:15, would we think of the kingdom of God as *the* central theme of Jesus' message? We would see it as *a* central theme, yes; but as *the* central theme? And without Mark 1:15 and 9:1, would we think of imminence as central to Jesus' teaching about the kingdom? And, more broadly, without the coming Son of man sayings and without Mark's reading of the kingdom, would we think of the heart of Jesus' message as the need for repentance because the eschaton was imminent?

If the kingdom is not to be understood within the framework of imminent eschatology, how then is it to be understood? I have not worked this out in a detailed way, but the following possibilities seem promising as an agenda to be explored. The list should not be seen as categories of sayings, but rather as resonances or nuances of meaning associated with Jesus' use of kingdom language:

> *Kingdom as* dunamis *of God.* Kingdom as the power of God seems clearly indicated in Matt. 12:28 = Luke 11:20.

Kingdom as presence of God. The kingdom is present, only people ordinarily do not "see" that. Such seems to be the meaning of sayings such as Luke 17:20, Thomas 3 and 113. To be in the experiential presence of God is to experience the kingdom, which is also suggested by the kingdom as "epiphany of God."[68]

Kingdom as life under the kingship of God. Kingdom as yoke, as "covenant." Such a life is radically different from other ways of living.

Kingdom as a reality one can be "in" or "out of." This is related to the previous two, and also may point to kingdom as community.

Kingdom as "theo-political." Here the emphasis is on kingdom as a political metaphor and the contrast to other kingdoms: there is the kingdom of God, and there is the kingdom of Herod, kingdom of Caesar, etc.[69]

Kingdom as the ideal state of affairs. Kingdom imaged as, e.g., the messianic banquet.

I do not know if a detailed exegetical study would substantiate all of these, or whether some would emerge as "most important" and others as peripheral. Here I want simply to suggest that the disappearance of kingdom-as-imminent-eschaton does not leave the phrase devoid of rich and plausible resonances.

Concluding Clarifications

Finally, I wish to conclude with four clarifying remarks about what is (and is not) being denied in my own non-eschatological understanding of Jesus.

First, I think that Jesus probably had some eschatological beliefs. It seems likely that he believed that God's promises to Israel would some-day be fulfilled. He probably believed in an afterlife (though I have no clear idea what it means to say this). Moreover, I think he occasion-ally talked about eschatological matters. The way he is reported to have done so is instructive. Restricting ourselves to Q and Mark (and ex-cluding special Matthew in particular), Jesus spoke about eschatology only infrequently, and then in ways that subverted popular eschatolog-ical notions.[70] The broader point, however, is that when I speak of a "non-eschatological Jesus," I do not mean that Jesus never said anything about eschatology. I mean, rather, that imminent eschatology is not to be the interpretive context for reading the Jesus tradition.

Second, I think that Jesus was concerned about "the future." I think he threatened the temple and Jerusalem (as the home of the ruling

elites) with destruction, much like the classical prophets of the Hebrew Bible did.[71] I think his alternative social vision is intended as
something to be embodied in the present and extended into the future. That is, to say Jesus was non-eschatological does not mean that
he was unconcerned about the future or about history or community. A
non-eschatological Jesus need not be imagined as an enlightened master living in a timeless present or as a radically individualistic Hellenistic
Cynic sage unconcerned with the future of his people.

Third, I think there is urgency in the Jesus traditions. One of the
virtues of the eschatological consensus is that it provided a plausible
explanation of the bell of crisis ringing throughout the tradition (and
much of the scholarship against which it was reacting at the end of the
nineteenth century did not): the urgency came from the imminent expectation of the eschaton. Time is short. But urgency can be accounted for
in other ways as well. There is the urgency of the wisdom teacher: what
is at stake in the choice between "the two ways" is nothing less than
the way of life and the way of death. There is the urgency of the social
prophet who speaks in a time of crisis, issues indignant indictments of
ruling elites, and warns passionately of coming catastrophe. To say that
Jesus is non-eschatological is thus not to deny the element of crisis in the
Jesus tradition. Rather, it leads to a different interpretation of the crisis.

Fourth and finally, I want to speak briefly about how a non-
eschatological understanding of Jesus can be correlated with the role
of eschatology in the early Christian movement, including the synoptic
gospels in particular. My intention is not to argue this case, but simply
to suggest what it would look like. For the sake of schematic clarity, I
will present it in a series of numbered statements.

1. Jesus' message and mission were non-eschatological. To put this
only slightly differently, what Crossan calls "apocalyptic eschatology"
was not part of Jesus' message or understanding of his mission or self-
understanding.

2. The Easter experience (and perhaps the Gentile mission as well)
introduced an eschatological element. Some (and perhaps many) in the
early community believed that they were living in "the end of days" and
that Jesus would return soon. But this was not the center of their understanding, and their message was not primarily, "The end is at hand,
repent!" Rather, it was one of the things they believed.

3. Intensifications of eschatological expectation occurred in response
to particular crises: in Palestine, around the year 70, and perhaps earlier
in 40; in Asia Minor near the end of the first century. Thus eschatological expectation varied in intensity at different times (and probably in
different places).

4. The gospel of Mark comes out of a period of intensified eschatological expectation.

5. Matthew basically takes over Mark's pattern; thus, like Mark, Matthew continues to expect the return of Jesus soon.

6. Luke's largely non-eschatological understanding of Jesus is an earlier and more historical image.

This last point requires further exposition. The role of eschatology in Luke's gospel is quite different from that of Matthew and Mark: there is little to suggest an imminent parousia. How should we see this difference? Within the framework of the previously dominant paradigm, Mark and Matthew were seen as continuing the emphasis of Jesus, and Luke was understood as adapting the tradition to the delay of the parousia. A non-eschatological understanding of Jesus would reverse this. If Mark and Matthew represent an intensification of eschatological expectation rather than Luke representing a diminishment, then the author of Luke, though writing later than Mark and perhaps "correcting" the imminent eschatology of Mark, actually represents an earlier non-eschatological understanding of Jesus.

As noted earlier, all of this is "suggested" rather than argued. It has a twofold purpose at the end of this essay. It shows that it is possible to sketch a plausible alternative account of the role of eschatology in the early Christian movement within the interpretive context of a non-eschatological Jesus. It also shows how far-reaching the eschatological question is: it deeply affects our understanding not only of the historical Jesus but of early Christianity as well.

Notes

1. It is one of the central themes in the two essays at the beginning of the present volume, and I have also written about it elsewhere. See "Jesus and Eschatology: A Reassessment," in *Images of Jesus Today*, ed. James H. Charlesworth and Walter P. Weaver (Valley Forge, Pa.: Trinity Press International: 1994), 42–67. For earlier treatments, see *Conflict, Holiness and Politics* (New York: Edwin Mellen Press, 1984), esp. 8–13, 201–76; "An Orthodoxy Reconsidered: The 'End-of-the-World Jesus,' " in N. T. Wright and L. D. Hurst, ed., *The Glory of Christ in the New Testament* (Oxford: Clarendon Press, 1987, 207–17; the essay was written in late 1984).

2. Chapter 2 above, p.19.

3. Including E. P. Sanders (treated later in this chapter); Geza Vermes, *The Religion of Jesus the Jew* (Minneapolis: Fortress, 1993); and probably John P. Meier. The second volume of Meier's *Jesus: A Marginal Jew,* in which he will treat the message and activity of Jesus, has not been published as I write this. However, his recent essay, "Reflections on Jesus-of-History Research Today," in James H. Charlesworth, ed., *Jesus' Jewishness* (New York: Crossroad, 1991), 84–107, suggests that he is likely to present a form of Jesus as eschatological prophet.

4. Gerhard Sauter, "The Concept and Task of Eschatology: Theological and Philosophical Reflections," *Scottish Journal of Theology* 41 (1988), 499–515; reference to Calov on p. 499. According to *The Oxford English Dictionary* (1971), the term is first used in English around the middle of the 1800s: it cites the first use of "eschatology" as 1844, and of "eschatological" as 1854.

5. I do not know if biblical scholars prior to Reimarus (1694–1768) used the term. Reimarus used it to refer both to the political eschatology that he ascribed to Jesus and to the more supernatural eschatology that he ascribed to the early church. See Albert Schweitzer, *The Quest of the Historical Jesus* (1906, 1910), chapter 2.

6. A point that is emphasized by N. Thomas Wright, *The New Testament and the People of God* (Minneapolis: Fortress, 1992); see, e.g., 208, 285–86, 298–99, 333. See also E. P. Sanders, *Judaism: Practice and Belief, 63 B.C.E.–66 C.E.* (Philadelphia: Trinity Press International, 1992), 368.

7. Eugene Boring, professor of New Testament at Texas Christian University and author of a number of important studies. The exception may be 2 Peter 3:10–12, which speaks of the meltdown and disappearance of the elements, and which might therefore be designated a "molecular eschatology."

8. In a number of my previous writings, I have used the phrase "end-of-the-world" expectation as "shorthand" for this notion, and the phrase "the end-of-the-world Jesus" to designate an image of Jesus in which the expectation of such a dramatic event is central. I did not intend to imply the end of the space-time world. To make this clear, in the present essay I will not use "end of the world" as a shorthand expression.

9. In appreciation of Dodd, I wish to add that he seems to me (and to many Jesus scholars today) to have been correct in his emphasis that Jesus spoke of the kingdom of God as a present reality. It is his use of the words "realized eschatology" that strikes me as infelicitous.

10. The stretching of the term nearly beyond recognition is illustrated in one of Norman Perrin's early works. In *The Kingdom of God in the Teaching of Jesus* (Philadelphia: Westminster, 1963), Perrin argued (and accepted) the claim that this century's scholarship had established that "kingdom of God" in the message of Jesus is to be understood in the eschatological sense affirmed by Weiss and Schweitzer. In the same book, Perrin also argued that Jesus' message may not be interpreted in terms of a linear understanding of time (chronological futurity is gone), that Jesus departed from an apocalyptic understanding of history in favor of a prophetic understanding, that Jesus' eschatological teaching did not necessarily involve the end of time or cosmic catastrophe, and that it yielded no guidance regarding the manner or time of consummation (see pp. 185, 176–78, 190, and 198.) With this many qualifications, does it make sense to say that Jesus was eschatological in the sense affirmed by Weiss and Schweitzer? How broad can the meaning of eschatology become without the word ceasing to be meaningful?

11. G. B. Caird, *The Language and Imagery of the Bible* (London: Duckworth, 1980), 243–71. He also proposed a subscript system for distinguishing them. His conclusions about use of end-of-the-world language in the Bible are illuminating: (1) The biblical writers literally believed the world had a temporal

beginning and would have a temporal end; (2) they regularly used end-of-the-world language to refer to that which they well knew was not the end of the world; (3) As with all use of metaphor, we must allow for the possibility of literalist misinterpretation by some hearers and of possible blurring between mode of communication and meaning on the part of the speaker.

12. Respectively, J. C. Beker, "Biblical Theology Today," in M. Marty and D. G. Peerman, ed., *New Theology Number Six* (New York: Macmillan, 1969), 27; and J. Carmignac, "Les dangers de l'eschatologie," *New Testament Studies* 17 (1970–71), esp. 388–90.

13. David E. Aune, *The Anchor Bible Dictionary (ABD)*, ed. David Noel Freedman (New York: Doubleday, 1992), 2:575–609. In this impressively clear, informative, and long essay (over thirty double-column pages), Aune treats the whole sweep of "biblical eschatology": Old Testament eschatology, early Jewish eschatology, and early Christian eschatology. Quoted words are from pp. 575, 576.

14. Ibid., 577.

15. Ibid., 583. See also p. 596, where he notes "the impropriety" of speaking of the pre-exilic prophets as eschatological.

16. John Dominic Crossan, *The Historical Jesus: The Life of a Mediterranean Jewish Peasant* (New York: Harper & Row, 1991), 238.

17. Ibid., 238; italics added.

18. To raise a question: I agree with Crossan that the items in his list are all forms of world-negation; but why use "eschatology" as a *generic term* for world-negation? Why not simply use "world-negation?" My point is not to engage in a terminological quarrel. Crossan is very clear, defining his terms with care and precision. Moreover, he and I are agreed that imminent eschatology (what he calls "apocalyptic eschatology") was not part of the message of Jesus. My point rather is to ponder whether anything is gained by broadening the meaning of "eschatology" this far.

19. For other comments on the confusion within the discipline caused by the imprecise ways in which "eschatology" and "apocalyptic" are used, see chapter 2 above, p. 31.

20. This does not completely preclude eschatology from the teaching of Jesus. I think Jesus occasionally addressed eschatological topics and probably had some eschatological beliefs, about which I will say more later in this essay. But I do not think eschatology in the narrow sense was important for him in any significant way.

21. John Koenig in the *New York Times Book Review,* cited on the back cover of the paperback edition of Sanders's book.

22. As will become apparent, Professor Sanders and I differ at a fundamental level. Yet, as is often the case, we learn a lot from those with whom we disagree. Interacting with his work has led me to a clearer understanding of why I see things differently.

23. Chapter 2 above, pp. 19–21.

24. See above, chapter 2, p. 20 and n. 8.

25. Sanders, *Jesus and Judaism* (Philadelphia: Fortress, 1985), 61–76.

26. It is important to note that the temple action and the accusation are not

in themselves evidence for an eschatological orientation. It was quite possible to speak of the destruction of the temple (as Jesus ben Hananiah did in the early 60s of the first century) without implying that the promises of Jewish restoration eschatology were about to be fulfilled; and "overturning tables" can mean something other than the impending eschatological destruction of the old temple. For a very different interpretation of the temple action, see chapter 5 below.

27. Sanders, *Jesus and Judaism*, 73.

28. Ibid., 77–119. See also Sanders, *Judaism: Practice and Belief*, 289–98.

29. Sanders, *Jews and Judaism*, 77–90.

30. Ibid., 95–106.

31. Ibid., 98. Italics in original.

32. Among scholars who see the choosing of twelve as going back to Jesus without setting it within the framework of imminent eschatology are C. H. Dodd and G. B. Caird; the latter also argues explicitly that Jesus was concerned with the restoration of Israel, even as he rejects imminent eschatology. My point is simply that there is no necessary connection between "the twelve" and imminent eschatology.

33. Sanders, *Jesus and Judaism*, 91–95. On p. 152 he indicates that this is the most important category of data: *more than any other single fact*, the imminent eschatological expectation of the early church "shows where the emphasis lay in Jesus' own message."

34. Caird, *Jesus and the Jewish Nation* (London: Athlone, 1965).

35. See Horsley, *Jesus and the Spiral of Violence* (San Francisco: Harper & Row, 1987), 129–45, 160; William R. Herzog, "The Quest for the Historical Jesus and the Discovery of the Apocalyptic Jesus," *Pacific Theological Review* 19 (1985): 25–39, esp. 32; David B. Batstone, "Jesus, Apocalyptic, and World Transformation," *Theology Today* 49 (1992): 383–97.

36. A fact that Sanders both obscures and acknowledges. In the text of his exposition, he says, "That John himself was an eschatological prophet of repentance is clearly implied in Josephus' account" (92). In his footnote to this sentence, he says, "That John was an eschatological prophet is less clear in Josephus, who here as elsewhere probably downplays eschatological features" (p. 371, n. 4). The point: Josephus does not speak of John as an eschatological prophet.

37. Crossan, *The Historical Jesus*, 237–38. Crossan has speculated that the change may have been triggered in part by the shock of John's death.

38. Sanders also notes that the two themes of judgment and repentance are typical of restoration eschatology. He therefore finds their relative absence in the message of Jesus surprising and not what one would expect from an advocate of restoration eschatology (Sanders, *Jesus and Judaism*, 112–19). Obviously, this is not surprising if one lets go of the restoration eschatology *Gestalt* of Jesus.

39. Ibid., 227–28.

40. I do not think it was *directly* subversive of political authority, that is, not an advocate of direct revolt. I think Sanders is right to emphasize this and to include this in his list of facts.

41. See Martin Hengel's comment that "the delay of the parousia" has become a "tired cliché" in Wright, *The New Testament and the People of God*, 462.

42. His argument for the authenticity of Matt. 16:27 requires setting aside the notion that it is a revision of its parallel in Mark 8:38 (p. 143). Most scholars would not be persuaded by this argument.

43. The logic is that language of a new temple (if seen as a literal replacement of the present temple in Jerusalem) intrinsically links up with restoration eschatology. I find this logic persuasive myself. Indeed, *if language of a new temple is authentic to Jesus and if he meant it literally*, then I think Sanders is basically right about Jesus. Sanders's exposition recognizes the importance of a saying about the temple being destroyed/rebuilt and then says that even if Jesus spoke *only* of destruction, it would still point to "new temple" eschatology. Here I disagree: I think he needs *both* "destroyed" and "rebuilt" if his case is to be persuasive. As noted earlier, it was possible in the first century (and earlier, for that matter) to speak of the temple's destruction apart from any eschatological expectation. It is a new (or renewed) physical temple in Jerusalem literally coming from God that connects to restoration eschatology.

44. In a helpfully illuminating remark at the 1988 annual meeting of the Society of Biblical Literature, Sanders suggested that he thought Jesus expected a divine intervention as dramatic as what is reported in the story of the walls of Jericho falling down in the time of Joshua.

45. Sanders, *Jesus and Judaism*, 307, 321–22, 324.

46. Recent studies of Q and Thomas have shown that both are dominated by wisdom, both as a form of speech and as a category of thought. I am not myself convinced that Q can be "layered" into successive redactions, as John Kloppenborg has argued in an important and influential book, *The Formation of Q* (Philadelphia: Fortress, 1987). And though it seems obvious to me that Thomas includes both earlier and later material, I am not confident that we can sort it into an early and later "edition." However, regardless of how one views the "layering" of Q and Thomas, it is clear even from their present form that the gospel tradition from a very early stage contained a large component of wisdom material.

47. I have treated the subversive wisdom of Jesus in a number of places. See chapter 8 in this book, chapter 6 in *Jesus: A New Vision* (San Francisco: HarperSanFrancisco, 1987) and chapter 4 in *Meeting Jesus again for the First Time* (San Francisco: HarperSanFrancisco, 1994).

48. Interestingly, this does not appear in Sanders's list of "facts" we can know about Jesus. Sanders might reply that parables and aphorisms belong to the sayings of Jesus and that he is seeking to avoid basing anything foundational on the sayings tradition. But it seems to me that a statement like "Jesus told parables and spoke aphorisms" is a "fact" we know about Jesus, quite apart from our uncertainty about the exact wording of particular parables and aphorisms.

49. Sanders is exempt from the possible caricature in this particular form. He does not think Jesus talked very much about judgment and does not think Jesus emphasized repentance.

50. It is important not to treat this issue as if it were simply a matter of the relationship between "wisdom" and "apocalyptic." If one reduces "wisdom" and "apocalyptic" to abstract categories without much specific content, then one does find the two being combined in documents of the time. It is when one moves beyond wisdom and apocalyptic as abstract categories and looks at the particularities of what is attributed to Jesus when he is seen as an eschatological prophet that the difficulties arise.

51. See my comment in note 48 about the absence of "Jesus as a teacher of wisdom" from Sanders's list of foundational facts.

52. Chapter 3, pp. 51–57.

53. The main debate was not about their authenticity, but about whether Jesus expected his own return as the Son of man or announced the imminent arrival of a supernatural Son of man (not himself).

54. For a description of his method, see chapter 2 above, pp. 33–34.

55. Crossan, *The Historical Jesus,* 243, 454–56.

56. Crossan points out another interesting result of his numerical analysis. If one broadens the category of "coming Son of man" sayings to *all* "Son of man" sayings, the numerical summary for *the phrase* "Son of man" is 40: 1 + 39 (40 complexes, with only one having plural attestation, and all the rest singular attestation). The one "Son of man" saying that has plural attestation for the phrase "Son of man" is "Foxes have holes...," a *present* Son of man saying and not a *future* Son of man saying (Q and Thomas: Luke 9:58 = Matt. 8:19–20, Gos. Thos. 86). Ibid., 255–56.

57. For his account of how this happened, see ibid., 245–55.

58. Douglas R. A. Hare, *The Son of Man Tradition* (Minneapolis: Fortress, 1990).

59. Ibid., x.

60. This is a theme running throughout his book. For one expression of it, see ibid., 257: "the phrase had denotative rather than connotative force; it referred to Jesus exclusively when used in sayings attributed to him but communicated nothing about his status in the divine plan."

61. About the apocalyptic Son of man sayings, Hare concludes, 277–78: "They conform so closely to the expectation of Jesus' Parousia that soon prevailed in the post-Easter church that all can be readily explained on this basis." It is thus puzzling to me that James Charlesworth cites Hare, as well as Barnabas Lindars (see above, chapter 3, p. 52), in a context that implies that both are affirming an understanding of the Son of man sayings different from my own. See Charlesworth and Weaver, *Images of Jesus Today,* 22.

62. My own sense is that the more comprehensive question of the "Son of man" sayings as a whole is in an unstable place. Though there is considerable agreement about what the phrase is unlikely to have meant (including that it is unlikely that Jesus used it in an eschatological or apocalyptic sense), there is as yet no persuasive explanation of why it is used so often in words attributed to Jesus.

63. See Sanders's helpful categorization of kingdom sayings into six groups, *Jesus and Judaism,* 141–50: (1) kingdom as "covenant"; (2) kingdom as yet to be fully established; (3) kingdom as an other-worldly unexpected event involv-

ing judgment; (4) kingdom as a decisive future event involving a new social order; (5) kingdom as present; (6) kingdom sayings that speak of the character of the kingdom or its king.

64. For my earlier analysis, see chapter 3 above, pp. 53–55.

65. An earlier generation of critics was virtually unanimous in seeing this verse as authentic and as pointing to imminent eschatology. More recent scholarship (represented by Norman Perrin's 1967 book, *Rediscovering the Teaching of Jesus* [New York: Harper & Row, 1967]) tends to see it as inauthentic.

66. Though Matthew takes over Mark's summary, the "inaugural address" of the Jesus of Matthew is the Sermon on the Mount (Matt. 5–7). Luke reports Jesus' inaugural address to have been, "The Spirit of the Lord is upon me, and has anointed me to preach good news to the poor" (Luke 4:18f). The point: each evangelist (including Mark) has a particular image of Jesus and uses the "inaugural address" of Jesus to point to that image. There is no *prima facie* reason for thinking that Mark 1:15 is more historical than what we find in Matthew and Luke.

67. For Mark as a "wartime gospel," see Daryl Schmidt, *The Gospel of Mark* (Sonoma, Calif.: Polebridge, 1970), 3–6. For an interesting case that Mark 13 is to a large extent the product of an earlier threat to the temple (in the year 40, when the Roman emperor Caligula planned to have a statue of himself erected in it), see Gerd Theissen, *The Gospels in Context: Social and Political History in the Synoptic Tradition* (Minneapolis: Fortress, 1991), 125–65.

68. For this meaning, see especially Bruce Chilton, *God in Strength: Jesus' Announcement of the Kingdom* (Linz: Plöchl, 1979).

69. Brian Rice McCarthy, "Jesus, The Kingdom, and Theopolitics," *SBL 1990 Seminar Papers* (Atlanta: Scholars Press, 1990), 311–21.

70. For further development of this point, see "Jesus and Eschatology: A Reassessment," 60–61; and *Meeting Jesus Again for the First Time,* 85. There I treat Mark 12:18–27 (the question from the Sadducees) and four Q sayings (Luke 10:12 = Matt. 10:15; Luke 10:13–14 = Matt. 11:21–22; Luke 11:31 = Matt. 12:42; Luke 11:32 = Matt. 12:41) to illustrate the way Jesus' eschatological sayings often involve a subversion of eschatological notions of the time. Two further points about the Q sayings: (1) Their purpose is not to affirm or proclaim a judgment; rather, they presuppose a belief about the judgment and subvert it. (2) They do not say anything about imminence. Though two of them refer to "this generation," the point is not that the judgment would come within "this generation"; rather, at the judgment, whenever it comes, Gentiles from the distant past will do better than some from "this generation."

71. See *Jesus: A New Vision,* chapter 8; and *Conflict, Holiness and Politics,* where I do an extensive analysis of the synoptic threat tradition, arguing that little of it is eschatologically oriented and that most of it is about evenly divided between threats of historical destruction and threats whose content is unidentified. See esp. 201–27, 265–76.

Chapter Five

Jesus and Politics
in Contemporary Scholarship

One of the most notable features of contemporary Jesus scholarship is a reopening of the question of Jesus and politics. As noted in chapter 2, significant voices in North American scholarship, in what could be an emerging majority position, are affirming that there was a sociopolitical dimension to the message and activity of Jesus.

This is a new development, even though the claim that Jesus was political goes back to the birth of the discipline over two hundred years ago. In a work commonly seen as the beginning of the quest for the historical Jesus, Hermann Samuel Reimarus argued that Jesus' message about the kingdom of God referred to a this-worldly kingdom that would involve liberation from Rome, and that Jesus' death resulted from his naive expectation that he could stir up a successful revolt.[1] Yet most often, scholars in the two centuries since have denied that Jesus was political.[2]

Why has this changed? The major reason is one of the central characteristics of the contemporary renaissance: the entry into the discipline of interdisciplinary models and perspectives. These provide new angles of vision for seeing the social world of Jesus. Social world is context, and these perspectives give us a fuller picture of the context within which the Jesus tradition receives its historical meaning. In this chapter, I will describe three of these perspectives, what they enable us to see about the social world of first-century Jewish Palestine, and their effects as lenses through which to see the Jesus tradition.

The Importance of Definition

As with eschatology, there is both a narrow and broad definition of politics, and whether one sees Jesus as political is greatly affected by one's definition. The narrow definition associates politics with "government": to be political is to seek to affect governmental policy, or to gain a position of governmental power, or to attempt to overthrow the government. The broader definition of politics builds on the semantic associations of its Greek root *polis*. *Polis* means "city," and politics concerns the shape and shaping of the city, and by extension the shape and shaping of a society's life.

If "politics" is used in the narrow sense, then Jesus was basically non-political. A few scholars since Reimarus have argued that Jesus sought a change in government by inciting a political rebellion against Rome, but their arguments have not persuaded many. Moreover, it seems evident that Jesus did not seek a position of governmental power or to reform governmental policy.

Yet, as I shall argue, Jesus both challenged the existing social order and advocated an alternative. That challenge involved social criticism, an alternative social vision, and the embodiment of that vision in the life of a community. This is "political" in the broad sense of the word. Indeed, in this broader sense, much of the biblical tradition is political. Ancient Israel's originating event involved liberation from the lordship of Pharaoh and creation of the alternative community of Moses. Much of the legal portion of the Torah concerns the structuring of community life, and not just individual virtue. The political character of the tradition continues in the second major division of the Hebrew Bible, the prophets. From King David onward through the time of the monarchies, a period of about four hundred years, the social prophets of Israel indicted the ruling elites (political, economic, and religious) in the name of an alternative social vision that they affirmed to come from God.

It is in this broader sense of the word "politics" that contemporary scholarship is increasingly affirming a sociopolitical dimension to Jesus. Before turning to that, it will be illuminating briefly to examine some of the reasons why Jesus has commonly been seen as non-political by both popular Christianity and academic scholarship.

The Exclusion of Politics

There are at least four major reasons for the denial of politics to Jesus. The first is because Jesus scholars have most often used the narrow definition of politics. Both proponents and critics of seeing Jesus as an advocate of the cause of Jewish liberation from Rome (what used to be called "the Zealot hypothesis"[3]) have tended to equate being "political" in first-century Palestine with anti-Roman revolutionary activity. Denying that Jesus was this, most scholars have concluded that Jesus was therefore non-political. It is striking how often one runs into this argument in the history of scholarship.[4]

Even more pervasive as a reason for the exclusion of politics has been the *Gestalt* of Jesus as an eschatological figure. The logic is straightforward: because Jesus expected the last judgment and the "end" of this world soon, or alternatively because he expected the transformation of this world through a supernatural act of God, he was not interested in social or political questions. What did they matter? Why be concerned to change the world if in its present form it was soon to end? From Albert Schweitzer at the beginning of this century through Rudolf Bultmann and Günther Bornkamm and (in some quarters) into the present, this has been a frequent refrain of scholarship.[5]

A third reason is the individualistic orientation of much of modern Jesus scholarship. It has taken several forms. Within the framework of traditional Christian piety, Jesus and the New Testament are seen as concerned with the eternal religious questions of the individual and his or her relationship to God and the neighbor, not with the specific social and political issues of a particular time and place. This way of seeing Jesus was especially common in nineteenth-century scholarship, though its effects linger into the present. In this century, existentialist interpretation of Jesus' eschatology has most commonly radically internalized and individualized his message. The individualistic reading of the tradition continues in our time in the picture of Jesus as a Hellenistic-type Cynic sage who spoke of a life-style for individuals, not for a community.

A fourth reason is the social location of Jesus scholarship. Since its beginnings in the Enlightenment, most of it has been done by northern Euro-American academics who have generally been white, male, and middle-class. Moreover, until recently, most of our academic positions have been in institutions related to the church.

Perhaps more than anything else, that social location affects how and what we see. It generates the perspectives through which we see the world, including the world behind the texts, and functions as both lens and blinders. Five factors are especially important:

1. The academy tends to be an individualistic milieu, and accounts in part for the individualistic orientation just described.

2. The churchly social location of much of scholarship has led to seeing the texts through Christian (or sometimes "anti-Christian") lenses: the focus is on the relationship of the texts to Christian teachings (beliefs and ethics) rather than on their relationship to the social environment out of which they came.

3. Within the framework of the modern separation of religion and politics, scholars have often concentrated on the "religious" meaning of texts, as if religion were separable from other matters in the first century.

4. The middle-class status of most academics has not been conducive to seeing a sociopolitical dimension in the Jesus traditions, just as the social location of much of the church during the centuries of Christendom made it unlikely that priests and preachers would find Jesus' message to be politically subversive. The social location of scholarship means that we often miss things in the text that the experience of poverty, marginality, patriarchy, or oppression might have led us to see.

5. Finally, unless we make special efforts to compensate for it, our seeing of texts is unconsciously shaped by our experience of the world that we know, namely, post-Enlightenment modern industrial society with its middle class and emphasis upon individualism.[6]

Seeing from New Perspectives

To some degree, the social location of scholarship remains much the same. The majority of us are still middle-class white male northern Euro-Americans in academic institutions. What then accounts for a more political reading of the Jesus traditions? The primary reason is the emergence of new perspectives from which to see the traditions. The change is not because we suddenly have new data; rather, for a number of reasons, familiar data are being seen in new ways.

New voices have entered the discipline, especially feminist and liberationist voices. The "view from below" provides an angle of vision on the texts quite different from the view "from the middle" or the "view from the top."

Many of us (probably a majority) now teach in secular or secularized universities and colleges. The change in institutional setting means that the questions brought to the texts are no longer shaped primarily by a Christian agenda. The focus has shifted to the relationship of the texts to their original historical setting, and/or to their relationship to other disciplines within a more pluralistic academy.

The final reason flows out of the previous one: the emergence of interdisciplinary and cross-cultural perspectives and models for seeing the traditions about Jesus.[7] These new perspectives and models make it possible to some extent to step outside our own social world by providing vantage points that enable us to enter imaginatively into the very different social world of first-century Jewish Palestine and to see meanings in the Jesus tradition we otherwise would not see.

I want to illustrate this claim by describing the perspectives generated by three social models. Each highlights a major characteristic of Jesus' social world and thereby provides a context within which to place many of the most central themes of his message and activity. Together, they enable us to see that Jesus was a sociopolitical critic as well as an advocate of an alternative social vision — in short, that he was "political" in the broad sense of the word.

Peasant Society and Politics in First-Century Palestine

The first perspective, providing a new way of seeing both the social world of first-century Palestine and the meaning of words and actions in that context, is the awareness that it was a peasant society. To say that it was a peasant society does not mean simply that there were a lot of peasants (though that is true). Rather, it is shorthand for a particular type of society, namely, "pre-industrial agrarian society," one of five types of society identified by Gerhard Lenski.[8]

According to Lenski, peasant societies are different not only from modern industrial societies but also from three other pre-modern types of society: hunting and gathering, simple horticultural, and advanced horticultural societies. The difference between peasant societies and horticultural societies is in part technological. The digging stick and hoe were replaced by the plow, increasing both the scale and efficiency of agriculture.

Even more so, the difference between peasant societies and earlier horticultural societies is socioeconomic organization: the emergence of centralized forms of government. Cities (and not simply towns) began to develop, made possible by greater agricultural production, to be followed by city-states, nations, and eventually empires. These more centralized forms of social organization were dominated by ruling elites who generally lived in cities or towns. The politically and economically dominant urban elites no longer worked the land, even though (as we shall see) they controlled much of the land. Thus in these societies, there were essentially two social classes: urban elites and rural peasants.

Between these two classes there was a huge gulf. Indeed, "marked social inequality" was the single most striking trait of pre-industrial agrarian societies.[9] This inequality was above all one of wealth. Where did the urban elites get their wealth? They did not manufacture anything or produce anything. In these societies, there was no significant generation of wealth through industry; manufacturing was small-scale and done by hand. Rather, in such societies the primary source of wealth was agriculture: land and the people who worked the land.

Thus, in a sentence, the elites got their wealth from the peasants. They did so through a "tributary mode of production" by means of which they extracted wealth from peasants in two ways.[10] The first was land rental. Through the process of land consolidation, the elites over time owned more and more of the land. Peasants who were small landholders easily acquired debt and often lost their land to the elites to whom they were indebted. Ownership of agricultural land generated income from land rent (paid in cash or kind) and the subsistence employment of agricultural workers.[11]

The second source of income was taxation, which was primarily on agricultural production. Through these two means, wealth flowed from the countryside to the city, from rural peasants to urban elites. Estimates vary and differ to some degree from society to society, but generally about two-thirds of the wealth generated by agriculture ended up in the hands of the urban elites.[12] The remaining one-third was left for the other 90 percent of the population, the rural peasants who were, of course, the primary producers of wealth.[13] To fill out the model, Lenski subdivides the primary twofold class division into nine more specific classes. The upper five comprised the urban elites. The first two of these were *the ruler* himself, plus *the governing class* (high officials and traditional aristocracies). Together, they were 1 to 2 percent of the population and generally received one-half of the wealth generated by agricultural production. Third, *retainers* were essentially a service class to the elites, in effect, their employees. The retainer class included soldiers, bureaucrats, scribes, tax collectors, etc. Fourth and fifth were a *merchant class* and (in many societies) a *priestly class.* These three groups typically comprised about 8 percent of the population and received about one-sixth of the society's income. The four lower classes (90 percent of the population) were peasants proper (agriculturalists), artisans, unclean and degraded classes (despised or downgraded occupations), and expendables (outlaws, beggars, etc.)

The above is not intended as a description of first-century Jewish Palestine *in particular.* Rather, in broad strokes, it describes most premodern agrarian societies with centralized forms of government. Indeed, this type of society characterized ancient Israel throughout much of its history, beginning with the emergence of the monarchy around 1000 B.C.E. Seeing this has great illuminating power. I can recall how it transformed my understanding of the classical prophets of ancient Israel. When I was in seminary and graduate school some twenty-five years ago, I was struck by the prophets' passion for social justice and their warnings of impending historical destruction because of injustice. Then and through the first half of my teaching career, I also took it for granted (as most scholars did, I think) that their indictments and warnings were directed at Israel "as a whole": *Israel* had become unjust and corrupt.

Then, some ten to fifteen years ago as models of peasant societies began to have an effect on biblical scholarship, the awareness that ancient Israel was a two-class society divided between oppressive urban elites and exploited rural peasants generated a very different perception of the prophetic message. Their indictments were directed not at *Israel,* but at the elites in particular. It was the elites (and not the population as a whole) who were responsible for the injustice and oppression that the prophets attacked.

The basic form of this type of society continued into the time of Jesus.[14] In Galilee, the elites were large landholders, the Herodian court, and retainers attached to both groups. In Judea, the elites were concentrated in Jerusalem: the high priestly families and the traditional aristocracy and, of course, their retainers. As in peasant societies generally, wealth flowed to these elites through ownership of land and taxation.

Though some peasants still owned small pieces of land, much of it was owned by absentee landlords living in cities and towns who typically collected from one-fourth to one-third of agricultural production as "rent."[15] Taxes on the agricultural production of peasants were paid to both civil and religious authorities. Though we do not have precise information about tax rates under Herod the Great, estimates place it between 10 and 20 percent,[16] a range that his sons presumably continued. When Judea came under direct Roman rule in 6 C.E., the Roman crop tax was apparently 12.5 percent.[17]

There was also taxation by religious authorities, namely, the tithes of the Torah, which amounted to taxes on agricultural produce. As understood in the first century, these included each year a first tithe, a second tithe, and, apparently, a third tithe every third year.[18] Though estimates can be only approximate, the combination of taxes and tithes probably amounted to 30 to 35 percent of agricultural production.[19] Added to the one-fourth to one-third paid in land rent by peasants not owning their own land, the portion of agricultural income flowing from peasants to the urban elites may have been as high as 60 percent to two-thirds.[20] Like other peasant societies, first-century Palestine was thus marked by pervasive economic exploitation and oppression.[21]

The recognition that the social world of Jesus was a peasant society with a two-class system and tributary mode of production provides a social context that illuminates many of the traditions about Jesus. Because it is not possible within the limits of this essay to provide a detailed exegesis or even a comprehensive listing of all relevant passages, I will cite only a few examples in order to illustrate the difference this fresh perspective on the social world of Jesus makes.

It casts Jesus' sayings about the poor and the rich, poverty and wealth, in a different light. "The poor" (to whom the "good news" comes and who are pronounced "blessed') are the economically oppressed class of a peasant society, just as the rich (against whom woes are spoken) are the wealthy urban elites. Poverty and wealth cease to be abstractions or metaphors. They also cease to be primarily qualities of individuals. Wealth was not the result of being an ambitious hard-working individual striving to advance in the world, but the product of being part of an oppressive social class that extracted its wealth from peasants; and poverty was not the result of failing to make use of one's opportunities.

Consideration of a particular saying illustrates the difference in meaning generated by setting it in the social world of a peasant society:

> No one can serve two masters; for a slave will either hate the one and love the other, or be devoted to the one and despise the other. You cannot serve God and wealth. (Matt. 6:24 = Luke 16:13)

If we hear this saying within the context of our social location — namely, the kind of social world most of us in the modern industrialized world know, in which there is a large middle class and considerable possibility of upward mobility — then we are likely to hear it as addressed to individuals faced with the choice of whether to serve God or wealth. Should I pursue affluence in my life, or the service of God? But such a choice did not exist for peasants living in the highly stratified social world of first-century Palestine. The statement is not advice directed to the undecided and deciding individual, but an indictment of a social class, the elites (you cannot be wealthy and serve God), even as it also hints at a way of life in which wealth is irrelevant. If we hear it only within our social world, we miss its social meaning in Jesus' social world.

There are many other sayings that are illuminated by the peasant society model. About the scribes, who were retainers of the elites, Jesus said:

> Beware of the scribes, who like to walk around in long robes, and to be greeted with respect in the marketplaces, and to have the best seats in the synagogues and places of honor at banquets! They devour widows' houses and for the sake of appearance say long prayers. They will receive the greater condemnation. (Mark 12:38–40)[22]

The reference to those who "devour widows' houses" apparently refers to a legal proceeding whereby homes were expropriated because of debt.

Jesus' threats against Jerusalem (which are quite well grounded in the tradition) are cast in a new light. It is not Jerusalem as the center or symbol of Judaism that is indicted, but Jerusalem as the home of the ruling elites.

The perspective provided by peasant society awareness also enables us to see more clearly where the responsibility for Jesus' death belongs. Given the popular Christian understanding of "the Jews" as having rejected Jesus, this is a perception of great importance for Jewish-Christian relations. The most likely scenario of Jesus' arrest, condemnation, and execution is that it involved cooperation between the Roman governor and the inner circle of the Jerusalem elite, namely, the high priest and what has been called his "privy council."[23] In the eyes of the elites, Jesus was a popular leader operating outside of established authority who had attracted a following. Such persons aroused suspicion (and often worse) among those concerned with maintaining the present order. The elites were not only accountable to Rome but also had their own self-interested reasons for preserving the existing order of a peasant society that benefitted them so greatly. Thus it was not "the Jews" or "the Jewish people" who rejected Jesus. Rather, it was a narrow circle of the Jewish ruling elite who, rather than representing "the Jews," are more accurately seen as oppressors of the vast majority of the Jewish population of Palestine at the time of Jesus.

To conclude this section, the perspective provided by understanding the dynamics of a peasant society suggests that, whatever else needs to be said about Jesus, he was a social prophet.[24] Indeed, when we realize that the social dynamics that operated in the time of the classical prophets of ancient Israel also operated in the time of Jesus, it is clear that he, like them, indicted the elites and championed the cause of an exploited peasantry.[25] I do not think that he sought to lead a peasant revolt or that his following can be described simply as a peasant movement. Nevertheless, and minimally, it is clear that he engaged in radical social criticism of the elites of his day. And, given what else can be known about him, social critique was accompanied by an alternative social vision.

Patriarchal Society and Politics in Palestine

A second perspective for seeing the politics of Jesus is provided by awareness of the social dynamics of patriarchal societies, brought into biblical scholarship mostly by feminist scholars. Two terms, "androcentrism" and "patriarchy," require definition. "Androcentrism" refers to a way of seeing, namely, seeing from a male point of view. "Patriarchy" refers to a way of structuring society with two characteristics: it is hierarchical and male-dominated.[26]

Jesus and the early Christian movement lived in a tradition and social world that generally was both. Written texts (including the sacred traditions of Judaism) were almost always produced by males and reflected a male way of seeing the world. A classic example is the book of Proverbs. Though there are many sayings about difficult or fretful wives, there are no sayings about difficult husbands. And though there is an adoring portrait of the ideal wife, there is no portrait of the ideal husband. The explanation is obvious: the book of Proverbs was written by men for other men. So also with the tradition as a whole: male images of deity are dominant, laws are written from a male point of view, and males are assigned all of the official religious positions.

Patriarchy was as omnipresent as androcentrism.[27] Hierarchies with males at the top were the normative forms of social organization (political, religious, and familial), both within Palestine and throughout the Roman empire. To put that only slightly differently, the peasant society with its urban ruling elites was also a patriarchal society. The ruler was typically male. Below him were high government and/or priestly officials (male) and the male heads of the traditional aristocratic families. Together, they ruled over all other men, as well as all women and children.

The patriarchal structure of the society was mirrored in the family. The patriarchal family was a microcosm of society as a whole. People lived in extended patriarchal families, in which the head male was the authority figure. All others were ultimately subject to him. Females were always embedded in some male: father, brother, husband, son. Moreover, it is important to underline how central the family was in that world compared to the modern world. It was the primary unit of economic production and security, as well as the primary center of identity and loyalty.

Together, androcentrism and patriarchy pervasively affected how women were seen and their roles in society. Texts, laws, and customs reflected how women looked through the eyes of men, including both male perceptions as well as projections. Male concerns about honor and shame, as well as anxiety about the legitimacy of heirs, shaped codes governing female behavior.[28] Women were radically separated from men in most arenas of life.[29] Respectable women were veiled in public, as they still are today in traditional parts of the Middle East. Access to religious institutions and traditions was limited. In the temple, they were restricted to the court of the women, which was further from the center — the holy of holies — than the court of the men. They were not to be taught the Torah, allegedly because they were not very bright and might be a source of temptation to a male teacher, but perhaps because the ability to interpret Torah was a form of power.[30]

Setting the traditions about Jesus in the context of a social world structured by patriarchy sheds light on a number of texts. All of the stories of Jesus' relationships to women involve ignoring or subverting the structures of patriarchy. The role of women in the early years of the Christian movement (and most likely already in his lifetime) is extraordinary in a patriarchal world. Behind it or undergirding it is a very different vision of social relationships.

Among the texts illuminated by this perspective are the familiar even if also difficult sayings about family. They are generally negative; Jesus was no champion of family values. People are invited to leave their families, indeed, to hate father and mother. Christians (scholars as well as ordinary folk) have often been perplexed by the negative attitude toward family and have sought ways of reconciling family life with taking Jesus seriously, most commonly by suggesting that Jesus basically meant that God must come first and family second. But such an approach abstracts the family sayings from their social context. Originally, they were directed not at "the family" in general, but at the patriarchal family in particular. The invitation was to break with the patriarchal family — an oppressive hierarchical structure mirroring the society as a whole.

Patriarchy as social context illuminates two other sayings related to family. To the woman who declared the mother of Jesus to be "blessed" because of the remarkable character of her son, Jesus said, "Blessed rather are those who hear the word of God and obey it" (Luke 11:27–28). Without the social context of a patriarchal society, Jesus' response sounds a bit opportunistic and perhaps even insensitive, as if he is simply using the woman's adoring exclamation as an occasion for telling the crowd what is really important. Within the context of a patriarchal society, however, it is a denial that identity for a woman comes from her embeddedness in a male. Rather, there is a source of identity outside of the structures of patriarchy, which thereby also subverts those structures.

Patriarchy as social context also provides a persuasive framework for understanding Matt. 23:9: "And call no one your father on earth, for you have one Father — the one in heaven." Abstracted from its context, it seems to have to do with "titles" and correct speech. In the context of a society structured around the patriarchal family, however, its meaning is clear and basically identical to the anti-family sayings: a subversion of patriarchy. Indeed, it is a fascinating use of a male image of God as a way of subverting a male-dominated social order: just as the lordship of God means one is to have no other lords, so the fatherhood of God means one is to have no other fathers.[31]

Purity Society and Politics in First-Century Palestine

A third perspective is provided by studies of purity societies. This is the vantage point that my own work on the politics of Jesus has emphasized: the realization that first-century Jewish Palestine was a purity society enables us to see the sociopolitical significance of sayings and actions connected to purity issues. Because I have exposited this at length elsewhere, here I will highlight what is most central in summary fashion and then make some fresh connections.[32]

Of first importance is the awareness of what a purity society is.[33] Found in many times and places, such societies are explicitly organized around the polarities of pure and impure, clean and unclean. Pure and impure apply to persons, behaviors, places, things, times, and social groups. Applying to persons and social groups, pure and impure may be the product of birth (as in hereditary caste systems), behavior (actions that render one impure), social position (often including occupation), or physical condition (whole versus not whole). The contrasts of pure and impure establish a spectrum ranging from most pure through degrees of purity to marginalized to the radically impure (who often are "untouchables" or "outcasts"). The social boundaries generated by the polarities and gradations of pure and impure are typically sharp and strong.

In purity societies, purity and purity laws have a significance much different from what they mean in the modern Western world. For us, purity is an individual quality, whether of a product (as when something is advertised as "100 percent pure"), or of a person (an especially innocent or devout individual), or of thoughts (pure and impure thoughts, often connected to sexuality). Purity laws within the religious life are generally viewed by us as relatively unimportant, certainly of less value than "moral" or "ethical" teachings. We see them as something only a particularly pious or overly meticulous individual might be much concerned about. Thus, to a large extent, for us purity has been trivialized, individualized, and internalized.

This way of seeing purity has affected the way scholars have seen texts pertaining to purity. It is instructive to read through commentaries on the gospels written more than twenty or thirty years ago to see how they treat texts that refer to conflicts over purity issues between Jesus and his critics (most often identified as Pharisees). Again and again, the concern of the Pharisees with purity is dismissed as trivial, or, worse, seen as mean-spirited righteousness; they are accused of being blind hypocrites preoccupied with the minutiae of the law; and purity disputes in general are seen as rather "stupid." Any decent person, it is implied, would know that purity laws do not matter very much. To say the obvious: this is the way purity concerns look through modern Western eyes.

But in a purity society, it is not so. In such societies, purity is the core value or paradigm structuring the social world. It becomes embedded in social structures and generates a purity system. Within a purity society, purity issues are neither trivial nor a matter of individual piety. Instead, purity is political.

Second, I have argued that first-century Jewish Palestine was a purity society. Its two centers and foundations were the temple and a particular interpretation of the Torah.[34] The temple's "holy of holies" was the geographical and cultic center of Israel's purity map, the point of greatest purity, and from it radiated outward concentric circles of decreasing degrees of purity, ending at the borders of "the holy land."[35] The other foundation of the purity system was a way of interpreting the sacred Scriptures of Israel that had become increasingly dominant in the centuries since the exile. Its core value was crystalized in a verse from Leviticus: "You shall be holy as God is holy" (Lev. 19:2). Holiness was understood as "purity," meaning separation from everything unclean. What it meant to be pure was spelled out especially by the purity laws of Leviticus and their elaboration.

Third, of major importance is the way purity and impurity applied to persons and social groups. It got attached to the contrast between righteous and sinners: the pure were the righteous, and the radically impure were sinners (within a purity system, sin often becomes a matter of being unclean). Though there was not strictly speaking an inherited caste of "untouchables,"[36] as in traditional Hindu society, there were persons whose impurity meant that one could acquire impurity by touching them; hence, there were "untouchables." Pure and impure got attached to other primary social polarities: intrinsically to the contrasts between whole and not-whole (the chronically ill and the maimed), Jew and Gentile; and associationally to the contrasts between rich and poor, male and female. As in purity societies generally, these contrasts generated sharp social boundaries.

All of this I have exposited before. What I wish to emphasize here are the connections between purity society, peasant society, and patriarchal society. Two connections are especially striking.

First, to a considerable extent and in a general kind of way, the gradations of the purity system correlated with the descending ladder of peasant society. At the top of the native elites were the ruler (the high priest) and governing class (largely the "chief priests," apparently leading male members of the high priestly families).[37] They were the purity elites as well as the political and economic elites. Politically, the internal affairs of Jewish Palestine during the centuries when the country was under the sovereignty of one foreign empire after another were generally in the hands of the high priest and his council. Economically, the high priestly families were large landowners.[38] This was so despite the Torah's prohibition against priests owning land, which they apparently interpreted *not* as meaning that they could not own land, but as meaning that they were not allowed to work it.[39] They could be landlords, but not agricultural laborers. Instead, peasants worked their land, as sharecroppers, renters, or day-laborers. Thus those at the top of the purity system were a traditional aristocracy, a political and economic (as well as religious) elite.[40]

Next came the retainers. Scribes and lawyers would have been advocates of the purity system, lower ranking soldiers probably less so. Among the retainers may have been the Pharisees. A strong strand of contemporary scholarship sees them as a "purity group" seeking to extend the rules of purity in public life and emphasizing tithing in particular.[41] If so, their interests and the interest of the high priestly governing class were similar. Wealthy urban merchants were probably committed to purity as well, simply because of their social proximity to the elites. The upper level of the peasant class (farmers who still owned small plots of land) were probably, with respect to purity, marginalized; some may have abided by the purity laws, whereas others did not or could not. Those at the bottom of peasant society — degraded classes and expendables — were generally not only impoverished but also impure.

Second, the purity system was the ideology of the ruling elites.[42] The claim is made plausible in part by the correlations between purity and class structures, as well as for additional reasons. One of the central functions of ideology is to legitimate the existing order. This the purity system accomplished by locating the temple at its center, thereby legitimating both the temple and the temple elites. Their place in society was divinely sanctioned.

Moreover, the purity system was the result of scribal activity. It was an interpretation of the Torah coming from a scribal class, that is, from a retainer class attached to the elites. The Torah of course contains purity laws. But the decision to make them central and to elaborate them into a system is the product of scribal interpretation. As noted earlier, the "purity system" resulted from a hermeneutic that made purity the paradigm for interpreting the Torah.

Finally, the income of the temple and the temple elites to some extent depended upon the observance of purity laws by others.[43] Namely, taxation (payment of tithes, which, as stated earlier, amounted to taxes on peasant agricultural production) was a purity issue. Untithed crops were impure and would not be purchased by the observant. We do not know if the demand for payment of tithe consistently or often involved physical coercion, though it sometimes did. There were, in any case, forms of social and economic coercion. Non-observant Jews were socially ostracized by those committed to purity, and the classification of untithed agricultural produce as impure and therefore not to be bought by the observant amounted to an economic boycott. Moreover, the aristocratic land-owning elite, because of their identity with or connections to the high priestly families, were committed to purity, and it is easy to imagine them refusing to accept produce from their sharecroppers unless the tithes were first paid, thereby effectively requiring payment. Whatever the details, it is clear that the elites had an economic interest in the purity system: it enforced taxation.

Thus I find it persuasive to see the purity system as the ideology of the ruling elites. It provided an ordering of society that established and legitimated the place of the temple elites — the native Jewish aristocracy — at the pinnacle of their social world.[44] This is what I mean when I have described first-century Jewish Palestine as dominated by a politics of purity. Its dominant social vision was a politics of purity in the sense that purity was the ideology of the elites.[45]

We do not know to what degree the ideology of the elites was affirmed by the peasant classes. Were the purity system and the sharp social boundaries engendered by it accepted as norms among peasants?[46] Would peasants, for example, have viewed an untouchable as an untouchable? Elites would have, of course. Would peasants have honored the purity system, whatever their ability to observe it and in spite of its negative effect upon them? Or would they have felt victimized by it and resentful toward it? Would they have seen the payment of tithes as a sacred obligation, or would they have seen it as an unreasonable and self-serving demand on the part of the elites? The latter is a real possibility, in part because tithes were originally commanded in the Torah because the Levites and priests had no land of their own and therefore had to be supported by others. But now that the high priestly families had become large landowners, their continuing demand that tithes be paid may have seemed unjustified and may have been met with resentment. It is quite possible that the politics of purity and the purity system in which it was embedded were not seen as normative by peasants.[47]

But whether the purity system was accepted by peasants or not, it was the dominant ideology of the social world of Jesus. Within this context, it is significant that conflicts about issues of purity constitute one of the central strands of the Jesus tradition. In this setting, such conflicts had sociopolitical intentions and consequences. To summarize material I have presented elsewhere, there are five primary categories of texts.

First, there are sayings explicitly referring to purity issues. In general, their effect is to say that purity is not a matter of external condition, but is internal.[48] In the context of modern Western culture, these are "of course" sayings: true purity is internal, not external. But in the context of a purity society, they are radical and subversive. To say that purity is not a matter of observing external boundaries is to challenge the central organizing structure of such a society.

Second, one of the main features of Jesus' activity was an inclusive table fellowship, or "open commensality."[49] Commensality was a purity issue. The purity system, with its sharp social boundaries generated closed commensality. The open commensality of Jesus subverted these boundaries, and embodied a radically inclusive social vision.

Third, purity issues were the central theme of conflicts with the Pharisees, a movement committed to purity in everyday life. Granted, the author of Matthew's gospel wildly accentuated and distorted these disputes, but they do not seem to be simply the creation of the early Christian movement or the evangelists.[50]

Fourth, purity issues are present in some of the healing stories. Jesus is reported to have touched people who were impure and, rather than being defiled himself, the person was "cleansed" or "healed."[51] Moreover, Jesus' practice of healing outside of institutional authority challenged the system centered in the temple.[52]

Fifth, I have argued that Jesus replaced the "politics of purity" with a "politics of compassion." In contexts where the dominant ideology of his social world spoke of purity as the paradigm for social life, Jesus spoke of compassion.[53]

In short, the evidence is very strong that Jesus mounted a pointed critique of the purity system of his day. Moreover, it does not seem adequate to suppose that he simply ignored purity. For a religious figure in the context of a purity system to ignore purity is in fact to challenge it.[54] To put that differently, for an ordinary peasant to have ignored purity may have been without significance; for a figure like Jesus, who spoke of the kingdom of God and who attracted a following, to ignore purity made a strong statement. It was a challenge to a social world organized as a purity system. Purity was not a question of piety, but of society.

Purity, Temple, and Politics

The perspectives of peasant, patriarchal, and purity society analysis provide a compelling social context for understanding Jesus' action in the temple. Periodically in the history of scholarship, scholars have made the temple act central to their understanding of Jesus. A generation ago, E. F. Scott did so in a book whose title refers to the temple act: *The Crisis in the Life of Jesus* (1952). In our time, E. P. Sanders uses it as the point of departure for his portrait of Jesus.[55]

The gospel accounts of what Jesus did in the temple (Mark 11:15–17 and John 2:13–22) report both an action and a saying, whose function is to interpret the action. For two reasons, it has become routine among scholars to treat the action and the words of interpretation separately. John and Mark both report the action of overturning tables, but report the words of interpretation quite differently.[56] Moreover, both use quotations from the Old Testament to do so, and many scholars systematically suspect the voice of the early movement (rather than the voice of Jesus) whenever Scripture is quoted.[57] Thus there is widespread skepticism or suspended judgment about whether the words go back to Jesus, even as there is general confidence that the action does.[58] Accordingly, we shall initially look at the action apart from the words of interpretation.

Jesus overturned the tables of the moneychangers and the seats of those selling sacrificial birds. What did this mean? To say the obvious, interpretation requires a context. Without a context, the meaning of an action (like a saying) ranges from ambiguous (it could mean many things) to opaque (impossible to discern what it means).

Most commonly, it is interpreted as a "cleansing," reflected in the widespread designation of the event as "the cleansing of the temple," even though the phrase does not appear in the story itself. Implicitly, the context is "purity," with Jesus an advocate of purity: the temple had become defiled, and Jesus wished to purify it. This interpretation sometimes sees the issue as the impropriety of commercial activity in the temple courts, and sometimes as excessive profiteering involving inflated prices for sacrificial animals and unfair rates of exchange.

In his review of previous research Sanders persuasively shows the inadequacy of seeing the action as a cleansing or an attempt to purify the temple.[59] He then suggests an alternative context for understanding it, namely, the context of restoration eschatology: the act of overturning tables symbolized the coming eschatological destruction of the temple and its replacement by another.[60]

Perhaps. But three matters are problematic. The first is Sanders's claim that the act of overturning tables intrinsically points to destruction.[61] This seems like a bit of a stretch. The most immediate associations of "overturning tables" would seem to be a mixture of anger, protest, and indictment. This leads to a second problem. The action seems to imply some kind of indictment, that something was "wrong." Yet on Sanders's reading, so far as I can see, there was no indictment of the present temple. The only reason Jesus symbolically enacted the destruction of the temple was because he was operating with an eschatological scenario that said, "Before the kingdom of God comes, the present temple will be destroyed." There was nothing "wrong" with it that would account for the threat of destruction. Third, for this reading, the meaning of the action had nothing to do with moneychangers or money. Rather, its meaning was extrinsic: it connected to a belief system outside of itself (namely, restoration eschatology), and could be understood only by somebody who knew enough to make that connection.

Thus Sanders sets the temple action in the context of a belief system, where its function was really to "signal" that set of beliefs. I have no doubt that Jesus had beliefs and that beliefs matter. But I am skeptical that Jesus had this particular set of beliefs, and that they explain the temple action. The social world sketched in this chapter provides a different context for interpreting the temple action. Rather than being understood within a belief system, it finds its meaning within the social-political context of a peasant, patriarchal, and purity society dominated by temple elites.

As Mark presents the story, the action in the temple was a deliberate act.[62] He describes Jesus going into the temple the day before, looking around at everything, and "as it was already late," leaving for the night. The other option is to regard it as unplanned, a spontaneous outburst of anger perhaps generated by Jesus' surprise at what was happening in the temple courts.[63] My own hunch is that Jesus had been to Jerusalem before, perhaps many times, and that he knew what was going on there.[64] As a planned action, it had an intention, and is best understood as a "prophetic act" in the tradition of the classic prophets of Israel.

According to Mark, the next day he returned:

> Jesus entered the temple and began to drive out those who were selling and those who were buying in the temple, and he overturned the tables of the moneychangers and the seats of those who sold doves; and he would not allow anyone to carry anything through the temple. (Mark 11:15–16)

Jesus overturned "money tables": the tables of moneychangers and the seats of sellers of sacrificial birds. Both were providing services to pilgrims. The latter sold to poor people, who were allowed to sacrifice birds rather than more expensive quadrupeds. The moneychangers facilitated payment of the temple tax by providing Tyrian shekels (the coinage with which the tax had to be paid) in exchange for other coins. Tyrian shekels were known for their high silver content and careful quality control.[65]

Both the moneychangers and sellers of birds were part of the temple system that stood at the center of the tributary mode of production, drawing money to the Jerusalem elites.[66] Within this context, the action of overturning "money tables" in the temple had the meaning intrinsic to it as an expression of protest. It was an indictment of what the temple had become: the center of an economically exploitative system dominated by ruling elites and legitimated by an ideology of purity grounded in an interpretation of Scripture. It was not an indictment of unscrupulous merchants, but of the elites themselves.

Interestingly, the meaning of the action that flows out of placing it in this context is consistent with the words of interpretation reported by Mark. As already noted, recent scholarship is skeptical that the words go back to Jesus. Behind the question of their authenticity are more questions. Did Jesus ever quote Scripture? Did he have the level of scribal awareness one would have to have in order to quote Scripture?[67] Without seeking to resolve these questions, I would like to suggest what the words of interpretation would mean *if* they go back to Jesus.

According to Mark, Jesus interpreted the meaning of his act by combining lines from two Old Testament passages:

> Is it not written: "My house shall be called a house of prayer for all the nations"? [Isa. 56:7] But you have made it "a den of robbers" [Jer. 7:11].

Together, they contrasted God's intention for the temple with its present state: the temple was meant to be "a house of prayer," but it had become "a den of robbers."

Both references are important. The line from Isaiah comes from one of the most inclusive visions of temple community in the Hebrew Bible. The temple was to include marginalized groups and outsiders: eunuchs, foreigners, and outcasts.[68]

The second phrase, "den of robbers," echoes a line from Jeremiah's famous temple sermon, in which he indicted the Jerusalem elites of his day.[69] It was they who had acted unjustly, oppressing the helpless (aliens, orphans, and widows), even as they also affirmed, in Jeremiah's mocking threefold acclamation, "This is the temple of the LORD, the temple of the LORD, the temple of the LORD." As the center of the ruling class (aristocracy and priesthood together), the temple had become "a den of robbers," or "a cave of violent ones" (as the phrase may also be translated). Thus it was the elites themselves who were indicted as "robbers" or "violent ones." Then, in classic prophetic fashion, Jeremiah followed the indictment with a threat: the sermon ended with the threat that, because of what the temple had become, it would be destroyed.

To move to the words of Jesus as reported by Mark: the allusion to Jeremiah's temple sermon does not suggest the illicit profiteering of merchants or the impropriety of their presence in the temple court, as if everything would have been fine if they had charged less or moved their activity elsewhere. Rather, the indictment was directed at the elites, not at the traders at their tables. As in the days of Jeremiah, the elites had made the temple into a den of robbers and violent ones. The "You" in "You have made it a den of robbers" referred not to the moneychangers, but to the temple establishment that they and their activity represented. The echo of Jeremiah may also suggest the threat of destruction: because the elites had made the temple into a den of robbers, it would be destroyed.[70] Read in this context, the words of interpretation cohere remarkably well with the action itself. Indeed, this coherence is a reason for seeing the words as historically plausible.[71]

But even without the words of interpretation, the act of overturning "money tables" in the temple is most plausibly seen as a protest against the temple as the center of an exploitative social-economic system. Action and meaning are intrinsically (rather than merely extrinsically) related.[72] It seems to me that the context generated by the perspectives described in this chapter yields a way of reading the story that is more satisfactory than its chief rivals. The temple action was not the invocation of eschatological restoration. Neither was it a cleansing, a purification of the temple, but virtually the opposite. It was anti-purity rather than pro-purity: a protest against the temple as the center of a purity system that was also a system of economic and political oppression.

Conclusions

The perspectives provided by patriarchal, peasant, and purity society analysis enable us to see meanings in the message and activity of Jesus that we otherwise would not. Together, they suggest that Jesus walked to the beat of a drummer very different from the dominant ideology of his social world. To say that God's will for human life was compassion rather than purity challenged the domination system of his time, and indeed of most times. Given the perspectives provided by these social models, it is difficult to imagine Jesus' message and activity as primarily concerned about the coming end of all things (the eschatological version of Jesus),[73] or as only concerned about the individual's relationship to God and other individuals (the politically domesticated version of the Jesus tradition).

Thus it seems apparent that Jesus engaged in radical social criticism. A Cynic Jesus might do this. But it is doubtful that Jesus was that individualistic. Moreover, the tone of his message had a sharper edge than a witty mocking of convention. The kind of passion one hears in Jesus' social critique suggests more of the social prophet. It is the same passion I hear in Abraham Heschel's exposition of the passion of the classical prophets of Israel.[74] Jesus was not simply concerned with the individual's freedom from the prison of convention, but with a comprehensive vision of life that embraced the social order.

I do not think he was interested in a "top down" change in the social order that involved taking over or replacing political leadership. Nor do I see him as a reformist, in the sense of seeking to improve or modify the present system.[75] Rather, I see him as having an alternative social vision that, even in his lifetime, may have been embryonically embodied in an alternative community. In his social criticism of the practice and ideology of the dominant classes and in his advocacy of an alternative social vision, we see the politics of Jesus.

Finally, when I say that Jesus was political, I do not mean "just political," as if we have been mistaken in perceiving him as a religious figure. He was more than political. To use general history of religions categories, he was also (as I have argued elsewhere) an ecstatic, a healer, and a wisdom teacher. He was thus to some extent an Elijah-type figure:

an ecstatic with paranormal religious experience, a healer, and a social prophet.[76] And he was also an "enlightened one" who taught a wisdom that both subverted the world of convention and imaged an alternative way of life.[77] Ecstatic, healer, social prophet, and wisdom teacher are combined.[78]

But he was not less than political. It seems to me that any adequate sketch of Jesus requires a sociopolitical stroke as one of three or four broad strokes. To construe Jesus primarily as an eschatological figure or primarily as a wisdom figure, two of the poles of scholarship in this century, leaves too much of the tradition unassimilated.

Notes

1. H. S. Reimarus, *On the Intention of Jesus and His Disciples.* Published in 1778 (and completed before 1768), it is available in *Reimarus: Fragments,* ed. C. H. Talbert (Philadelphia: Fortress, 1970).

2. The sociopolitical dimension of Jesus' message and activity has been a persistent theme of my own work, beginning with my doctoral thesis (1972), "Conflict as a Context for Interpreting the Teaching of Jesus," which was the germ of my *Conflict, Holiness and Politics in the Teachings of Jesus* (New York and Toronto: Edwin Mellen, 1984). See also *Jesus: A New Vision* (San Francisco: HarperSanFrancisco, 1987), esp. chapters seven through nine; and *Meeting Jesus Again for the First Time* (San Francisco: HarperSanFrancisco, 1994), chapter 3.

3. Most recently in the work of S. G. F. Brandon, who published a trilogy of books in the 1960s arguing that Jesus was a Zealot sympathizer; see especially his *Jesus and the Zealots* (New York: Scribner's, 1967). Scholars now generally do not speak of "Zealots" in the time of Jesus because of the evidence that "Zealot" as a term designating a revolutionary Jewish group did not come into use until the beginning of the great Jewish revolt against Rome in 66 c.e. See my "The Currency of the Term 'Zealots,'" *Journal of Theological Studies* 22 (1971): 504–12; Richard Horsley, "The Zealots: Their Origin, Relationships and Importance in the Jewish Revolt," *Novum Testamentum* 27 (1986): 159–92.

4. See my *Conflict, Holiness and Politics,* 5–8.

5. The erosion of the eschatological consensus described in earlier chapters is among the reasons for the question of Jesus and politics being reopened.

6. That same social location may also insensitize us to the meaning of community, the role of ritual, and the experience of the sacred, but that is another set of issues.

7. For an introduction to the use of models and perspectives from the social sciences, with a superb bibliography, see John H. Elliott, *What Is Social-Scientific Criticism?* (Minneapolis: Fortress, 1993). See also Bruce J. Malina and Richard Rohrbaugh, *Social-Science Commentary on the Synoptic Gospels*

(Minneapolis: Fortress, 1992), and Bengt Holmberg, *Sociology and the New Testament: An Appraisal* (Minneapolis: Fortress, 1990).

8. Gerhard E. Lenski, *Power and Privilege: A Theory of Social Stratification* (New York: McGraw Hill, 1966). Further description of the pre-industrial agrarian type of society comes from the same volume. See also John H. Kautsky, *The Politics of Aristocratic Empires* (Chapel Hill: University of North Carolina Press, 1982). Within North American Jesus scholarship, Richard Horsley and John Dominic Crossan have been most responsible for introducing the discipline to the illuminating power of peasant society analysis.

9. Lenski, *Power and Privilege,* 210.

10. The phrase "tributary mode of production" comes from Norman K. Gottwald, "Social Class as an Analytic and Hermeneutical Category in Biblical Studies," *Journal of Biblical Literature* 112 (1993): 5, who attributes it to Samir Amin, *Class and Nation, Historically and in the Present Crisis* (New York/London: Monthly Review, 1980), 46–70. See also Gottwald's "Sociology of Ancient Israel" in *Anchor Bible Dictionary,* 6:79–89. Gottwald has been one of the pioneers in applying this mode of analysis to the Old Testament; see esp. *The Tribes of Yahweh* (Maryknoll, N.Y.: Orbis, 1979), and *The Hebrew Bible: A Socio-Literary Introduction* (Philadelphia: Fortress, 1985).

11. See Robert B. Coote and Mary P. Coote, *Power, Politics, and the Making of the Bible* (Minneapolis: Fortress, 1990), 15, who describe the various ways agricultural workers could be related to the land they worked: "A villager might be a cultivating small owner, a cultivator paying fixed rent in cash or kind, a cultivating head of a work team, a sharecropper possessing some productive aids like an ox or ass, a sharecropper with only labor to sell but with a regular position on a work team or attached to a parcel of land, a worker with a regular wage paid in cash or kind, a part-time seasonal worker, an indentured servant (debt slave), a slave at forced labor (corvee or statute labor), or a simple slave. Few villagers actually owned their own land." The volume as a whole makes use of peasant society analysis.

12. Lenski reports that a sixteenth-century ruler of Japan abolished all other taxes and rents and substituted a land tax of two-thirds of crops, which Lenski sees as typical: it is "probably the best indication we have of the *total* take" of the elites in agrarian states (Lenski, *Power and Privilege,* 267; also cited by Crossan, *The Historical Jesus: The Life of a Mediterranean Jewish Peasant* [Harper: San Francisco, 1991], 45–46).

13. If one were to represent visually the economic class structure in such societies, it would not be with the familiar pyramid (large lower class at the bottom, then a smaller middle class, and finally a yet smaller upper class at the apex), but with an oil can with its long narrow needle-like spout (the elites) rising vertically from a broad base (the peasants).

14. For a diagram that very helpfully illuminates the class structure of first-century Jewish Palestine, see Dennis Duling, "Matthew and Marginality," *Society of Biblical Literature Seminar Papers 1993* (Atlanta: Scholars Press, 1993), 651.

15. Douglas Oakman, *Jesus and the Economic Questions of His Day* (Lewiston/Queenston: Edwin Mellen, 1986), 72. Pages 17–91 provide a detailed

analysis of economic conditions in first-century Palestine. See also David Fiensy *The Land Is Mine: The Social History of Palestine in the Herodian Period* (New York: Edwin Mellen, 1990).

16. Oakman, *Jesus and the Economic Questions,* 68–71. Herod the Great was (to put it mildly) a big spender, undertaking massive building projects both in his own kingdom as well as elsewhere. Though Herod had other sources of income (taxes on trade, land of his own, and the production of peasants working it), much of his income had to come from taxes on agriculture.

17. E. P. Sanders, *Judaism: Practice and Belief, 63 B.C.E.–66 C.E.* (Philadelphia: Trinity Press International, 1992), 167.

18. For a readily accessible account of the tithing system, see ibid., 146–69. The first tithe was to be paid to the Levites, the second tithe was to be consumed by the farmer and his family in Jerusalem, and a third tithe (every third year) given to the poor. In addition, there was an annual temple tax of approximately two days' wages. Sanders argues that the second tithe was not really a tax because the farmer himself got to consume it in Jerusalem. This typically involved converting it into money that was then spent in Jerusalem: "Second tithe counted as festival and holiday money, and it was probably not felt to be a tax" (167). For further comment, see the next note.

19. Sanders argues that many scholars (including Horsley and me) have exaggerated the burden of taxation on Jewish peasants. He notes that many of us have counted the "second tithe" as a tax, when in fact it was to be consumed by the farmer himself (see previous note). In particular, he objects to my estimate (derived from F. C. Grant) of tithes and taxes adding up to around 35 percent. Yet on his own accounting, tithes and taxes added up to 28 percent (*Judaism: Practice and Belief,* 166–67), and this does *not* include the second tithe. True, it might have been a treat for a peasant to spend a tenth of his annual production on holiday in Jerusalem; but the expectation that one would do so was most likely experienced by most peasants as a heavy and probably impossible burden.

20. And thus remarkably close to the two-thirds rate reported by Lenski as the best indication of what is typical in such societies; see note 12 above.

21. Sanders strongly objects to portrayals of the economic situation of peasants in first-century Palestine as particularly oppressive, arguing that their situation was probably not much different from earlier periods and from other places in the empire (see especially *Judaism: Practice and Belief,* 161–62). He may well be right. But this misses the point (or at least the point I am making). The point is not that Palestine was worse than elsewhere; the point is that this is typical of pre-industrial agrarian societies. See also his article, "Jesus in Historical Context," *Theology Today* 50 (1993): 429–48, where he also makes a case that things were not so bad.

22. For indictments of scribes who were experts in the law ("lawyers"), see Luke 11:45–52.

23. The phrase is from Ellis Rivkin, *What Crucified Jesus?* (Nashville: Abingdon, 1984). That Jesus' death involved not exclusively Roman authority but also cooperation from the Jerusalem elite is widely accepted.

24. Richard Horsley (for bibliography, see chapter 2) emphasizes the "so-

cial prophet" dimension of Jesus perhaps more than any other contemporary scholar, arguing that Jesus not only indicted elites but also sought to reorganize the life of peasant villages into communities of solidarity. Horsley sets a number of specific traditions within this context. For example, he argues that the mutual forgiveness of debts should be understood quite literally as "debt forgiveness," and that the saying about love of enemies should be understood to refer to reconciliation of enemies within peasant communities. Though I have learned much from Horsley and find his emphasis on the illuminating power of peasant society analysis completely persuasive, I am not persuaded by some of his more detailed claims. I am not convinced that Jesus sought to reorganize the life of local communities, and I see Jesus as more than a social prophet. It is unclear to me how much Horsley's portrait would be affected by adding the dimensions of wisdom teacher and spirit person/healer.

25. See Norman Gottwald's comment in *The Anchor Bible Dictionary* 6:86: One can locate Jesus within "the field of political economy. Jesus led a movement among the heavily taxed and indebted peasantry of Palestine that went on to directly challenge the temple economy and thus the very core of the native tributary mode of production."

26. Elisabeth Schüssler Fiorenza, *In Memory of Her: A Feminist Theological Reconstruction of Christian Origins* (New York: Crossroad, 1983), 29.

27. See Schüssler Fiorenza's remarks about there being other voices within Judaism, *In Memory of Her,* 106–18. It is remarkable that there are some biblical and deutero-canonical works about women. Ruth and Judith are especially striking.

28. See Crossan's treatment of the politics of sexual honor, *The Historical Jesus,* 8–15.

29. This varied somewhat by class. Within the peasant class, women were not as separated from men in public life, largely because of economic necessity (working alongside men in fields, selling produce in markets, etc.). See the helpful discussion, with bibliography, by Kathleen E. Corley, "Jesus' Table Practice: Dining with 'Tax Collectors and Sinners,' including Women," *Society of Biblical Literature Seminar Papers 1993,* 444–59. Corley concludes, however, that this fact should not obscure the great limitations on the lives of peasant women, including gender limitations.

30. There are many Jewish sayings from around or shortly after the time of Jesus that reflect very negative perceptions of (and/or projections upon) women. As C. E. Carlston, "Proverbs, Maxims, and the Historical Jesus," *Journal of Biblical Literature* 99 (1980): 95–96, has shown, these can be paralleled in Roman and Hellenistic authors of the time. The point is that these attitudes are not characteristic of Judaism in particular, as if it were worse than other cultures in this respect. There is no reason to think it was. Rather, such statements and attitudes are generally characteristic of cultures in the first-century Mediterranean world (and, in differing variations, of most cultures throughout history to the present time).

31. See Schüssler Fiorenza, *In Memory of Her,* 149–51.

32. See works cited in note 2 of this chapter.

33. Within New Testament and Jesus scholarship, the work of anthropologist

Mary Douglas has been particularly important, especially her *Purity and Danger: An Analysis of Concepts of Pollution and Taboo* (London: Routledge and Kegan Paul, 1966). She defines "purity system" very broadly as an orderly system of classifications, lines, and boundaries, which makes "purity system" and "culture" virtually synonymous. I prefer to define "purity system" and "purity society" more narrowly: a cultural system of classification *that makes explicit use of the language of purity.*

34. The phrase "particular interpretation" is important. I do not see "purity system" as intrinsic either to the Torah or to Judaism, and I do not equate Judaism itself with "purity laws" or "purity system." Rather (a point to which I return below), "purity system" was what happened when "holiness" or "purity" became the core value (and hence hermeneutical lens) for expounding the Torah, an interpretation that made the purity laws central. There were other hermeneutical lenses through which Judaism's sacred traditions could be seen. For example, a number of popular prophetic movements in the first century made the exodus story central to their understanding of the Torah.

35. See Jerome Neyrey, ed., *The Social World of Luke-Acts* (Peabody, Mass.: Hendrickson, 1991), 278–79. Neyrey provides one of the clearest and most accessible expositions of the purity system of Jewish Palestine; see pp. 271–304 of the volume just cited, and his "The Idea of Purity in Mark's Gospel" in *Semeia 35*, ed. John H. Elliott (Decatur, Ga.: Scholars Press, 1986), 91–128. See also William Countryman, *Dirt, Greed, and Sex* (Philadelphia: Fortress, 1988), esp. 11–65. Countryman focuses his treatment on the relationship between the purity system and sexuality.

36. This needs slight qualification. There were conditions of birth that placed one very low within the purity system. Illegitimacy or a birth defect that left one "not whole" are examples.

37. There is some ambiguity about who the "chief priests" were. "Chief priests" translates a Greek word that is simply the plural of "high priest." Because there was only one high priest at a time, the Greek plural cannot precisely mean "high priests." It could mean "former high priests," or it could mean priests from "the high priestly families," namely, aristocratic priestly families from whom high priests were traditionally appointed. For discussion and a preference for the latter meaning, see Sanders, *Judaism: Practice and Belief,* 327–28.

38. Outside of the high priestly families, many priests (probably the majority) belonged to the poorer classes and were more often among the exploited than they were exploiters.

39. Sanders, *Judaism: Practice and Belief,* 77, 147. I trust that it is not cynical to see class interest at work here: this is the kind of interpretation one would expect from economic elites (I should note that Sanders does not draw this inference).

40. That the high priestly families enjoyed an opulent standard of living is confirmed by recent archaeological excavations of their residences in Jerusalem. They were spacious villas, paved with mosaics, equipped with ritual baths and elaborate bathing installations, and filled with luxury goods. See N. Avigad, *The Herodian Quarter in Jerusalem* (Jerusalem: Keter Publishing, 1989), 10.

41. The quest for the historical Pharisees is as plagued with uncertainty as the quest for the historical Jesus. See the excellent survey by A. J. Saldarini, *Anchor Bible Dictionary* 5:289–303, and the balanced treatment by James D. G. Dunn, "Pharisees, Sinners and Jesus," in *The Social World of Formative Christianity and Judaism,* ed. Jacob Neusner et al. (Philadelphia: Fortress, 1988), 264–89.

42. See the very helpful discussion of ideology by Ched Myers, *Binding the Strong Man* (Maryknoll, N.Y.: Orbis Books, 1988), 17–19. With Myers, I do not see ideas/ideology solely as epiphenomena of the economic base; rather, there is generally a dialectical or reciprocal relation between ideology and socioeconomic conditions. The study of how ideology functions socially always includes the question, "On whose behalf"? (Myers, *Binding the Strong Man,* 18). Ideology can function to legitimate the social order ("hegemonic ideology") or to subvert it. My claim is that the purity system, grounded in elite interpretation of the Torah and centered in the temple, was the hegemonic ideology of the first-century Jewish social world.

43. I say "to some extent" because both the temple and priesthood had other sources of income. The temple elites (the high priestly families) no doubt drew most of their income from the production of peasants working their land. They (and the rest of the economic elite) also got income from lending money. Though the Torah prohibited interest on loans and also required that debts were to be forgiven every seventh year, ways of getting around both regulations were found: the imposition of fines (not interest) if loans were not repaid on time, and the *prosbul* (which effectively nullified the sabbatical cancellation of debt). Martin Goodman, "The First Jewish Revolt: Social Conflict and the Problem of Debt, *Journal of Jewish Studies* 33, 422–34, argues that the economic elites instituted these because of their accumulation of excess capital during the first century and their desire to make money off of that capital through loans.

44. Sanders strongly objects to this portrayal of the social world of Jesus, on two grounds. First, he argues that economic conditions in first-century Palestinian Judaism were not worse than elsewhere (see n. 21 above). Second, he argues that some (and perhaps many) among the elites were good people, and he protests against what seems to him to be a scholarly tendency to equate "rich" with "bad," and "poor" with "good" (see, for example, *Judaism: Practice and Belief,* 336–40). But this misses the point. The issue is systemic, not individual; it is not about the virtue of individuals, but about the effects of the economic system of a peasant society. Elites as individuals can indeed be good people: devout, responsible, courageous, kind, gentle, generous, charming, intelligent, faithful to spouses, loving to children, loyal to friends, etc. To repeat, the issue is not the moral character of elite individuals, but a social system that places over half of the society's wealth into the hands of a few (1 to 2 percent), with crushing consequences for the many. Finally, I wish to emphasize that all of this is not a fault or characteristic of *Judaism*. Not only is the same systemic structure the norm in other cultures of the time, but the emphasis upon purity as the ideology of an exploitative system is a *particular interpretation* of the Jewish tradition: namely, the way the elites interpreted it.

45. The combination of the ideology of purity with the dynamics of a peas-

ant and patriarchal society has been called by Walter Wink "the domination system" of first-century Jewish Palestine, a system that Wink sees in various forms as the most common type of social organization over the last several thousand years. See his essay, "Jesus and the Domination System," *Society of Biblical Literature Seminar Papers 1991*, 265–86; also found in slightly revised form in his *Engaging the Powers* (Minneapolis: Fortress, 1992), 109–37. It is the most persuasive and powerful chapter-length treatment of the politics of Jesus known to me. See also Wink's essay, "Neither Passivity Nor Violence: Jesus' Third Way," *Foundations and Facets Forum* 7 (1991): 5–25, where he argues that Jesus was an advocate of active (though non-violent) strategies of political resistance (also found in *Engaging the Powers*, 175–93).

46. There is disagreement between two of the most eminent scholars of first-century Judaism as to whether the common people would have observed the purity laws. Sanders thinks they did; Jacob Neusner thinks they did not. See Sanders, *Judaism: Practice and Belief*, 229.

47. There is considerable evidence of peasant unrest in first-century Jewish Palestine. This seems to have been directed against the Jewish elites as much as it was against the Romans. Indeed, one should not make too great a distinction between Jewish elites and Roman authority, as they were closely related to each other and, from a peasant point of view, were collaborators in the maintenance of what Wink calls "the domination system" (see note 45 above). For a compact listing of incidents of peasant unrest, see Crossan, *The Historical Jesus*, 451–52.

48. These include sayings about the ritual washing of hands (Mark 7:1–5), inside versus outside (Luke 11:37–41 = Matt. 23:25–26), what comes out of a person versus what goes into a person (Mark 7:14–15), true purity as "of the heart" (Matt. 5:8).

49. Jesus' inclusive table fellowship was one of the main themes of my 1972 thesis and 1984 book, *Conflict Holiness and Politics*, 73–121, and "open commensality" a main theme of Crossan's *The Historical Jesus*.

50. They are found in both Q (Luke 11:37–44, with parallels in Matthew) and Mark, and even once in Thomas. Some scholars, accepting John Kloppenborg's analysis of Q into redactional layers [*The Formation of Q* (Philadelphia: Fortress, 1987)], see them as inauthentic because they belong to the second layer of Q rather than the first layer. I am skeptical about our ability to sort Q into layers; moreover, as Kloppenborg himself had said, there is no presumption that material found in the second layer of Q is less authentic than material found in the first layer.

51. Examples include the story of the leper in Mark 1:40–45, the hemorrhaging woman in Mark 5:25–34, and the Gerasene demoniac in Mark 5:1–20. Clearly there are symbolic elements in the last story, but it is noteworthy that their effect is to paint a picture of radical impurity: tombs, Gentile territory, pigs. The story is a shattering of purity taboos.

52. A point especially emphasized by Crossan with his provocative designation of Jesus' healings as "magic." Magic is "religious banditry," analogous to social banditry: a denial of the authority of established religious institutions. See chapter 2 above.

53. See *Conflict, Holiness and Politics*, chapter 5; *Jesus: A New Vision*, chapter 7; *Meeting Jesus Again*, chapter 3.

54. To cite somewhat distant but I think appropriate analogies: for a religious figure in traditional Hindu society to ignore the caste system was in fact to challenge it, just as it would have been for a public figure to ignore the pre-1960 segregation system of the American South.

55. See chapters 2 and 4 above.

56. There are also two differences in how they report the action. One is *when* they locate it in the ministry: John has it at the beginning, and Mark (followed by Matthew and Luke) places it in the last week of Jesus' life. A second difference concerns *what* Jesus did. Though both agree that Jesus overturned tables, John also has Jesus driving out sheep and cattle. Both the *when* and *what* of Mark's report are to be preferred. His placement of the action near the arrest of Jesus (indeed, as its immediate cause) makes historical sense, and Sanders's argument that sheep and cattle were unlikely to be in the temple courts is persuasive (*Judaism: Practice and Belief*, 87–88).

57. In Mark, it is Jesus himself who reportedly quotes the Old Testament in a saying that combines Isa. 56:7 and Jer. 7:11; in John, the quotation is from Ps. 69:9, and it is not attributed to Jesus, but to his disciples who "remembered" this verse.

58. There are exceptions. Burton Mack, *A Myth of Innocence: Mark and Christian Origins* (Philadelphia: Fortress, 1988), 291–92, and David Seeley, "Jesus' Temple Act," *Catholic Biblical Quarterly* 55 (1993): 263–83, argue that it is a Markan creation. Robert Miller, "The (A)Historicity of Jesus' Temple Demonstration: A Test Case in Methodology," *Society of Biblical Literature Seminar Papers 1991*, 235–52, describes the difficulties involved in reaching a decision about its historicity, though he does not draw a conclusion himself. Nevertheless, that Jesus did something like this is generally accepted. The voting of the Jesus Seminar, a group of scholars who as a whole are on the skeptical side of contemporary scholarship, is instructive: over two-thirds affirmed that Jesus performed an anti-temple act; see Robert W. Funk, Roy W. Hoover, et al., *The Five Gospels: The Search for the Authentic Words of Jesus* (New York: Macmillan, 1993), 97–98.

59. Sanders, *Jesus and Judaism* (Philadelphia: Fortress, 1985), 61–68.

60. See chapter 4 above, p. 75, p. 81.

61. Sanders, *Jesus and Judaism*, 70, where he reports his correspondence with C. F. D. Moule.

62. I do not think that Mark gives us an exact report simply because Mark is earlier than John, but I know of no other place to begin than with the earlier account.

63. So, for example, it is presented in the movie *The Last Temptation of Christ*. Jesus sees the money tables in the temple, seems surprised by their presence, says, "What?," and in rage overturns them. If one sees it as a spontaneous act of anger (as some scholars also do), the question of its "meaning" is muted, whereas seeing it as planned implies a deliberate intentionality.

64. That Jesus had been to Jerusalem before (perhaps many times) is almost certain. He seems to have been a "religious quester" (how else does one explain

his going to the Jordan to hear John the Baptizer and then becoming part of John's movement?), and as a Jewish male who was serious about the religious life, it seems intrinsically probable that he had gone on pilgrimage to Jerusalem.

65. Peter Richardson, "Why Turn the Tables? Jesus' Protest in the Temple Precincts," *Society of Biblical Literature Seminar Papers 1992*, 507–23, esp. 514–18. He notes that the silver content of coins minted in Antioch averaged about 80 percent, and Tyrian shekels about 90 percent. Before reading Richardson, I had mistakenly assumed that the issue was "imageless" coins, and that Tyrian shekels were required because they were free of images. As Richardson points out, they in fact had images of a pagan deity (Melkart) on them. Richardson reads the incident otherwise than I do: he sees the issue as whether the tax was to be paid only once in a person's life or annually, with Jesus taking the former position. Even so, the issue was still protest against economic aggrandizement by the temple elites, though in a softer form.

66. This is true whether they were actually employees of the temple or high priestly families, or private entrepreneurs. Even if the latter, they were nevertheless in the retainer class, as dependent upon the temple system as the elites themselves.

67. Though I will not argue the point here, my hunch is that the answer to both questions is yes.

68. Isa. 56:1–8. See Myers, *Binding the Strong Man*, 302.

69. The temple sermon is in Jer. 7:1–15. Another version is in 26:1–6, followed by the story of Jeremiah being seized by the temple authorities and threatened with death. Peasant society awareness is relevant for the reading of this material. It was not all of Judah (peasants and elites alike) who were guilty of these offenses, but the Jerusalem elites in particular.

70. Mark clearly understands the temple action as portending destruction; note how he frames it with the story of the cursing of the fig tree (11:12–14, 20–23). Other traditions make the threat explicit: as noted earlier, the warnings of Jerusalem's coming destruction are threats against Jerusalem as the center of the elites, not against Jerusalem as the center of Judaism.

71. To which I would add one more reason for finding them plausible: prophetic acts in the Old Testament were most often accompanied by words interpreting their significance. On the hypothesis that the temple action was an intentional prophetic act and not an unplanned outburst of anger, it is likely that it was the occasion for a teaching.

72. There is both continuity and discontinuity between this position and my earlier work (reflected in my 1972 thesis, 1984 book, and still to some extent in my 1987 book). Both then and now, I saw the temple as the center of the politics of purity and the temple action as a protest against the politics of purity. However, then I saw the politics of purity (and the temple) as the ideological ground of the national liberation movement; now I see the politics of purity (and the temple) as the ideology of the native ruling elites. Thus my understanding of the temple action (and more generally, of the politics of Jesus) has developed and, in an important respect, changed from my earlier work.

73. Here I use "eschatological" in the narrow sense argued in chapter 4. If the word is broadened to include "utopian," I would be willing to say Jesus

was eschatological in that sense — but not if "utopian" is used in the sense of dreamily irrelevant. I would prefer to speak about the historical relevance of a utopian vision.

74. Abraham Heschel, *The Prophets* (New York: Harper & Row, 1962).

75. Myers, *Binding the Strong Man,* 80–87 (esp. 85–87), insightfully criticizes the tendency of modern scholars (following Ernst Troeltsch) to see non-reformist movements as politically passive and then argues that there are "sectarian" movements that are radically critical of dominant culture, non-reformist, *and* politically engaged. I understand such a movement, in other language, as an alternative community with an alternative social vision. Myers sees the community behind Mark's gospel as such a group, and his analysis can equally well apply to the Jesus movement during the lifetime of Jesus.

76. Horsley often refers to Jesus as an Elijah-type social prophet, though I am uncertain whether he would emphasize healing and paranormal religious experience as integral to the type.

77. I have developed a picture of Jesus as subversive sage in a number of places: *Jesus: A New Vision,* chapter 6; *Meeting Jesus again for the First Time,* chapter 4; and chapter 7 of this volume. My use of "enlightened one" to describe Jesus is meant to suggest that an "enlightenment experience" lies behind his subversive and alternative wisdom. I think Stephen Mitchell in his *The Gospel according to Jesus* (New York: Harper Collins, 1991) is most likely right: to suppose that Jesus had an enlightenment experience (presumably more than one) seems the most satisfactory explanation of the transformed perception that we find in the wisdom teaching of Jesus.

78. It is interesting to speculate about the relationship between enlightenment experience and prophetic passion. The former characteristically relativizes all cultural distinctions by disclosing their artificial character as a "grid" imposed upon reality. Such an awareness would complement and thereby in a sense temper Jesus' indictments of the elites. Because the distinction between elites and peasants is finally relative, even the elites are to be loved (which seems to me a plausible meaning of "Love your enemies"). Yet there is also a strong affirmation that the oppressive character of the relation between elites and peasants matters. It is reasonable to imagine that the passion of a social prophet and the wisdom of an enlightened one interact in some such way.

Chapter Six

Root Images and the Way We See: The Primordial Tradition and the Biblical Tradition

Ideas matter. One would only expect an academic to say this, so let me add at once that some ideas do not matter very much. But some do, deeply affecting our lives. Of the ideas that do affect us, perhaps none does so as much as the root images of reality which lie deep in our psyches. A root image is a fundamental image of how reality is, our most basic "picture" of reality. Perhaps most often called a "world-view," it consists of our most taken-for-granted assumptions about what is possible. It is an idea (a mental construct) with immense power. Very importantly, a root image not only provides a model of reality, but also shapes our perception and our thinking, operating almost unconsciously within us as a dim background affecting all of our seeing and thinking. A root image thus functions as both an image and a lens: it is a picture of reality which becomes a lens through which we see reality.

Much of Huston Smith's work throughout his career has centered on the fundamental importance of root images. In particular, he has been concerned to describe and contrast two very different root images of reality: the pre-modern world-view, which he calls "the primordial tradition," and the modern world-view. Though this emphasis can be seen

This chapter was originally published in Arvind Sharma, ed., *Fragments of Infinity: Essays in Religion and Philosophy, A Festschrift in Honour of Professor Huston Smith* (Bridport, Dorset, U.K.: Prism Press, 1991; Lindfield, N.S.W., Australia: Unity Press, 1991): 31–45. Huston Smith is widely known as the author of the best-selling *The Religions of Man,* first published in 1958, and revised and updated in an inclusive-language edition as *The World's Religions* (Harper: San Francisco, 1991). In this essay, I describe Professor Smith's contribution to my own thinking about the significance of world-views, or "root images" of reality, for our understanding of the biblical and Jesus traditions.

in many of his publications, it is most systematically treated in *Forgotten Truth: The Primordial Tradition* (New York: Harper & Row, 1976).

Many scholars have described the contrast between the modern world-view and a more traditional world-view, of course, but Professor Smith has done so with unusual lucidity and precision. And passion: he has persistently emphasized the pervasive effects of the modern world-view not only in our culture but also within the academy. One of the most far-reaching realizations of my own intellectual journey was the discovery of how deeply the modern way of seeing reality has affected my own mind, accompanied by a perception of how deeply it has affected the academic discipline in which I was trained and continue to work. For me, Professor Smith has been one of those "bridge people," scholars in disciplines other than one's own who become significant in one's own work. Indeed, among such scholars, none has been more important to me.

In this tribute, I wish to describe the effect his treatment of the primordial tradition has had on my practice and perception of my own discipline of biblical studies. In particular, I will make the argument that the biblical tradition is a form of the primordial tradition, describe reasons why this has not commonly been given due regard in this century's scholarship, and then suggest the importance of taking this claim seriously.

Defining the Primordial Tradition

Whether one sees the biblical tradition to be a form of the primordial tradition depends, of course, upon how one defines the latter. Central to Professor Smith's description of it are three elements.

First, the most essential element of the primordial tradition is a map of reality as having more than one level. The key or fundamental claim is that reality has minimally two levels or layers, the visible (or "terrestrial") world of our ordinary experience, plus another level, a world of "spirit" or "God" or "being-itself," normally not visible and yet charged with energy and power, actual even though non-material, and "more real" than the terrestrial or visible.

This basic division of reality into two levels is often elaborated into multiple levels (a "third heaven," or a "seventh heaven," etc.). Professor Smith speaks of four levels that are explicitly or implicitly affirmed in most pre-modern traditions: the "terrestrial" plane of the visible space-time world; the "intermediate" plane between the terrestrial and the higher non-material planes (the level of dreams, archetypes, good and evil spirits, etc.); the "celestial plane" in which the gods (or God) are experienced as personal beings; and the level of the "infinite," where the infinite "ground" or "source" is experienced without attributes or differentiation.

Secondly, the levels of reality are not completely separate from each other, but are connected. This notion of connectedness is seen in the nearly universal claim that the visible world has its source or ground in the non-visible: the two worlds are connected as creator and creation, as source and product, as ground and plant. Moreover, the two worlds are connected not simply at "the beginning" in an initial act of creation, but continually: in each moment, the terrestrial world depends upon the other world for its existence. The other world "floods" this world with its reality; the terrestrial vibrates with divine reality.[1] Connectedness is also affirmed in the notion of "sacred moments" in which the other world is experienced, "sacred places" which function as connectors between the two worlds, "sacred times" which become openings to the transcendent, and "sacred persons" who become connectors between the two worlds in exceptional or ritualized moments. In short, the other levels of reality are not completely separate from the terrestrial, but interpenetrate it.

In very simple language, these two characteristics of the primordial tradition are expressed in a current exhibition recounting the history of King's College chapel in Cambridge, England. The text accompanying the exhibition begins, "The people who built this chapel thought of the universe, the whole of what there is, as twofold." It then continues, "These two worlds are not sealed off from one another," rather "there are places which are thresholds between them" and "people in whom the two worlds join" (then are listed Mary, Jesus, prophets, saints, bishops, and kings). In short, reality is minimally twofold, and there are connectors or mediators between the two worlds.

The third defining element of the primordial tradition is the claim that the other levels of reality are experienced or known. They are not simply elements of belief. In every culture known to us, there are people who have vivid subjective experiences of another world. These experiences cover a broad spectrum: moments of mystical union, visions, theophanies and hierophanies, nature mysticism, extraordinary dreams, good and evil spirits (Professor Smith even includes a vivid exorcism in his exposition of this point).[2] If the word "shaman" is not defined too narrowly, this is the "shamanic universe," a root image of a multi-leveled reality generated by intense experiences of an extraordinary kind. Thus the notion of other realms is not simply the speculative creation of our pre-modern ancestors, arising out of pre-scientific curiosity or primal anxiety, but is grounded in experience. Indeed, Professor Smith's four levels of reality can usefully be understood as a categorizing of the kinds of experiences people have. The primordial tradition, as a way of imaging reality, is the natural result of these kinds of experiences.

Thus the primordial tradition is most essentially constituted by three elements: a "tiered" understanding of reality, with the levels connected in various ways, all capable of being experienced. This is the way people both pictured and experienced their "world" prior to the modern period. As Professor Smith stresses, the primordial tradition was the virtual "human unanimity,"[3] a root image that was almost culturally universal.

Smith's characterization of the primordial tradition can also be clarified by means of contrast. The essential contrast, of course, is the way of imaging reality that constitutes "modernity" and "the modern mind." Its central characteristic is a "one-leveled" understanding of reality. Only the terrestrial plane is "real"; only the visible world of our ordinary experience and as disclosed by science belongs to the category of "what is."

This one-layered root image flowed out of the new way of knowing that emerged in the Enlightenment, namely, through observation and verification. The new way of knowing led rather naturally (though not necessarily) to an inference about what is real: only that is real which is knowable in this way. Epistemology shaped ontology, lens shaped image.

What began among a bold intellectual elite in the seventeenth and eighteenth centuries has become the dominant consciousness of our culture, the foundation of the "modern mind."[4] The polemic in Smith's writings is directed against this modern understanding of reality, as both image and lens. To use a metaphor important to him, the modern worldview sees only two dimensions of what is in fact a "three-dimensional cross," only a world of space and time and not a world of spirit.[5] Or, to use an image that he borrows from Karl Popper, the modern way of knowing is like a searchlight scanning the night sky: it can illuminate only that which comes within its beam and casts no light on that which is outside of its sweep.[6] In the modern mind, science as a way of knowing (which Smith describes with wonder and admiration) becomes "scientism," the presumption that only what can be known in that way is real.[7] Thus the modern world-view denies, and in a sense cannot "see," that which is most central to the primordial tradition.

To conclude this section on defining the primordial tradition, one further point merits mention. Describing the primordial tradition as we have may be considered a broad definition. Sometimes the notion is given a narrower connotation (perhaps unintentionally) by its association with "the great chain of being," an association which Smith has frequently made himself. The association comes about by taking the notion of connectedness in the direction of plenitude and gradation: the notions that reality "overflows," filling every possible potentiality; and that reality is "gradated" from the top downward in a descending chain of being: the infinite, God, archangels, angels, humans, lower animals, rocks, etc. When this happens, something very like Neoplatonism results.

Yet it seems to me that it is a mistake to identify the primordial tradition very closely with the great chain of being. True, one might argue that the great chain of being is the most intellectually elegant expression of the primordial tradition; one might also argue that it is the esoteric core of most or all religious traditions. But to identify the great chain of being and the primordial tradition too closely conflicts with the claim that the primordial tradition is nearly universal; the implication that all pre-modern cultures are forms of Neoplatonism seems rightfully suspect. Rather, as a near cultural universal, the virtual "human unanimity" found at the core of all pre-modern cultures, the primordial tradition embraces and is expressed in a vast array of cultural forms, indeed in as many forms as there are cultures, a root image underlying both esoteric and exoteric traditions. It is therefore not to be identified with any particular map of reality. Rather, as a root image it is a "concept of structure," an underlying pattern whose elements can vary considerably in their specific content.

The Primordial Tradition and the Biblical Tradition

When the primordial tradition is defined in this broad way, then it becomes immediately apparent that it is the root image of reality which we find in the biblical tradition. The notion that there are minimally two levels of reality — the world of our ordinary experience and "another reality" — lies at the core of the biblical tradition. It speaks of (and presupposes) a multiple-leveled understanding of reality. Though there is not much precision to the levels, the other world itself is portrayed as including different kinds of spiritual beings: angels, archangels, principalities, powers, cherubim, seraphim, councils of gods.

At the ultimate level of the world of Spirit and spirits is, of course, God. God is "the lord of both heaven and earth." As in the primordial tradition, God can be imaged both as the supreme being at the apex of the celestial plane, and as infinite encompassing Spirit. As a personal transcendent being on the celestial plane, God is spoken of as a distinct being "up in heaven." As the immanent omnipresent Spirit, God is spoken of as that "in which we live and move and have our being" (Acts 17:28), as the Spirit from whose presence we can never depart (Psalm 139), as the one who fills both earth and heaven and the highest heaven (1 Kings 8).

As in the primordial tradition, the two worlds of the visible and the invisible are connected in many ways in the Jewish-Christian Scriptures. The terrestrial world has its origin and ground in God: God is the creator of heaven and earth. Moreover, the created world is sometimes spoken of as the manifestation of God, as in passages which speak of God's "glory" manifest on the terrestrial plane: "The whole earth is full of God's glory" (Isa. 6:4). "Glory" in the Hebrew Bible is associated with the presence of God and connotes "radiant presence": thus, the earth is filled with the radiant presence of God.[8] God can show through the face of nature, and nature itself can become a sacrament, a vehicle of the sacred.

The two worlds are connected in other ways as well. As the institutionalized place of God's presence, the temple on Mount Zion was the "navel of the earth," the *axis mundi* joining this world to the world which gave it birth. Other sacred places are referred to as thresholds or gates or doors into the other world, as in Jacob's exclamation after his night vision of angels ascending and descending on a fiery ladder: "Truly this is the gate of heaven" (Gen. 28:17).

The two worlds are also connected in the extraordinary kinds of experiences which are reported throughout the biblical tradition. There are experiences of journeying into the other world. Paul speaks of being "caught up into the third heaven" (2 Cor. 12), and stories are told of Elijah, Ezekiel, and Jesus "journeying in the Spirit." Throughout both testaments, people have visions in which they momentarily "see" into the other world. The book of Ezekiel's prophecies begins with, "The heavens were opened and I saw visions of God" (1:1). The visions of the last book of the Christian Bible are introduced with the affirmation, "I looked and behold in heaven an open door" (Rev. 4:1). Indeed, most of the major figures of the tradition are visionaries: Abraham, Jacob, Moses, the prophets, Jesus, Peter, Paul, John of Patmos. There are also theophanies and hierophanies, manifestations of "God" or "the holy." Sometimes these may take visionary forms; at other times, they involve a momentary transfiguration of ordinary reality.

The accounts of the two most central figures of the tradition, Moses and Jesus, presuppose the root image of reality found in the primordial tradition in an especially clear way. Both function in the accounts as "holy persons," i.e., people experientially in touch with the sacred who become mediators between the two worlds, delegates from the tribe to the other world, to use an anthropological characterization. Moses regularly ascends Mount Sinai (symbolically, the sacred mountain connecting the two worlds) where he encounters God and becomes the revealer of the divine will. He is also mediator of divine power in the stories of the mighty deeds accompanying the exodus. He was one who "knew God face to face and mouth to mouth" (Deut. 32:10; Num. 12:8).

The accounts of Jesus' ministry similarly presuppose the primordial tradition's map of reality. He had visions and indeed undertook a vision quest (the forty-day fast in the wilderness). In his healings and exorcisms he became a connector between the realm of Spirit and the terrestrial world. Stories report that people experienced the "cloud of the numinous" around him.[9] In his teaching, he spoke from the vantage point (and with the authority) of one whose perception had been transformed by the experience of another reality.[10] And, of course, the framework for the story of his life speaks of two worlds: born of a virgin by the Spirit and raised to the right hand of God after his death, Jesus came from the world of Spirit and returned to the realm of Spirit.

In short, at the heart of the biblical tradition is a root image of reality radically different from our own. Indeed, seeing the way the biblical tradition is permeated by the primordial tradition's image of reality as minimally two-fold yields a highly compact but illuminating definition of the former: Scripture is the story (and stories) of the relationship between the two worlds.[11] More precisely, the Hebrew Bible is ancient Israel's story of the relationship between the two worlds as perceived in her own experience, and the Greek New Testament is the early Church's story of the relationship between the two worlds as perceived in Jesus and their post-Easter experience.[12] It is a definition of Scripture which takes seriously what is in the texts themselves.

Biblical Scholarship and the Modern Root Image

Yet this understanding of Scripture has not, for the most part, significantly informed modern biblical scholarship. Indeed, quite the opposite is the case. To a large extent, the defining characteristic of biblical scholarship in the modern period is the attempt to understand Scripture without reference to another world. Born in the Enlightenment, which radically transformed all academic disciplines, modern biblical scholarship has sought to understand its subject matter in accord with the root image of reality that dominates the modern mind.

As noted earlier, a root image functions as both a picture of reality and a lens. When the biblical tradition is seen through the lens which accompanies the modern world-view, then the "other world" is either denied or "bracketed," that is, set aside. In the battle between supernaturalism and rationalism which reached its peak in the early 1800s, the reality of the other world (or at least its interaction with this world) was essentially denied. "Rational" explanations — that is, "rational" within the framework of a one-dimensional understanding of reality — were offered for texts which spoke of "supernatural" phenomena. Treatments of the miraculous provide the best known instance of this. Texts reporting miracles were either understood psychosomatically or as mistaken perceptions of quite "natural" events. They were to be understood wholly within the framework of interactions within the terrestrial world.

In biblical scholarship in our century, the aggressive denial of the two-foldness of reality has largely been replaced by a "bracketing" or ignoring of the question. The major sub-disciplines which have emerged in the past several decades are those which can be done without reference to other levels of reality: studies of the way the biblical writers redacted the tradition which they received, the form and functions of various literary and oral genres, the rhetorical structure of texts, social factors shaping or reflected in texts, the development of early Christian tradition expressed in the texts, etc. All share in common the fact that they focus on the "this-worldly" aspects of the texts: their sources, forms, functions, social and historical "rootedness," etc. They treat the kinds of questions and claims that are intelligible within the framework of the modern world-view.

All of this is legitimate. The texts do indeed have "this-worldly" features. Indeed, in an important sense, the texts are completely "this-worldly": they are human creations, the products of historical communities and individuals over a long expanse of time. Biblical scholarship's focus on the this-worldly aspects of the texts has been immensely illuminating, interesting, and important. Yet, for the most part, modern biblical scholarship has left something out. Though the texts as texts are completely "this-worldly," they often speak about another reality, the "other world" of the primordial tradition. In modern scholarship, what the texts say about that other reality is seldom the subject of study. The effects of modernity can be seen not only in the types of sub-disciplines which have emerged, but also in the dominant modes of interpretation operative in biblical scholarship through much of this century. The two most influential hermeneutical approaches in mainstream Protestant biblical scholarship have both stressed the historical and this-worldly meanings of the texts.[13]

Within that scholarship, the interpretation of the Hebrew Bible was dominated by a "covenant-historical" model. What is important, it was affirmed, is what the Old Testament says about the world of history. Indeed, the centrality of history in the Old Testament was seen as its defining characteristic. Sometimes this emphasis was even seen as unique, allegedly distinguishing it from all other religious traditions (and thus also from the primordial tradition). What mattered was not what the Old Testament might say about another world, but its concern with historical existence in this world.

To some extent, of course, this emphasis flows out of a central feature of the Hebrew Bible: it is organized around a historical narrative involving the experience of a people through time. It does assign more importance to historical and political existence than many religious traditions do. But one suspects that the hermeneutical emphasis upon history is also because of the importance that the world of history has come to have in the modern period: it is the world we think of as "real," the visible world of space and time. We are led to see the texts in a particular way by our root image of reality.

Within New Testament scholarship, a similar dynamic can be seen. Here the most influential hermeneutic permeating the discipline has been existentialist interpretation, seminally (and also most fully) represented by Rudolf Bultmann. Bultmann's work has an ironic dimension. More clearly than most, he recognized the very different world-view found in the texts of the New Testament; his famous essay speaking of the "three-story universe" has become a classic.[14] But then, in a hermeneutical move which graphically exemplifies the modern mind, he sought in his program of demythologizing and existentialist interpretation to translate that language into what it says about life in this world. Language about another world is to be understood in terms of its reference to human existence, its actualities and possibilities. The other world is vividly recognized, only immediately to be demythologized.

As with the covenant-historical model for interpreting the Hebrew Bible, this hermeneutic does illuminate central features of the texts. In a sense, the language of the New Testament does need "demythologizing." Its cosmology of heaven above and Hades below is simply part of an earlier world-view. Language about another world is a different kind of language and is certainly not to be taken literally. Moreover, to a large extent the New Testament is sharply focused on human existence, its bondage and liberation. The existentialist interpretation of Paul is very impressive. Much of the message of Jesus can be powerfully understood in this way, as existentialist interpretation of his wisdom teachings (parables, aphorisms, proverbs) shows.

Thus the two dominant hermeneutics are not mistaken in what they affirm. Rather, their limitation lies in what they overlook. By seeking to translate biblical language about another world only or primarily into language about human existence in history, they effectively eliminate that language as language about another world, or about experiences of another world. Yet it is possible to take this language about another world seriously, even though not literally. To a large extent, it is the language of the "imagination," that part of us that creates and responds to symbols and images. The crucial question is, "What are these images and symbols about?" Are they simply an oblique way of talking about existence in this world? Or are they a way of speaking about realities and energies that people have actually experienced? It is this latter possibility that is largely overlooked. In much of mainstream biblical scholarship, what is "demythologized" is not simply language about another world, but the very notion of another world at all. What disappears is what is arguably most central to the texts: the world of Spirit.

Modern biblical scholarship's concentration on the this-worldly characteristics, functions, and meanings of the texts points to the fact that what is at work is not simply a collection of modern methods, but also a lens, a way of seeing. That lens is, of course, the one that accompanies the modern root image of reality. It enables us to see much, but at the same time circumscribes what we look at. We pay attention to what it says is real. That which falls outside of that image of reality, which is not contained within the perimeter it inscribes, is not "real." The modern lens calls our attention to particular features of the texts, but leads us to overlook or avoid others. It defines what the legitimate areas of study are: those which can be addressed within the canons and spirit of modernity.

Re-viewing Scripture through the Lens of the Primordial Tradition

In short, the dominant thrust of biblical scholarship since the Enlightenment has been the effort to understand the biblical tradition within the framework of the modern world-view. We have been attempting to see *their* world through *our* lens. However, what is needed as an essential complement to the rich results of modern scholarship is a way of seeing the biblical texts that does not immediately reduce them to their this-worldly dimensions. We need to "re-view" the biblical tradition with a different lens, one that reflects and refracts the radically different understanding of reality contained in the texts.

Of potentially great value in this effort is an emphasis which has emerged strongly in biblical scholarship in the last decade: the interdisciplinary study of the "social world" of the biblical texts.[15] Using insights and models derived from the social sciences and cultural anthropology, these studies seek to re-create the "social world" or "life world" of the communities whose experience the biblical tradition reports.

Some of these studies limit themselves to illuminating an aspect of the social world of the texts, as when studies of peasant societies or purity/impurity societies are used to disclose and explore similar dynamics in much of Scripture. Even these sharply focused studies illustrate the value of a different lens: we are led to "see" things we otherwise might not see if we looked only through our cultural lens.

But it is especially when "social world" is defined in a comprehensive sense that we can see the value of this approach and the importance of the primordial tradition to it. When "social world" is defined as the *total* social environment of a people, it includes their shared root image of reality. In the case of the biblical tradition (and most pre-modern traditions) that shared root image of reality was of course the primordial tradition. Moreover, the model of reality limned by the primordial tradition was not simply one element in a belief system, but it was the image of reality which structured their life world — their perception, experience, thought, practices, social organization, and political institutions. It was foundational to their way of seeing and being.

Taking this alternative model of reality seriously enables us increasingly to see their world through their lens. Doing so completely is impossible, of course; we never cease to be twentieth-century persons. But by imaginatively reconstructing their mental and experiential world, we are enabled somewhat to see from within their perspective. It is an exercise in "passing over" from one culture to another; not just seeing one culture through the lens provided by another, but the ability to enter into another perspective and to "see" from that vantage point.

Re-viewing the biblical tradition through the lens provided by the primordial tradition would generate questions in addition to those which have dominated modern scholarship. Texts which report paranormal religious experiences could be studied not only for their literary structure or redactional history, but also for what they may say about religious experience, and the role of that experience in generating the tradition. Vision texts could be studied not only for their literary characteristics and historical rootedness, but also for what the vision may be saying about experiences of another reality.[16] Healing and exorcism texts could be studied not only for their redaction and literary form, but also for what they may say about an experiential tradition.[17]

It is important to note that taking material like this seriously does not require an ontological affirmation. One does not need to affirm the ontological actuality of another world in order to take seriously the fact that people had experiences which they believed to be experiences of another world. One may ask, "What do these texts say about those experiences?," while still leaving the ontological question in brackets; that is, unresolved. However, taking this material seriously does require a momentary bracketing of the modern world-view. So long as we do not set aside the modern root image, our vision remains limited by it. Our own image of reality circumscribes what we can *imagine* the texts to be saying.

Some ways of seeing and some models of reality enable us to see more than others. The primordial tradition provides a way of seeing the biblical tradition that enables us to see more clearly the world of the texts. It is a world very different from our own, one not simply or exhaustively to be understood in categories drawn from our world. There is an "otherness" in the texts — not only the otherness of a distant culture, but the otherness of an image of reality radically different from our own. An approach to the texts which does not see this does not see them fully.

Operating within us at the level of the imagination, a level deeper than the discursive intellect, root images of reality involve the imaging or intuiting of a whole *Gestalt* in light of which everything else is seen. As the root image of reality of the biblical writers themselves, the primordial tradition enables us to see Scripture through their lens rather than simply through our lens: as the story of the intersections between the two worlds, a narrative of creation and history, of epiphanies and incarnation, of encounter and response, all occurring in a world which is filled with the glory of God.[18]

Notes

1. For Smith's powerful description of Pascal's famous vision of fire as a moment when reality as a whole "vibrated" with a radiance that was both transcendent and immanent, see *Forgotten Truth: The Primordial Tradition* (New York: Harper & Row, 1976), 33.

2. Ibid., 43–46.

3. Ibid., x, 5, 18.

4. In Smith's own words, "the final definition of modernity" is "an outlook in which this world, this ontological plane, is the only one that is genuinely countenanced and affirmed" (*Forgotten Truth*, 6).

5. The "three-dimensional cross" is the central image (and title) of the second chapter of *Forgotten Truth*, 19–33.

6. Ibid., 8–9.

7. Ibid., 16.

8. The passages which speak of God's glory being manifest on the terrestrial plane are probably not enough to establish the notion of plenitude; though the notion of "gradation" can be found in a few texts, there is no indication that it was a central conviction of the biblical writers.

9. A point stressed by Rudolf Otto in *The Idea of the Holy* (New York: Oxford University Press, 1958), 155–59.

10. For an account of the ministry and message of Jesus within the framework of the primordial tradition, see my *Jesus: A New Vision* (San Francisco: Harper & Row, 1987), esp. chapters 3, 4, and 6.

11. This definition of Scripture as the story of the relationship between two worlds is very consistent with the work of Mircea Eliade, another "bridge person" important in the development of my perception. See especially his *The Sacred and the Profane* (New York: Harcourt, Brace & World, 1959); *Myth and Reality* (New York: Harper & Row, 1963); and his technical study *Shamanism: Archaic Techniques of Ecstasy* (New York: Pantheon, 1964).

12. "Scripture as Story" is a growing hermeneutical movement in contemporary biblical theology. For a popular-level introduction, see John Shea, *Stories of God* (Chicago: Thomas More, 1978).

13. Until recently, mainstream biblical scholarship was primarily Protestant and, to a lesser extent, Jewish. For the most part, Roman Catholic scholars entered the stream only after World War II.

14. Originally published in German in 1941, the essay may be found in H. W. Bausch, ed., *Kerygma and Myth* (New York: Harper & Row, 1961), 1–16.

15. So important is this emphasis that it is one of the central characteristics of the resurgence in historical Jesus studies. See my essay "A Renaissance in Jesus Studies" from *Theology Today* 45 (October 1988): 280–92 [chapter 1 in this volume].

16. Not all biblical vision texts should be taken as reflecting actual visionary experience; some seem to be consciously contrived literary creations designed to carry a particular message. But, unless we are inclined to deny that visions "happen," it seems likely that some vision texts do reflect actual visionary experiences.

17. A few studies have already done this. In my own field of historical Jesus studies, two important recent studies are Geza Vermes, *Jesus the Jew* (New York: Macmillan, 1973); and James Dunn, *Jesus and the Spirit* (Philadelphia: Westminster, 1975). Vermes takes seriously the gospel texts which locate Jesus in the experiential stream of charismatic Judaism, with its paranormal phenomena of healings, exorcisms, visions, and auditions. Dunn treats many of the "Spirit" texts in the gospels as reflecting actual experiences of Jesus. In the field of Pauline studies, James D. Tabor's *Things Unutterable* (Lanham, Md.: University Press of America, 1986), locates Paul's ecstatic experience in 2 Cor. 12 in the context of other "heavenly journey" texts. But such studies are few compared to the vast number that basically bracket the fact that the texts contain a root image of reality radically different from our own.

18. In a personal note to Professor Smith a few years ago, I described *Forgotten Truth* as "the best work in religious apologetics" known to me. By that I meant something very specific. His work is not religious apologetics in the common sense of seeking to persuade one of the truth of a particular religious tradition, often at the expense of other traditions. Rather, by exposing the root image of reality common to the primordial tradition and by exposing the modern root image as a limited way of seeing, his work makes religious traditions in general credible by making their central claims *imaginable*.

Part Three

Contemporary Jesus Scholarship and the Church

Chapter Seven

New Understandings of Jesus and Motives for Contemporary Evangelism

The topic for this year's Beattie Lecture, "New Understandings of Jesus and Motives for Contemporary Evangelism," provides me with an opportunity to combine the two worlds in which I live. As a historical Jesus scholar, I work primarily in the world of the secular academy, teaching in a state university supported by public finds and active in professional organizations committed to the non-sectarian study of Jesus and the origins of Christianity. As a committed Christian, I live in the world of the church and have been deeply involved in its life for decades. Indeed, I am even married to a priest, which I must admit was not one of my childhood fantasies.

It is very satisfying to be invited to put those two worlds together because, though the historical study of Jesus has an intrinsic fascination, it is the significance of this study for the life of the church that seems most important for me. Furthermore, it has been fruitful for me to think about the topic. Its phrasing ("*New* Understandings of Jesus and Motives for Contemporary Evangelism") implies a contrast to older understandings of Jesus. Indeed, it implies a pair of parallel contrasts: an older understanding of Jesus that went with an older understanding of evangelism, and a newer understanding of Jesus that goes with a new understanding of evangelism. The contrast provides me with my starting point. I shall begin by speaking of an older understanding of Jesus and the motive for evangelism that went with it.[1]

This is the text of the Beattie Lecture, given at the University of the South in Sewanee, Tennessee, on April 18, 1991. It first appeared in the *Sewanee Theological Review* 36, no. 1 (Christmas 1992): 136–51. © 1992. *STR* is published quarterly by The School of Theology of the University of the South.

An Older Image of Jesus and the Motive for Evangelism

It was not very long ago that the motive for Christian evangelism was very clear. Moreover, this motive was tied to a particular understanding of Jesus. I want to illustrate this connection by sharing a childhood memory that came back to me while preparing this lecture.

I grew up in a small town in northeastern North Dakota near the Canadian border in the 1940s. My family and I were Lutherans, and church was important to us. From time to time there was a mission Sunday in our parish, and on one of those occasions the speakers were a missionary couple from China.

I was probably about six or seven. The day was one of those balmy sunny Sundays in early summer, and I can still remember — as I sat with my parents in the church waiting for the service to start — feeling mildly sweaty from playing in the churchyard with the other children. I don't remember what the missionary couple said, though I'm sure they talked about the successes and difficulties of the mission to China and, above all, about the importance of bringing people to Christ. What I do remember with great vividness is a hymn that we sang during the service:

> O Zion haste, thy mission high fulfilling;
> To tell to all the world that God is light.
> That he who made all nations is not willing
> One soul should perish, lost in shades of night.
> Publish glad tidings, tidings of peace,
> Tidings of Jesus, redemption and release.[2]

And in that assembly, still secure in the womb of a small-town Lutheran world of a generation (or two!) ago, I remember being very moved. It was obvious to me in that sun-filled, white wooden church that the most important thing in the world was bringing the Christian gospel to others. Nothing could be more important, and the motive for evangelism was utterly clear. At stake was nothing less than the prospect of souls perishing, lost in shades of night.

This understanding of the motive for evangelism was tied to a particular understanding of Jesus. It was the image of Jesus that I (and I think most of us) learned in childhood, which I have since come to call the popular image of Jesus. Its answers to the questions of Jesus' identity, purpose, and message were simple: Jesus was the only Son of God whose purpose was to die for the sins of the world and whose message consisted of the importance of believing in him. John 3:16 summarized it perfectly: "God so loved the world that he gave his only begotten Son that whosoever believes in him should not perish but have everlasting life."[3]

Jesus was indispensable, the only way of salvation, and from this followed the importance of bringing people to Christ and into the church. Globally, it meant foreign missions and, locally, it meant witnessing and church growth. "Each one reach one" was one of our parish evangelism slogans.

That world now seems very far away — not just the world of small-town North Dakota in the 1940s, but the set of convictions that seemed so certain then. To some extent the passing of that world was the result of a process of growing up and being exposed to a larger world, which for me (and I expect for most of us) led to a greater secularization of consciousness and to an awareness of cultural relativity and religious pluralism.

The passing of that world was also a result of what many of us learned from the academic study of the Christian tradition in college or seminary. Some of this learning was about Jesus. We learned that his own message was not about himself or the importance of believing in him. Such has been the claim of mainstream Jesus scholarship for over a century: Jesus did not speak of himself with the exalted titles of John's gospel, nor did he speak the great "one way" verse of John 14:6: "I am the way, the truth, and the life; no one comes to the Father but by me." Jesus' own understanding of evangelism did not consist of seeking to convert people to believe certain things *about him.*

Some of our learning was about the Christian tradition in relation to other religious traditions. We learned that the Christian tradition itself (including the Scriptures) is a historically conditioned and relative human product, not a divine product containing a unique repository of absolute truth. In this respect it is like other religious traditions, which seem also to be witnesses to the human experience of God and to be "means of salvation." The cumulative effect was to undermine the conviction that Christianity is the only way of salvation. For many Christians in mainline churches, the old motive for evangelism — saving souls for heaven through belief in Jesus Christ — is no more.

So what then can be the motive for contemporary evangelism? In an age (and church) that no longer sees the Christian tradition as the only and indispensable revelation of God, and that no longer sees knowledge of Christ as necessary for salvation, what is the motive for evangelism? That is my task in the rest of this lecture: to talk about "new understandings of Jesus" and "motives for contemporary evangelism."

A Renaissance in Jesus Scholarship

Before I turn directly to that task, I want briefly to report some news from contemporary Jesus scholarship. The biggest news is that there is news to report. The "quest for the historical Jesus" went out of scholarly fashion soon after the beginning of this century. It became a commonplace within New Testament scholarship (and in related theological disciplines such as Christology) to say that we cannot know much at all about the pre-Easter Jesus. The historical difficulties were felt to be so great so as to render any claims about him highly problematic. Moreover, the pre-Easter Jesus was also declared to be theologically irrelevant. This disinterest in historical Jesus research dominated New Testament study throughout much of this century, channeling the energy of scholars in other directions and generating the decades-long period in the history of Jesus research known as the time of "no quest."[4]

Thus the big news is that there has been a renaissance in historical Jesus scholarship. In a field largely neglected throughout much of this century, the 1980s saw a striking burst of new growth. Several new professional organizations focusing on the pre-Easter Jesus have come into existence, including the highly visible (and in some circles controversial) Jesus Seminar, whose multi-colored edition of the gospels will soon be published.[5] There has been a flood of new research and publishing on Jesus and on the first-century Jewish social world, much of it utilizing new methods.[6] And the last ten years have seen a large number of fairly comprehensive sketches of the historical Jesus.[7]

The second major news item concerns a paradigm shift within the discipline: namely, the eschatological consensus which had dominated much of this century's Jesus scholarship has seriously eroded. That consensus, which had its roots in the work of Johannes Weiss and Albert Schweitzer near the beginning of this century, affirmed that Jesus' message about the coming kingdom of God was to be understood in an imminent "end-of-the-world" sense.[8]

In the 1980s, it became clear that a majority of scholars no longer held this view.[9] Indeed, as a consensus, the imminent eschatological image of Jesus has ceased to exist. James M. Robinson of the Claremont School of Theology describes this development as "the fading of apocalyptic" and sees it as a "paradigm shift" and "Copernican revolution" in Jesus scholarship.[10] The collapse of the imminent eschatological consensus makes possible asking about the historical Jesus anew: if his message and mission were not dominated by imminent eschatological expectation, then what was his message and what was he up to?

New Understandings of Jesus and Contemporary Evangelism

What insights that may be important for our thinking about evangelism flow out of this recent research? If it is true that the older understanding of evangelism generated by the popular image of Jesus — converting people to believing in Jesus now for the sake of heaven later — is no longer persuasive and compelling, what then can be the motive for our evangelizing and, for that matter, the motive for people to respond to our evangelizing? To state my central claim in advance, the motive for contemporary evangelism which flows out of recent Jesus research is the vision of life that we find in the message and mission of Jesus. We can see that vision of life by looking at three central and related features of the pre-Easter Jesus: his alternative wisdom, his relationship to the Spirit, and the alternative community which formed around him. Because of limitations, I shall focus primarily upon the first, and I shall say just enough about the second and third to underline their importance and to show the relatedness of the three to each other.

One: A Vision of Life Lived by an Alternative Wisdom

We can see this vision initially by exploring contemporary scholarship's understanding of Jesus as a teacher of wisdom. This is the claim about which there is the strongest consensus among today's Jesus scholars: whatever else can be said about the pre-Easter Jesus, he was a teacher of wisdom, a "sage," as teachers of wisdom are called.[11] Moreover, as we shall see, both the "how" and the "what" of Jesus' wisdom teaching are relevant to evangelism.

The "How" of Jesus as a Wisdom Teacher

To begin with the "how," Jesus' most favored forms of speech as an oral teacher were aphorisms and parables. Aphorisms are short memorable sayings, great "one-liners." Parables, of course, are short stories. Together, aphorisms and parables are considered by scholars to be the bedrock of the Jesus tradition. It is striking that the most certain thing we know about Jesus is that he was a speaker of great one-liners and a teller of stories.

Importantly, both of these forms of speech function in a particular way. Most centrally, they are invitational. Aphorisms are arresting crystallizations of insight which invite further insight. "You cannot serve two masters," "You cannot get grapes from a bramble bush," "If a blind person leads a blind person, will they not both fall into a ditch?" "Leave the dead to bury the dead" — all are short provocative sayings which invite the hearers to further insight, that is, to see something that they otherwise might not.[12]

Jesus' parables work in a similar way. The very short parables function very much like aphorisms, saying something provocative which plays upon the imagination, teasing it into thought: the kingdom of God is like a weed (which is what a mustard plant was); the kingdom of

God is like a woman (often regarded as impure) putting leaven (which was impure) into flour. The longer parables are invitational in yet another way. They are genuine stories which could be spun out at varying lengths, depending upon what the occasion permitted or called for. It is useful to think of the texts of the parables in the gospels as "plot summaries" of stories that Jesus told many times. As I have heard colleagues say, "No great storyteller tells a great story only once." As stories of some length, they invite the hearer to enter and experience the world of the story and then to see something in the light of that story. "Judge for yourself what is right," Jesus says, and then a parable follows; or "What do you think ?" Jesus asks, and then a story begins: "There was a man who had two sons.... [13]

Thus both parables and aphorisms are invitational forms of speech. They address the imagination, which is both that "place" within us where our images live (images of reality, of ourselves, and of life itself) as well as our capacity to imagine things being different. Their appeal is not to the will, not "Do this," but rather, "See it this way." They invite a different way of seeing.

Finally, it is worth noting that the forms of Jesus' wisdom teaching are non-authoritarian. They do not invoke divine authority as do the speech forms of the divine lawgiver ("Thus says the Lord, 'You shall...'") and the inspired prophet ("Hear the word of the Lord..."). Rather, their authority rests in themselves, that is, in their ability to involve and affect the imagination. "Consider the lilies of the field" functions very differently from "Here are God's requirements for salvation." The voice is invitational rather than imperative.

That is the "how" of Jesus as a wisdom teacher. There is, it seems to me, an obvious lesson for evangelism here, perhaps so obvious that it need not be named. Evangelism which takes seriously the "how" of Jesus' own teaching will be invitational in style. By this I do not simply mean that evangelism should include a warm and hospitable invitation to become part of the community of Christ and that its voice should be invitational and not imperative. I also mean that evangelism should recognize the importance of the images which live in our psyches and seek ways to invite another way of seeing. Few (if any) of us will be able to do this in aphorisms and short stories as Jesus did, but the purpose which his rhetorical genius served can be honored: he invited people to see differently. "The eye is the lamp of the body," Jesus said, a saying which I have always found puzzling, but whose meaning I think I have now partially glimpsed: how we see makes all the difference in how we live our lives. Thus, in form, an evangelism shaped by what we can know of Jesus will be an invitation to see differently — to see reality differently, our lives differently, and ourselves differently.

The "What" of Jesus' Wisdom Teaching

Jesus used these invitational and provocative forms of speech to subvert conventional ways of seeing and living and to speak of an alternative vision of life. As a teacher of wisdom, Jesus was not primarily a teacher of information, nor of religion and morals (what to believe and how to behave), but a teacher of a way or path of transformation. A way of transformation from what to what? To provide a conceptual crystallization in advance, he taught a way of transformation from life in the world of conventional wisdom to a life centered in God.

The Problem: Conventional Wisdom

We need to begin by describing at some length the opposite of Jesus' subversive and alternative wisdom, namely, conventional wisdom. It is an exceedingly useful notion, illuminating our own lives and illuminating the Christian message, important for our self-understanding and as a hermeneutical tool.

Conventional wisdom is the heart or core of every culture. It consists of a culture's taken-for-granted understandings about how things are (its "world-view" or image of reality) and how to live (its "ethos" or way of life). It is "what everybody knows" and what everybody learns as they are socialized into a culture through the process of growing up. It is a culture's social construction of reality and the internalization of that construction within the psyche of the individual.

Though its specific content varies from culture to culture, conventional wisdom has a number of general features in common across cultures. Not only do these further define conventional wisdom, but they illustrate how it functions in our lives. It is these that enable us to see that living in accord with conventional wisdom was not only the dominant consciousness of the first-century Jewish social world, but is also the dominant consciousness in our time and culture.

First, conventional wisdom embodies the central values of a culture, its understanding of what is worthwhile and its images of the good life. In our culture these values are affluence, achievement, and appearance; in Jesus' social world, they were wealth, family, honor, purity, and religiosity. As the embodiment of a culture's ethos, conventional wisdom thus provides practical guidance about how to live covering everything from manners and etiquette to the central goals of life.

Second, conventional wisdom is intrinsically based on rewards and punishments. You reap what you sow, live this way and all will go well, the righteous will prosper — these are the constant messages of conventional wisdom. The notion of rewards for living the right way is found in religious forms (Eastern notions of karma and popular Western notions of a last judgment) and secular forms (work hard and you will succeed). Life becomes a matter of requirement and reward, failure, and punishment.

Third, conventional wisdom has both social and psychological consequences. Socially, it creates a world of hierarchies and social boundaries. Different roles are assigned different cultural values, and some people are more successful than others at living by the standards of conventional wisdom. Psychologically, it becomes the basis for both identity and self-esteem: I am who I am according to the world of conventional wisdom, and I shall feel positively or negatively about myself depending upon how well I measure up to its standards.

There is an image of God that goes with the world of conventional wisdom. When the notion of God is integrated into a system of conventional wisdom, God is imaged primarily as lawgiver and judge. God becomes the one who sets up the requirements and the one who enforces them. God becomes the one who must be satisfied. This happens repeatedly in religious traditions, including Christianity, whose most common forms have been forms of Christian conventional wisdom. It leads to an image of the Christian life as a life of requirements, whether many or few. Indeed, most forms of Christian evangelism have operated within this framework: "Here's what you must do (or believe) to be saved."

Thus, conventional wisdom, whether in secular or religious form, creates a world in which one lives. Life in that world can be and often is grim. It is a life of bondage to a dominant culture in which we become automatic cultural persons, living out the messages of culture. It is a life of limited vision, in which we see what our culture sees and pay attention to what our culture says is worth attending. It is a life of anxiety and anxious striving, seeking to measure up, and feeling "okay" or "not okay" to the extent that we do or do not. It is a life of judgment, of self and of others, in a world of comparisons. It is life according to the performance principle (which, ironically, is also life according to the conformity principle) in which everything depends upon how well I do. It is the life of preoccupation with self and its concerns, and thus deeply selfish. It is life under the lordship of culture, in which we live in relation to the standards of culture and not in relation to the one in whom we live and move and have our being. It is, thus, a life of exile and alienation from God. To use biblical symbols, it is life in Egypt and life in Babylon, a life of both bondage and exile.[14]

Strikingly, this way of being is not unusual. Rather, it is pervasive. Indeed, it is normal adult consciousness, both in Jesus' time and in our own time.[15] It is what we are socialized into. In an important sense becoming an adult means internalizing the conventional wisdom of one's culture. It is what faith-development researchers variously call the "conventional-synthetic" stage (James Fowler), the stage of "the adult" (Sam Keen), or the "conformist" stage (Elizabeth Liebert).[16]

The Alternative Wisdom of Jesus

Jesus spoke of a very different vision of life. His message as a wisdom teacher contained a twofold dynamic: subversion of the central convictions of conventional wisdom and invitation to a path of transformation that led to an alternative way of life.[17]

First, with several strategies Jesus subverted the voice of conventional wisdom in his day. Like most sages, he spoke of two ways, a narrow way and a broad way, a wise way and a foolish way, a way of life and a way of death. For most sages, the wise way was the way of conventional wisdom itself, and the foolish way was the path of disregarding conventional wisdom. Jesus reversed this: he spoke of the broad way which led to destruction, not as gross wickedness or flagrant foolishness, but as the way of conventional wisdom. He consistently undermined the focal points of his social world's conventional wisdom (wealth, honor, the patriarchal family, purity, religiosity), sometimes gently mocking and other times sharply ridiculing the concerns which animate and imprison people. He subverted conventional wisdom's image of God as lawgiver and judge and regularly spoke of God as gracious and generous, as the intimate *Abba* and as womb-like compassion.[18] Both his message and behavior proclaimed that God does not observe the standards and boundaries of conventional wisdom.

Second, Jesus not only subverted conventional wisdom, but spoke of an alternative wisdom. Put most simply, he spoke of a way of transformation that led from life centered in the world of conventional wisdom to life centered in God.

The content of that way is indicated by a number of images. He used imagery of "the heart" to speak of the need of an internal transformation. In biblical psychology the heart is the self at its deepest level. When hearts are hardened, what is needed is a new heart or an open heart. Such a heart is centered in God. In imagery which the evangelists emphasize and extend, but which also goes back to Jesus himself, Jesus spoke of his alternative wisdom as the way of death.[19] This too is a metaphor for an internal transformation, a dying to the world of conventional wisdom as the center of identity and security, and a dying to the self as the center of one's concern and preoccupation. It is a striking and evocative metaphor for the path of spiritual transformation. Not only is death the ultimate "letting go," but the process may often involve the stages we have come to associate with dying: denial, anger, bargaining, depression, and acceptance. The path of death was also, of course, the path to new life — to a life centered in God.

To begin to draw this section together, I think the alternative wisdom of Jesus can be a powerful centerpiece in the evangelism of our time. It is a challenging message, but also very attractive. The world of conventional wisdom continues to be pervasive in our time. Life in modern secularized culture is deeply marked by bondage and exile. It is frequently experienced as burdensome and deeply unsatisfying. The work is hard and the rations are often meager, and even when they're abundant, we may have the experience of being satiated and yet not full. The signs that people in modern culture often yearn for something more are many and encouraging.[20]

The gospel of Jesus — the good news of Jesus' own message — is that there is another way of being. The path of transformation of which Jesus spoke leads from the life of requirements and measuring up (whether to culture or to God) to the life of relationship with God. It leads from the life of anxiety to trust. It leads from the bondage of self-preoccupation to the freedom of self-forgetfulness. It leads from life centered in culture to life centered in God.

Two: Jesus, the Spirit, and Evangelism

A central feature of my own work on the pre-Easter Jesus is the claim that he was a "spirit person."[21] By this I mean what Rudolf Otto meant with the earlier non-inclusive term "holy man." Put compactly, my claim is that Jesus was one of those figures in human history who had vivid and frequent experiences of that reality which has variously been called "the numinous," "the Holy," "the Sacred," "the Spirit," or simply "God." Such figures frequently become mediators of the Spirit to their community, whether as healers, inspired prophets, clairvoyants, game-finders, charismatic warriors, divine lawgivers, movement founders, or enlightened teachers.

When one realizes that there really are people like this and that the Jewish tradition prior to and contemporary with Jesus knew such figures, it seems obvious that, whatever else one needs to say about Jesus, he was one of these. He was a spirit person in the charismatic stream of Judaism, a God-intoxicated Jew, a Jewish mystic and healer. He was one of those people William James referred to as "religious geniuses," persons whose perceptions of God and life are based on firsthand religious experience rather than on the secondhand religion of received tradition and belief.[22] My own claim is that Jesus' experiential relationship to the Spirit of God was the source of everything else he was — his activity as a healer, his perception as a teacher of wisdom, his passion as a social prophet, and his vision as a community founder.

Thus, "the Spirit" was an experiential reality for Jesus. This claim has three dimensions of significance for contemporary evangelism. First, we live in a time when the reality of God is no longer taken for granted. Indeed, for many people popular beliefs about God have become highly problematic. In this situation what can be known about Jesus can become a powerful testimony to the reality of the Spirit, not as a problematic article of belief, but as an element of experience. The experience of Jesus (and of others like him) calls into question the secularized consciousness of the modern psyche.

Second, the centrality of the Spirit in Jesus' own life underlines what should always have been obvious to us: Christian evangelism should make the experiential reality of the Spirit the foundation and center of our message. Without God at the center, the Christian life makes no important sense. If we are uncertain about the reality of God, we have no really important message.

Third, Jesus' experience of the Spirit amplifies our understanding of Jesus' alternative wisdom. His alternative wisdom of centering in God was not a message about "Believe strongly in God," and neither should ours be. Rather, the message of Christian evangelism today should be, like his, an invitation to enter into a relationship with the Spirit of God. That relationship, as it deepens and grows over time, is the experiential content of living in accord with the alternative wisdom of Jesus. The path of transformation is life in the Spirit.

Three: Jesus, Community, and Compassion

The final element in the vision of life which we find in the message and mission of Jesus is community. This is especially important for us to remember and emphasize, given that we live in an age of individualism. In such an age the alternative wisdom of Jesus as life in the Spirit can easily be understood in an individualistic mode.

But the message of Jesus was not individualistic, as if he were concerned primarily with the solitary seeker after God. Rather, consistent with the emphasis of the biblical tradition in which he stood, his message contained an alternative vision of human life in community. This vision is embodied in his teaching and behavior, as well as in the movement which came into existence around him.[23]

The community of Jesus in Palestine in the decades after Jesus' death was marked by a remarkable social radicalism.[24] Indeed, the more we learn about the social world of first-century Jewish Palestine, the more clearly we can see the extent to which the Jesus movement was an alternative community. First-century Jewish Palestine presented a social world with sharp boundaries, rigidly divided along lines of wealth, purity, gender, and ethnicity. It was constructed in accord with a purity system in which the polarities of pure and impure got attached to the other central polarities of the society: righteous and sinners (the worst of whom were "outcasts" or untouchables, which is what happens when sin is defined by a purity system), healthy and ill, whole and maimed, men and women, rich and poor, Jew and gentile.[25] In a world with sharp social boundaries, the inclusiveness of the Jesus movement was remarkable. As a boundary-shattering movement, it was a new social reality with an alternative vision of human life in community. This, too, is connected to the Spirit: there is something boundary-shattering about the activity and experience of the Spirit.[26]

The central quality of the community of Jesus can also be seen in the paradigm or core value which was meant to shape its life. The dominant paradigm structuring his social world was, "Be holy as God is holy" (Lev. 19:2) with holiness understood as purity. Jesus echoed this passage even as he deliberately contrasted it by substituting compassion: "Be compassionate as God is compassionate" (Luke 6:36). Compassion has particularly rich connotations because of its etymology: its root in both Hebrew and Aramaic is "womb."[27] To be compassionate is to be "like a womb," with its evocations of nourishing, life-giving, and encompassing. It is the opposite of purity in many ways, perhaps most notably in its inclusiveness. Concern with purity intrinsically creates boundaries; the life of compassion intrinsically reaches across boundaries. Like the Spirit, of which compassion is the primary fruit, compassion shatters boundaries. In short, the Jesus movement was a community of compassion, and to take Jesus seriously means to become part of such a community.[28]

Conclusion

This emphasis upon community and compassion completes my brief sketch of the vision of life we find in Jesus. As I move toward a conclusion, I want to return to my central claim: the motive for evangelism suggested by new understandings of Jesus is the vision of life we find in Jesus. That is what we have to offer the world. I have been speaking of that vision as a vision of life in an alternative community living by an alternative wisdom in relationship to an alternative lord. As I conclude, I wish to crystalize that vision with two statements.

First, it is a vision of the Christian life as a relationship with God. As simple and familiar as this statement sounds, it actually leads to an image of the Christian life quite different from many popular forms. The older image of Jesus led to an image of the Christian life as *believing* and of evangelism as *leading others to belief*. This newer (and more historical) image of Jesus leads to an image of the Christian life as a *relationship* to the same Spirit which Jesus knew and evangelism as *inviting people to enter into that relationship*.

To put the contrast another way, the older approach to evangelism emphasized *believing the Christian story,* and the approach I am suggesting emphasizes *living within the Christian story.* That story will be lived within community. The message of evangelism is an invitation to enter into the community that tells these stories, sings these songs, celebrates these liturgies, and sees itself as living in relationship to the reality pointed to by these Scriptures, these symbols, and these sacraments. Thus, the story, rather than being the object of belief, becomes an icon, a window into the sacred and a mediator of the Spirit. The call of evangelism — to those of us inside of the church as well as to those outside of the church — is to enter into a relationship with the Spirit of God as mediated by the tradition so that our consciousness, perception, identity, and way of living are shaped by this story. The call of evangelism is to a deepening relationship with the Spirit.

Second, it is a vision of the Christian life as a journey of transformation. The relationship to the Spirit of God changes us as that relationship endures and deepens through time. It puts us on a journey. Indeed, it is striking how central journey images are to the biblical tradition — the journey from the land of bondage to the land of promise, the journey from the place of exile to the place that is home. So also in the New Testament: the Christian life is a journeying with Jesus, as the rich image of discipleship suggests. To be a Christian is to be part of the community that travels with Jesus, more and more shaped by him and by his vision and way of life.

In that life together, our life with God and with each other, we shall be changed. This is the message of that difficult but glorious passage from Paul in 2 Corinthians 3:18:

> And all of us, with unveiled faces, seeing the glory of the Lord as though reflected in a mirror, are being transformed into the same image from one degree of glory to another — and this comes from the Lord, who is the Spirit.

This is the vision of life we see in Jesus. This is what we have to offer the world. And so our message is: come with us, for we have found a way. "Taste — and see that it is good." "Take, eat, lest the journey be too great for you."

Notes

1. A preliminary clarification: in Christian usage, the word "Jesus" has two referents. On the one hand, it refers to "the pre-Easter Jesus," that is, to Jesus as a figure of history before his death. On the other hand, it refers to "the post-Easter Jesus," that is, to the Jesus of Christian tradition and experience. The first is the historical Jesus, Jesus as the particular human being he was. The second is Jesus as a divine reality who is spoken about in the tradition of

the church and who continues to be known as a living spiritual reality in the experience of Christians. Throughout this lecture, I shall be speaking about the *pre-Easter* Jesus and what can be known with some degree of probability about him.

2. Quoted from Lutheran memory. The Episcopal *Hymnal 1982* has the fourth line as "one soul should fail to know his love and might," a change that perhaps reflects a changed understanding of the "stakes" of evangelism.

3. Verse is quoted in non-inclusive language. I believe gender-inclusive language is very important and I am committed to its use, but I wanted to quote this verse in the familiar form in which most of us learned it.

4. For a compact lucid history of Jesus scholarship and the terminology of "no quest," see W. Barnes Tatum, *In Quest of Jesus* (Atlanta: John Knox, 1982), 66–79. See also the excellent article by N. Thomas Wright, "Jesus, Quest for the Historical," in the new *Anchor Bible Dictionary,* ed. David Noel Freedman (New York: Doubleday, 1992), 3:796–802.

5. The Jesus Seminar has been meeting since 1985 for the purpose of assessing the degree of scholarly consensus on the historical authenticity of all the sayings attributed to Jesus in early Christian sources written before 300. Members of the seminar vote on each saying, a method that has attracted a lot of publicity. Voting involves casting one of four differently colored beads (red, pink, gray, or black) into a ballot box, with the four colors representing a descending degree of historical probability: a red vote means that a saying is thought to be close to the voice of Jesus, a black vote that it is thought to be the voice of the community (and not Jesus), with pink and gray being "in between" votes. The results will be published by Macmillan in August 1993 as *Five Gospels, One Jesus.* Already in print is Robert Funk and Mahlon Smith, *The Gospel of Mark: Red Letter Edition* (Sonoma, Calif.: Polebridge, 1991), which includes helpful essays introducing the work of the seminar and its "rules of evidence."

6. For a more detailed account, see my "A Renaissance in Jesus Scholarship," *Theology Today* 45 (1988): 280–92 [chapter 1 in the present volume]; James H. Charlesworth, *Jesus within Judaism* (New York: Doubleday, 1988), 9–29, 187–207, and 223–43 (includes extensive bibliography); and N. Thomas Wright and Stephen Neill, *The Interpretation of the New Testament: 1861–1986* (New York: Oxford University Press, 1988), 379–403. Wright speaks of the 1980s as having brought forth a "third quest" of the historical Jesus. See also the article by Wright referred to in note 4 above.

7. See my "Portraits of Jesus in Contemporary North American Scholarship," *Harvard Theological Review* 84 (1991): 1–22 [chapter 2 in the present volume]. There I treat five portraits from the 1980s: Ed Sanders's picture of Jesus as an eschatological temple restoration prophet, Burton Mack's construal of Jesus as a considerably Hellenized Jewish Cynic, Elisabeth Schüssler Fiorenza's *Gestalt* of Jesus as an egalitarian anti-patriarchal wisdom prophet, Richard Horsley's image of Jesus as a radical social prophet and community organizer, and my own sketch of Jesus as a Spirit person, subversive sage, social prophet, and movement founder. Since then, two more major works have appeared: John Dominic Crossan's *The Historical Jesus: The Life of a Mediter-*

ranean Jewish Peasant (San Francisco: Harper, 1991), and volume one of John Meier's *A Marginal Jew: Rethinking the Historical Jesus* (New York: Doubleday, 1991), initially announced as a two-volume work but now projected to be three volumes.

8. Parenthetically, I might note that this understanding of Jesus had a strong impact on the role of Jesus in Christian preaching, at least among clergy educated in mainline seminaries. What we learned about Jesus was that we cannot know much about him, and what we can know is that he was wrong about a very major matter. To put it mildly, this negatively affected thinking about the relation between the historical Jesus and Christian evangelism today. The "imminent end-of-the-world Jesus" was somewhat of an embarrassment rather than an aid.

9. See my "A Temperate Case for a Non-Eschatological Jesus," *Foundations and Facets Forum* 2, no 3 (1986): 81–102 [chapter 3 in the present volume].

10. In a paper presented at the international meeting of the Society of Biblical Literature in Vienna in August 1990, Robinson described the imminent eschatological understanding of Jesus as an "old model which is frayed and blemished, with broken parts, a Procrustean bed in which the discipline squirms." He suggests instead a sapiential (wisdom) model for "gestalting" the message of Jesus.

11. This conclusion is the result of two converging lines of research over the last twenty years: intensive research on the oral forms of Jesus' teaching (primarily aphorisms and parables, both wisdom forms of speech), and persuasive analyses of the Q tradition which argue that its early layer is dominated by wisdom forms. Emergent understandings of the *Gospel of Thomas* corroborate the centrality of wisdom to the early Jesus tradition (and thus to Jesus himself): in the judgment of an increasing number of scholars, parts of *Thomas* are as old as anything in the synoptic gospels, and *Thomas* (like Q) is a wisdom document.

12. The most important comprehensive scholarly work on the aphorisms of Jesus is John Dominic Crossan, *In Fragments: The Aphorisms of Jesus* (San Francisco: Harper & Row, 1983).

13. Of the many important books published on the parables in the last twenty years, the most comprehensive scholarly work is Bernard Brandon Scott, *Hear Then the Parable* (Minneapolis: Fortress Press, 1989).

14. The way of life I have been describing as "life in the world of conventional wisdom" also connects to other biblical language. It seems to me to be the central meaning of Paul's life under the law — living in the world of requirements, performance, rewards, and boundaries (between those who "measure up" and those who do not). I think it is also what Paul means by "the wisdom of this world" (which he contrasts to the wisdom — or foolishness — of God) and what James means by "the wisdom from below" (contrasted to the wisdom from above). That is, the usefulness of the notion of conventional wisdom as a hermeneutical tool extends beyond the message of Jesus.

15. That is, these are not characteristics of Jewish conventional wisdom in particular, but of conventional wisdom in whatever form it is found, including the secular conventional wisdom of late twentieth-century North America.

16. James Fowler's stage understanding is found in many works; his *Becoming Adult, Becoming Christian* (San Francisco: Harper, 1984) is especially useful. See also Sam Keen, The *Passionate Life* (San Francisco: Harper, 1983), and Elizabeth Liebert, *Changing Life Patterns: Adult Development in Spiritual Direction* (New York: Paulist Press, 1992).

17. For a fuller exposition, see chapter 6, "Jesus as Sage: Challenge to Conventional Wisdom," of my *Jesus: A New Vision* (San Francisco: Harper, 1987), 97–124.

18. In order to avoid possible misunderstanding, I want to stress that I am not claiming or implying that Judaism intrinsically sees God as lawgiver and judge. Rather, it is conventional wisdom (whether in Jewish or Christian form) that images God as lawgiver and judge. To make the same point differently, the image of God as gracious and compassionate is found in the Jewish tradition just as much as it is found in the Christian tradition. My point is that it is common for the dominant voice of both traditions to be accommodated to conventional wisdom.

19. The path of following Jesus as the path of death is a structural component in both Mark and Luke. Mark's central section (8:22–10:52) essentially defines discipleship as following Jesus on the road to Jerusalem and death. Luke's "travel narrative" (9:51–18:14) similarly speaks of journeying with Jesus to Jerusalem and death. Many scholars have suspected the imagery of death to be the post-Easter creation of the community and to be the product of the community's reflection about the death of Jesus as embodying the way which he taught, yet it may well be that death imagery as imagery for "the way" goes back to Jesus himself. It is found in both Mark and Q, which suggests at the least very early tradition.

20. Among other things, the popularity of M. Scott Peck's *The Road Less Travelled* is remarkable. As I write this, it has been on the *New York Times* best-seller list for over 460 weeks. Without implying that Peck is talking about exactly the same thing as Jesus was, his image of "the road less travelled" is akin to "the narrow way" of Jesus. Both are alternative wisdoms which seek to lead people beyond "the broad way" of convention.

21. For further elaboration of this whole section, see *Jesus: A New Vision,* chapters 2–4, pp. 25–75.

22. For James's exposition of religious genius, firsthand religion, and secondhand religion, see chapter 1 of his classic *The Varieties of Religious Experience,* first published in 1902 and available in many different editions.

23. We do not know the extent to which the pre-Easter Jesus founded a community in the sense of seeking to create an enduring group. He certainly did not intend to establish "Christianity" or "the church" in the sense of a new religion. Might he, however, have intended to found a defined group within Judaism? It is impossible to know. His public activity was so brief (one year? three years?) that significant community formation may not have occurred during his lifetime. Yet we do know that a community came into existence around him, and it is reasonable to imagine that it had its beginnings in his public ministry. Moreover, whether or not Jesus founded a group, his teaching frequently indicates a concern with the community of Israel — i.e., with the "shape" of

his social world. Thus, an alternative vision of community is central to Jesus, whether or not he "founded" a community himself.

24. The social radicalism of the Jesus movement in Palestine is also characteristic of the communities of Paul in the broader Mediterranean world. For the sake of compactness, however, I shall speak only of the movement in Palestine.

25. On purity systems, see my *Conflict, Holiness, and Politics in the Teachings of Jesus* (New York: Edwin Mellen, 1984); Jerome Neyrey, "The Idea of Purity in Mark," *Semeia* 35 (1986): 91–128, and two of his essays in Neyrey, ed., *The Social World of Luke-Acts* (Peabody, Mass.: Hendrickson, 1991), 271–304, 361–87; William Countryman, *Dirt, Greed and Sex* (Minneapolis: Fortress Press, 1989). See also chapter 5 above, pp. 107–16.

26. See Paul's famous statement in Galatians 3:28, as well as the many stories in Acts about the Spirit shattering the boundaries of the established social world, of which the story of Philip and the Ethiopian eunuch (8:26–40) is especially interesting and illustrative.

27. See *Jesus: A New Vision,* 102, 130–31. For this realization, I am indebted originally to Phyllis Trible, *God and the Rhetoric of Sexuality* (Philadelphia: Fortress Press, 1978), 31–59, esp. 33, 38–53.

28. It is worth noting that compassion as the core Christian value also has political implications. For Jesus compassion was not simply an individual virtue, but was meant as an alternative paradigm for the shaping of his social world. Just as one may speak of the paradigm of purity as leading to a politics of purity, so one may speak of Jesus's emphasis upon compassion as leading to a politics of compassion. In societies where Christians have political influence, this becomes an important paradigm for social policy. *See Jesus: A New Vision,* 131–42, 196–97.

Chapter Eight

The Jesus Seminar and the Church

By the time this essay is published, a significant event in the history of Jesus scholarship will have occurred. In December of 1993, accompanied by considerable media attention and a major advertising campaign, a new multi-color edition of the gospels was published. Entitled *The Five Gospels: The Search for the Authentic Words of Jesus,* it is the product of a a group of scholars known as "The Jesus Seminar."[1]

The feature of *The Five Gospels* that will catch the most public attention is its printing of the sayings of Jesus in four colors: some will be red, some pink, some gray, and some black. The colors represent the Jesus Seminar's historical judgments about whether a given saying is "authentic" (that is, goes back to Jesus himself), or is more the product of the early Christian movement.

The colors are the results of voting by the seminar, an aspect of its work that has generated both publicity and controversy since it began in 1985. After analysis and discussion of a saying attributed to Jesus, members of the seminar voted on whether they thought the saying goes back to Jesus himself by casting one of four differently colored beads into a ballot box. A red vote means, "I think these are the authentic words of Jesus"; pink means, "A close approximation of what Jesus said"; gray means, "Not Jesus' words, though they may reflect his ideas"; and black means, "Inauthentic; definitely not spoken by Jesus."

Media attention surrounding the publication of *The Five Gospels* is likely to emphasize the more sensational results. This is only to be expected; no criticism is intended, for media people, after all, report "the news." Among these are that only 20 percent of the sayings attributed to Jesus in the gospels will be printed in red or pink, with the other 80 percent in gray or black. Some of the most familiar and beloved words thought by millions to come from Jesus will be in black, including essentially all of John's gospel. Also in black will be all passages in which Jesus is reported to have spoken of himself with exalted titles (such

160

as "son of God," "messiah," all of the great "I am" sayings), and all passages that speak of his death as having a special purpose or saving significance as a redemptive death for the sins of the world. All of this is likely to be seen as a negative judgment on the reliability of the gospels and by some as a threat to the historical basis of Christianity.

Thus *The Five Gospels* will be perceived in some quarters (within churches as well as elsewhere) as anti-Christian and anti-church, in intention or results or both. Yet it is not intended, and need not be seen, that way. There is no intrinsic incompatibility between taking the results of the Jesus Seminar seriously and being a Christian. In this essay, as one who is both a "Fellow" (as members of the seminar are called) and a committed Christian deeply involved in the life of the church, I wish to reflect on the possible significance of *The Five Gospels* for Christians. As I do so, I do not speak on behalf of the seminar, which has no official position on the theological or churchly significance of its work. Rather, I write as a Christian who is also a Fellow and suggest some of the ways this volume can be of value for Christians and in the educational program of churches. I begin by providing basic information about the Jesus Seminar and its results, which should be of interest to Christians and non-Christians alike. I then turn to comments on how *The Five Gospels* can be an ally in our quest within the church to gain a clearer understanding of Jesus, the gospels, Christian origins, and (more broadly) the Bible itself.

The Jesus Seminar at Work

The Jesus Seminar first met in March of 1985 at Pacific School of Religion, a Protestant interdenominational seminary in Berkeley, California.[2] It was founded and continues to be led by Robert Funk, a prominent North American New Testament scholar, former director of the Society of Biblical Literature, and author of numerous scholarly books and articles on Jesus and the gospels.[3]

At its opening meeting, Funk described the project the group was undertaking:

> We are about to embark on a momentous enterprise. We are going to inquire simply, rigorously, after the *voice* of Jesus, after what he really said. In this process, we will be asking a question that borders the sacred, that even abuts blasphemy, for many in our society.... Our basic plan is simple. We intend to examine every fragment of the traditions attached to the name of Jesus in order to determine what he really said — not his literal words, perhaps, but the substance and style of his utterances. We are in quest of his *voice,* insofar as it can be distinguished from many other voices also preserved in the tradition.[4]

The purpose was thus to assess the degree of scholarly consensus about the historical authenticity of each of the sayings attributed to Jesus in the New Testament and other early Christian documents written before the year 300. As the first systematic and collaborative examination of the totality of the Jesus tradition ever undertaken, the Jesus Seminar is unprecedented in the history of scholarship. Well over a hundred scholars were involved over a six-year period.[5] Fellows reflected a spectrum of contemporary scholarship. Requirements for membership were not "ideological," but formal: typically a Ph.D. in relevant areas of gospel research. Most were professors in universities, colleges, and seminaries. Almost all were from North America for a very practical reason: the cost of travel made regular participation by scholars from other continents prohibitive. Most were men, simply because there are relatively few women working in the discipline.[6]

Fellows also reflected the spectrum of mainline denominations. Though the seminar had no connection to any church body and no records of church membership of Fellows were made (so far as I know), my impression was that there were about equal numbers of Catholics, Protestants, and non-religious. Many were ordained. A few Jewish scholars were involved. Though fundamentalist scholars were welcome, none became members, presumably because their understanding of Scripture as a "divine product" made the activity of the seminar unnecessary and irrelevant (and perhaps even blasphemous). A few Southern Baptist scholars took part until pressure from within their denomination forced them to withdraw.

Typically, thirty to forty Fellows were present at the twice-yearly meetings.[7] Each meeting focused on a particular collection of sayings (e.g., the parables, the kingdom of God, the Sermon on the Mount, etc.). Papers were written and circulated by mail beforehand so that time at the meeting would not need to be spent reading papers to each other. Rather, the meetings were dominated by discussion of the sayings one-by-one until a point was reached when nobody had anything further to say that would count one way or the other toward the authenticity of the saying.[8] Then the vote was taken by secret ballot, with each Fellow casting a colored bead into a ballot box.

In more colloquial language than that used earlier, the meanings of the votes can be understood as follows:[9]

Red = "That's Jesus!"

Pink = "Sure sounds like him."

Gray = "Well, maybe."

Black = "There's been some mistake."

The votes for each saying were then tabulated, and the result was a "weighted average." Sayings with a high weighted average are "red," those with a low weighted average "black," and those in between "pink" or "gray."

The seminar is aware, of course, that one cannot actually determine what Jesus said by voting. Voting cannot settle historical questions, and majorities (even consensus majorities) are sometimes wrong. Moreover, we know that the votes on some of the sayings would likely be quite different ten or twenty years from now (just as the votes on some would have been different twenty or thirty years ago). What the voting does do, however, is to measure current scholarly opinion. It discloses the degree to which there is presently a consensus within this group of scholars.

The colors provide a visual representation of this. Red and pink both indicate a quite solid positive consensus. The Jesus Seminar was a skeptical group, reflecting the methodological rigor and skepticism that (quite properly, given the nature of the sources) define modern Jesus scholarship generally. A few Fellows voted black most of the time, with a gray vote being a major event. Many voted gray much of the time, only occasionally venturing a pink or red vote. Therefore, for a saying to receive a weighted average in the pink range indicates a considerable degree of positive consensus (and, of course, even more so in the case of red). Similarly, a quite strong negative consensus is indicated by black.

Gray, however, is a more mixed and ambiguous category. Given that the color scheme corresponds to a descending scale of historical authenticity, it is natural to think of gray as pointing to a moderately negative consensus (as "probably not"). However, gray frequently functioned as an "I'm not sure" vote; indeed, one of its agreed-upon meanings in the seminar was, "Well, maybe." Gray may thus point to uncertainty. Or, rather than meaning "The consensus is gray," gray may point to absence of consensus, indicating that the distribution of votes was "all over the place." Thus rather than meaning "Jesus probably didn't say this," gray often means that this is a saying about which there is considerable uncertainty and/or division in the discipline. Gray material is perhaps best understood as being in a "historical suspense account":[10] the verdict is not clear. Gray may also signal likely directions of research in the next several years as scholars turn their attention to this material about which no reasonably firm scholarly judgment has yet formed.

When the Jesus Seminar began, we saw our task as the examination of the sayings or teaching of Jesus. When after six years that task was completed, we decided to undertake a second phase, namely, examination of and voting upon the historicity of the events associated with the life of Jesus in the gospels, a process that will take about five years. We now refer to the analysis of the sayings tradition as the first phase of our work and the analysis of the "deeds tradition," as we call it, as the second phase.

The Five Gospels displays the results of the first phase of the seminar's voting. It does so in a new translation of the gospels. Known as "The Scholar's Version" and done by a group within the seminar, it seeks to express the particular characteristics of the original languages in fresh and contemporary English. The object is a faithful and yet unfamiliar rendition of familiar texts (a few examples will be reported later in this essay). In addition, it uses gender-inclusive language, except when the original languages refer to God as "father" or specifically to male human beings. The volume includes an extended introduction and hundreds of pages of commentary on the four-color gospel texts, describing why the seminar voted as it did.

A Sampling of Results

A few of the "more sensational" results were briefly reported at the beginning of this essay: the seminar does not think Jesus spoke of himself as "messiah" or "son of God," does not think Jesus saw his own death as the purpose of his life, and put (essentially) all of John's gospel in black. Later in this essay, I shall return to these points. For now, I wish to report some examples illustrative of the seminar's conclusions and of interest to Christians as well as to others. Some of these were already public knowledge before the publication of *The Five Gospels* because of news stories appearing in connection with each of the seminar's meetings.

The Gospel of Thomas

One of the striking features of the new volume is that it contains five gospels rather than the familiar four. The fifth gospel is Thomas, unknown until 1945 when it was discovered in upper Egypt buried in the ground with fifty other early Christian manuscripts.[11] For the study of the teaching of Jesus, it has turned out to be the most significant manuscript discovery ever made.

Thomas is a "sayings collection," containing 114 sayings attributed to Jesus. They fall into roughly three categories. A significant percentage resemble passages also found in the synoptic gospels. Sayings in a second category strike one as "odd" and suggest that the tradition behind Thomas was developing in a particular direction with a distinctive perspective. A third category includes sayings not found in the other gospels, but sound as if they could come from Jesus.

The scholarly analysis of Thomas took several decades. A foundational question concerned its age and whether it was dependent on or independent from the other gospels (that is, whether the author of Thomas knew one or more of the other gospels as written gospels, or whether Thomas represents an independent stream of oral tradition). By the 1980s, a generally (though not universally) accepted twofold conclusion was being reached: Thomas is independent of the canonical gospels and contains some material as early as anything in them.[12]

The Jesus Seminar built on this history of Thomas research and contributed significantly to it with its consistently careful consideration of Thomas texts. Our deliberations seemed to confirm the twofold conclusion reported above: Thomas is independent, and some of it is very early. In some cases, a saying from Thomas was found to be earlier than a similar saying within the canonical gospels. To cite a few examples: the parables of the mustard seed, wedding banquet, and wicked vineyard tenants in Thomas were voted to be more original than their parallels in the synoptic gospels.[13]

Likely to be of greatest public interest are a few sayings found only in Thomas to which the seminar gave pink votes. If the seminar is correct, these are authentic words of Jesus unknown for over 1500 years until their rediscovery in this century. They include two short parables, both of which refer to "God's imperial rule" (the phrase used in the Scholar's Version for the more familiar "kingdom of God"):

> *The Empty Jar* (Thomas 97): God's imperial rule is like a woman who was carrying a jar full of meal. While she was walking along a distant road, the handle of the jar broke and the meal spilled behind her along the road. She didn't know it; she hadn't noticed a problem. When she reached her house, she put the jar down and discovered that it was empty.

> *The Assassin* (Thomas 98): The Father's imperial rule is like a person who wanted to kill someone powerful. While still at home he drew his sword and thrust it into the wall to find out whether his hand would go in. Then he killed the powerful one.[14]

A third pink passage is a provocative saying about the kingdom of God or "imperial rule of God." The disciples ask Jesus *when* the kingdom will come, thereby implying that it is a future reality that is not yet here. Jesus responds (Thomas 113):

> It will not come by watching for it. It will not be said, "Look here!" or "Look there!" Rather, the Father's imperial rule is spread out upon the earth, and people don't see it.

In more familiar language, the passage affirms that the kingdom of God is already here, spread out upon the earth — only people typically do not have the eyes to see it.[15]

Eschatology ("Last Things")

The seminar consistently voted as "black" all sayings in which Jesus is reported to have spoken of "the end of the world," a last judgment, the coming of "the Son of man," or his own second coming. For scholars, this result is news because it constitutes a thorough rejection of the eschatological consensus that had dominated Jesus scholarship for much of this century.[16]

For the larger Christian and non-Christian public, many of whom are unaware that mainstream scholarship thought Jesus expected an imminent eschaton, what will probably be more surprising is the consistent black votes on second coming and last judgment texts. The seminar does not think Jesus spoke of his own second coming. Rather, it sees language about a second coming originating in the early community after Jesus' death.

So also with all passages that speak of an eternal judgment. The threats of being cast into a furnace of fire, or into the outer darkness where there will be weeping and wailing and gnashing of teeth, or of a harvest of wheat and a burning of weeds, are in black, as is the famous last judgment parable about the sheep and goats, the former to be given everlasting life and the latter condemned to everlasting fire. As a group, we do not think Jesus' message was about how to gain heaven and avoid hell.

The Kingdom of God

Our negative verdicts about an imminent eschaton and last judgment are also reflected in our voting on kingdom of God texts. Texts that speak of the kingdom as a future reality soon to come (which were one of the pillars of the eschatological understanding of Jesus) are black. These include Mark's well-known summary of the message of Jesus (Mark 1:15), which I quote first in the more familiar language of the Revised Standard Version and then in the language of the Scholar's Version:

> The time is fulfilled, and the kingdom of God is at hand; repent, and believe in the gospel.

> The time is up; God's imperial rule is closing in. Change your ways, and put your trust in the good news!

On the other hand, we regularly voted pink on sayings and parables that speak of the kingdom as present, such as Luke 17:20–21, Thomas 113 (quoted earlier in this essay), and Luke 11:10 = Matt. 12:28. According to the seminar, Jesus thought of the kingdom of God as a present reality, all around us, but difficult to discern.[17]

The Lord's Prayer

To the surprise of the seminar, our voting on the Lord's Prayer attracted more media headlines than any other vote taken, appearing as a front-page story in over one hundred Sunday newspapers. Put simply, we concluded that Jesus did not teach the Lord's Prayer *as a connected whole,* but that parts of it probably go back to him. The basis for this conclusion was threefold. First, the Lord's Prayer appears in three different forms in early Christian documents: in Matthew 6:9–13, Luke 11:2–4, and in Didache 8.2–3 (a collection of teachings attributed to the twelve disciples, probably written around the year 100). If one thinks the whole of the prayer goes back to Jesus, one is immediately faced with the question, "Which whole — that is, which version?" Clearly, they cannot all go back to Jesus. Indeed, once one sees the three forms, it seems clear that the Lord's Prayer is part of the community's developing tradition rather than going back in one of its present forms to Jesus himself.

Second, we were skeptical that Jesus taught his followers a rote prayer to be memorized and thought it more likely that the early movement created the Lord's Prayer for use in community worship. Matthew's formal liturgical opening, "Our Father who art in heaven" seems clearly to reflect such use. Yet, third, the elements found in common in the three versions seem early and may very well reflect "prayer fragments" going back to Jesus himself. These include the introductory use of the informal and intimate "Abba" (Aramaic for "Papa," an unusual even if not unique way of addressing God), and four petitions: the hallowing of God's name (as Abba!), the kingdom petition, bread for the day, and the forgiveness of debts. Thus, does the Lord's Prayer go back to Jesus? No. Do portions of it reflect prayer concerns of his? Yes.

Parables and Aphorisms

Two categories of material consistently received the greatest number of positive votes. Many of the parables of Jesus in their earliest form will be in red or pink: the Good Samaritan (Luke 10:30–35), the Dishonest Steward (Luke 16:1–8a), Workers in the Vineyard (Matt. 20:1–15), the Lost Coin (Luke 15:8–9), the Lost Sheep (Luke 15:4–6), the Corrupt Judge (Luke 18:2–5), the Prodigal (Luke 15:11–32), and others. On the other hand, some familiar parables will be in gray or black: the Rich Man and Lazarus (Luke 16:19–31), Wheat and Weeds (Matt. 13:24–30), Wise and Foolish Virgins (Matt. 25:1–13), Sheep and Goats (Matt. 25:31–46).

Also in red and pink will be many of the aphorisms of Jesus, short memorable sayings that colloquially can be described as "great one-liners." Eight of these received the highest number of red votes (and thus the highest weighted average) of any votes taken. At the top (and in descending order) are turn the other cheek (Matt. 5:39 = Luke 6:29a), coat and shirt (Matt. 5:40 = Luke 6:29b), blessed are the poor (Luke 6:20), go the second mile (Matt. 5:41), love of enemies (Luke 6:27b), woman leavening bread (Luke 13:20–21 = Matt. 13:33), emperor and God (Mark 12:17b = Thomas 100:2b), and give to beggars (Matt. 5:42a = Luke 6:30a). Approximately another fifty aphorisms will also be red or pink.

The earliest forms of the parables and aphorisms are thus seen as the bedrock of the Jesus tradition. Both are wisdom forms of speech, and taken together they point to Jesus as a "wisdom teacher." About this, there is the greatest consensus within the seminar

Considerable publicity accompanied the work of the seminar, especially during its first few years. Reporters from National Public Radio, the Canadian Broadcasting Corporation, *Time,* and *U.S. News and World Report* have attended meetings, as well as reporters from both national and regional newspapers. It is unusual, to put it mildly, for biblical scholars to have their deliberations covered by the media, and afterwards to have microphones thrust before them for interviews.

Generally the press has done a good job of reporting difficult material.[18] Headline writers, on the other hand, seeking to draw attention to the stories with telegram-size messages, have often highlighted the sensational. Headlines from the early years include, "Scholars Challenge Statements Attributed to Jesus," "Scholars Say Jesus Was Often Misquoted," "Bible Re-Write Progressing," "Scholars: Jesus Didn't Speak of Second Coming." Some had more of an edge to them: "Scholars Question Roots of Scripture" and "Scholars Seek to Discredit Christ." One conservative denominational magazine carried a story under the headline, "The Second Coming of Christ Has Been Cancelled," and another asked, "Why Do These Scholars Call Themselves Christian?"

The Five Gospels and the Church

These headlines (as well as many of the "negative" results reported) raise the question to which I will now turn. What connections are there to the life of the church? Does the work of the seminar essentially amount to a tampering with Scripture, as has sometimes been suggested? Is what we've been doing basically sensationalistic and destructive? Or does *The Five Gospels* have potential significance for Christians? Does it have a fruitful use within the church? My own answer (as already announced) is yes. Properly understood, the new volume can be of real value within the life of the church.

The Value of the New Translation

The Scholar's Version translation can help us to hear familiar texts in fresh ways. Words sometimes become old through habituated hearing. Words found in sacred texts in particular easily acquire a revered status that obscures the tone of the "street Greek" often found in the gospels. The substitution of new expressions for familiar phrases can sometimes revivify a text. Examples include (RSV followed by SV):

> For "kingdom of God": "God's imperial rule," "imperial rule of God," "God's domain," or "heaven's domain," depending upon context.

> For "Woe to you" (as in Matthew 23): "Damn you!"

> For "He who has ears to hear, let him hear": "Anyone here with two good ears had better listen."

> For "Do you not yet perceive or understand? Are your hearts hardened?": "You still aren't using your heads, are you? You still haven't got the point, have you? Are you just dense?"

> For "Blessed are you poor, for yours is the kingdom of God": "Congratulations, you poor! God's domain belongs to you."

In addition to fresh phraseology, the Scholar's Version also seeks to catch the vividness of narration created by the style of the evangelists, exemplified especially in Mark's gospel. Mark frequently narrates events in the present tense and also uses the imperfect tense to indicate typical or customary behavior. Most English translations convert all of this into simple past tense, as in the RSV translation of Mark 4:1–2, 9:

> Again Jesus *began* to teach beside the sea. And a very large crowd *gathered* about him, so that he *got* into a boat and *sat* in it on the sea; and the whole crowd was beside the sea on the land. And he *taught* them many things in parables, and in his teaching he *said* to them [parable of the sower follows] And he *said,* "He who has ears to hear, let him hear."[19]

The Scholar's Version preserves Mark's alternations between present and imperfect:

> Once again Jesus started to teach beside the sea. An enormous crowd *gathers* around him, so he *climbs* into a boat and *sits* there on the water facing the huge crowd on the shore. He *would teach* them many things in parables. In the course of his teaching, he *would tell* them [parable of the sower follows] And *as usual he said* [imperfect tense, suggesting Jesus typically said this], "Anyone here with two good ears had better listen."

Note two effects of the changes. The SV catches the present tense "storyteller" style of the original and suggests that this is typically the way Jesus would teach, rather than it being an account of what Jesus did once on a particular occasion.

Thus SV has advantages. Like any good new translation, it can enable the English reader to hear texts in a new way. And, unlike most translations, it preserves features of the Greek text even when, to some ears, they might sound clumsy in English. Because SV makes available nuances of meaning not found in most translations, it can very usefully complement other versions of the gospels, especially for study purposes.[20]

The Use of the Color Coding

I begin with a cautionary note: the color-coding of *The Five Gospels* should not be used as a new authority. As already mentioned, we in the seminar know that historical questions cannot be decided by voting and that elements of the consensus will change over time. Moreover, within the seminar itself, we are not agreed about everything; indeed, we are not unanimous about anything, except for many black votes. Gray is a large category, which (as also indicated earlier) is best understood in many cases as "undecided." I myself would move many of the gray sayings into pink or red. Thus the seminar's work should not be treated as an authority but seen as what it is: a reflection of historical judgments by a particular (though large) group of contemporary Jesus scholars. As such, *The Five Gospels* can be of value in the teaching mission of the church, especially in adult education settings.

First, it has great potential as a vehicle for teaching the scholarly understanding of the gospels that, despite the fact that it has been taught to mainline clergy for much of this century, is not widely known among lay people. Seeing the sayings of Jesus in four colors and realizing that the colors reflect voting done by scholars can be used to raise the question,"How does this make sense?" (The idea of voting on the sayings of Jesus often strikes people as bizarre, or at least as a bit odd. My brother-in-law jokingly said to a friend who asked how his sister's husband — me — was doing, "Well, he's flying around the country voting on the Lord's Prayer.")

The framework within which this activity makes sense is the understanding of the gospels that has developed in the last two hundred years of scholarship. Rather than being seen as straightforward historical documents, they are seen as the developing traditions of the early Christian movement put into their present form in the last third of the first century, some forty to seventy years after the death of Jesus. As such, to put it most simply, they contain two kinds of material: some material goes back to Jesus, and some is the product of early Christian communities in the decades after Easter.

During those decades, to use an organic metaphor, the traditions about Jesus grew. His followers modified and created sayings for at least two reasons: they adapted early material to new situations and settings;

and they created new material, either to address new situations, or to express new convictions about the significance of Jesus.

To move from an organic-developmental metaphor to an archaeological metaphor, one might think of the gospels as having layers, ranging from very early (close to the time of Jesus) to late (the time of the writing of the gospels themselves). The voting is a way of sorting out these layers: red is early and relatively undeveloped, black is later and the most developed, with pink and gray referring to intermediate layers.

The Five Gospels can thus readily be used to teach Christians about this view of the gospels. At a glance, the four colors illustrate the phenomenon: the gospels are the developing traditions of the early Christian movement. The awareness that the movement's traditions about Jesus grew and changed over time is central to an informed understanding of the gospels. They are not primarily historical reports that are to be believed, but rather they contain both the community's memories of Jesus and their understanding of the significance and role of Jesus in their own lives in their own time. To put that compactly, the gospels contain both the voice of Jesus and the voice of the community, and to be able to hear both voices enriches rather than impoverishes our understanding of the gospels.

Second, awareness of the distinction between the voice of Jesus and the voice of the community leads immediately to a further awareness: the distinction between the pre-Easter Jesus and the post-Easter Jesus. The pre-Easter Jesus is, of course, the historical Jesus: Jesus as a figure of history before his death, a Galilean Jew of the first third of the first century, a flesh-and-blood human being limited in time and space, finite and mortal, and executed by the empire that ruled the colonial society in which he lived.

The post-Easter Jesus, on the other hand, is what Jesus became after his death: the Jesus of Christian tradition and experience (and both nouns are important). This is the Jesus whom his followers continued to experience in the decades (and centuries) after his death, and whom they knew not as a finite mortal human being, but as a living spiritual reality who increasingly was seen as having all the qualities of God. The post-Easter Jesus is thus a divine reality. In most fully developed theological form, it is the Jesus of the great Christian creeds of the fourth and fifth centuries: only begotten Son of God, begotten and not made, of one substance with the Father, light of light, very God of very God, and so forth. The seeds of this development are already present in the gospels in their finished form, especially John. They are testimonies to the post-Easter Jesus, even as they also preserve traditions about the pre-Easter Jesus.

Both for historical and theological understanding, the distinction between the two is crucial. When it is not seen, then the historical Jesus is seen as having the qualities of the post-Easter Jesus, with several consequences. He ceases to be human, which is neither good history nor good theology. Moreover, the pre-Easter Jesus (it seems to me) ceases to be a credible figure if attributes properly belonging to the post-Easter Jesus are ascribed to him. Finally, we lose sight of the historical Jesus if we see him only through the screen of the post-Easter Jesus.

This leads to a third educational use of the color-coding in *The Five Gospels:* it can provoke curiosity about the historical Jesus and can provide a glimpse of him as seen by this group of scholars. Such curiosity is fruitful, it seems to me. The message of the pre-Easter Jesus is at least as interesting as the early Christian movement's message about him.

The glimpse provided by the red and pink passages highlights Jesus as a wisdom teacher who used parables and aphorisms. As used by Jesus, both were most commonly invitational forms of speech. As stories, the parables invited hearers to see something in light of the story. As crystallizations of insight, the aphorisms invited new insight. Moreover, Jesus regularly used both in a particular way: to subvert conventional (and religious) ways of seeing and being, and to suggest a radically alternative way of seeing and being. Rather strikingly, the most certain thing we know about Jesus according to the current scholarly consensus is that he was a teller of stories and a speaker of great one-liners whose purpose was the transformation of perception. At the center of his message was an invitation to see differently.[21]

Thus the consensus points to a central dimension of the pre-Easter Jesus. But it may be a glimpse of a part and not necessarily of the whole, for there may have been other central dimensions to Jesus as well. The seminar's large number of gray votes leaves this undecided. In particular, sayings of Jesus that suggest that he was a social prophet with an alternative social vision of life in community, or that suggest conflict with other Jewish groups about the direction of Israel, or that suggest that a movement came into existence around him during his lifetime, are generally in gray. Jesus was a teacher of a subversive and alternative wisdom, almost certainly, but it would be a mistake to conclude that this is a complete picture or an adequate *Gestalt*. The quest for the historical Jesus remains open. By identifying where there is a consensus, *The Five Gospels* is a starting place for understanding contemporary Jesus scholarship and is not intended as a final word that settles the matter.

Fourth, it is important to understand the nature and value of sayings printed in black. This must be emphasized, simply because there is a natural tendency to devalue (and perhaps even discard) black sayings on the grounds that they are inauthentic, that is, not said by Jesus. But they are valuable and illuminating precisely because they enable us to hear the voice of the community. Just as sayings in red and pink can help us to hear the voice of Jesus, so also sayings printed in black can help us to recognize and understand the voice of the community.

The voice of the community is a mixed bag. To be less colloquial, it contains a variety of material. Some of it is practical adaptation of the sayings of Jesus to new situations or to the needs of the community. For example, the saying in Mark 10:1–12, which declares the Torah's divorce law to be "because of hardness of heart," becomes in Matthew 19:9 a new rule, complete with an exception. Some of it represents the return of religious conventional wisdom, that is, an understanding of the relationship with God as based upon requirements and rewards.[22] Though found to some extent in all of the gospels, the return of conventional religious wisdom is especially characteristic of Matthew's redaction. Matthew often puts a "spin" on the teaching of Jesus that turns it into a new set of requirements, with eternal rewards or punishments for meeting them or failing to do so. Matthew often domesticates the message of Jesus by subverting his subversive teaching. And when the subversive is subverted, we are back to the conventional.

But some of the material in black is also quite wonderful. To put that differently, some of black bears witness to what the risen living Christ became in the experience of the community in the decades after Easter. It is difficult to know (or even to surmise) what happened at Easter, or even if we should think of Easter as a particular day or a particular set of events within a limited number of days. What one can say is this: after his death, the followers of Jesus became convinced that "Jesus still lives," though in a new way. This conviction was expressed in the language of visions (Paul), or appearances (the gospels), or in the affirmation that the spirit that was known in Jesus continued to be and to operate. Jesus after his death, as the post-Easter Jesus, was known as still present and active.

Much of black speaks about this. The "exalted titles" ascribed to Jesus in the gospels flow out of what the community experienced of Jesus after his death. It is in the light of Easter (again, not necessarily meaning a particular day or event, but the strong conviction that God had vindicated Jesus and that Jesus still lived) that the community affirmed that Jesus was messiah and son of God.

Even more powerfully, the great "I am" statements at the heart of John's gospel (all black) express what the post-Easter Jesus had become in the life of the Johannine community. These statements, using first-person language, affirm the most extraordinary things about Jesus: "I am the light of the world," "I am the bread of life," "I am the resurrection and the life," "I am the way, the truth, and the life," "Before Abraham was, I am," plus several more: I am the door, the vine, the good shepherd.

According to *The Five Gospels* (and mainstream biblical scholarship throughout this century), the pre-Easter Jesus didn't say any of this. Rather, this is the voice of an early Christian community, namely, the community in which the author of John lived and for which he wrote. Why did he (and they) speak of Jesus in all of these ways, even though the pre-Easter Jesus did not speak this way about himself? The most plausible answer is because of their experience. They experienced the post-Easter Jesus in all of these ways: as one who had brought them out of the darkness into the light, as one who nourished them with spiritual food in the midst of their journey, as the way that had led them from death to life, as the truth which had set them free, as the vine of which they were branches, and so forth.

It seems to me that this is a great gain in understanding. When the "I am" statements are understood as Jesus' own words, they become very problematic. What would we think of a first-century Galilean Jew (or anybody else, for that matter) who said about himself, "I am the light of the world," "I am the bread of life," etc.? But when they are understood as the voice of the community, as statements flowing out of the community's experience of the living risen Christ, they become a powerful witness to the reality, presence, and function of the post-Easter Jesus in their lives.

Thus black sayings are often of great value. They testify to the intensity and vividness of the early Christian community's experience of the post-Easter Jesus. For them, Jesus was not just a figure of the past, but a figure of the present, a living spiritual reality whom they still knew in their own experience. The risen Christ, the post-Easter Jesus, was for them (to move from black sayings in John to black material in Matthew) "Immanuel," that is, "God with us," God in their (and our) midst: "For I am with you always, even to the end of the age."

A Broader Issue: Raising Biblical Consciousness

The Five Gospels can also be used within the church as a springboard for reflecting about the nature and authority of the Bible. Indeed, this is one of the stated purposes of the Jesus Seminar: to raise consciousness about the Bible by making modern biblical scholarship public in a highly visible way. Although its voting and the publication of its results in four colors serve very practical purposes (what better way to determine and display the degree of scholarly consensus?), it is also intended to be provocative. The seminar has deliberately sought publicity, not for self-serving ends, but in order to provoke discussion about what the Bible is and how to understand it.

The Problem

Such a discussion is important because of widespread biblical illiteracy in our time. For many people the Bible has become a closed book. By this I mean two things. Awareness of basic biblical content has radically declined over the last generation or two. I have had college students ask me, "Who's Moses?" and "What is Judaism," and the last time I made a passing reference to "casting pearls before swine," I realized that my students felt vaguely insulted rather than recognizing it as an allusion to a saying of Jesus. Even more centrally, however, by biblical illiteracy I mean the inability to read the Bible with understanding (for literacy includes understanding what one reads, not simply the ability to recognize words). For many in our time, the Bible is opaque rather than translucent.

A historical perspective can help us see why. A major reason (and to me, it seems like *the* major reason) is that a way of understanding the Bible that worked for centuries has recently disappeared, and for great numbers of people, nothing satisfactory has replaced it.

Natural Literalism

Until perhaps a hundred years ago, most people living within Western culture (the world of Christendom) heard the Bible in what might be called a state of natural literalism.[23] In a state of natural literalism, a number of things are apparent about the Bible:

1. *It is divine product.* Such is the "natural" or "immediate" meaning of how the Bible is spoken about in Christian circles: as the Word of God, inspired by the Holy Spirit, sacred Scripture. This book is not a human product, but comes from God in a way no other book does.

2. *It is therefore true and authoritative.* Because it is a divine product, it is guaranteed to be true. Its statements can not only be taken as trustworthy but must be taken seriously as the ultimate authority about what to believe and how to live.

3. *It is literally true.* In a state of natural literalism, it is taken for granted that what the Bible says "happened" really happened (unless the language is manifestly metaphorical, such as "mountains clapping their hands with joy"; natural literalists can recognize and appreciate metaphor). This way of hearing the Bible takes it for granted that Adam and Eve were the first two people, that there really was a Garden of Eden, that the walls of Jericho really fell, that Jesus was born of a virgin, that Jesus really said and did all of the things reported about him, and so forth. Believing all of this literally takes no special effort; in this state, there is no reason to think otherwise.

4. *The Bible (and therefore Christianity) is uniquely and exclusively true.* It is taken for granted that the Bible is the unique revelation

of God, and that Jesus is the only way of salvation. Here — in the Bible — saving knowledge of God is found as nowhere else.

This way of seeing the Bible was dominant in Western Christian culture until very recently. It is familiar to us in part because it is so recent, virtually omnipresent within both culture and church until about a century ago. Most of our ancestors two or three generations back were natural literalists. And it is familiar because for most of us who grew up in the church, it is the image of the Bible we formed as children. We took it for granted that the Bible came from God and that what it said was true. As children, it never occurred to us to ask about the story of Noah and the ark, or about the virgin birth, "Now, is this literally or symbolically true?" No — we just took it for granted that it was literally true. Why would we have thought otherwise? Indeed, "taken for granted" is the key phrase for understanding natural literalism's approach to the Bible: in this state, *the distinction between literal and non-literal has not yet arisen.* There is no reason for it to do so. To put it more technically, there is no cognitive dissonance.

For the most part, Christians in Western culture lived in this state until the great divide in modern intellectual history known as the Enlightenment. Beginning in the 1600s among a few intellectuals and accelerating through the 1700s and 1800s, Enlightenment ways of thinking began to call into question the picture of the Bible as a literally true divine product. The loss of natural literalism produced a crisis in how to understand the Bible, its nature and authority.

Conscious Literalism

In the nineteenth century, the crisis gave birth to a new kind of literalism, conscious literalism, and a battle over the Bible began. It was no longer self-evident, for example, that the Genesis stories of creation described how the earth and life really began. Moreover, the cognitive dissonance between geology, evolution, and the Bible was but one instance of a new phenomenon: the emergence of sharp differences between traditional ways of understanding the Bible and what seems to be known on other grounds. The taken-for-granted literalistic reading of the Bible became impossible; a literal reading now had to be defended against non-literal readings, and literalism became a conscious choice. The difference between natural literalism and conscious literalism is large. Whereas the former did not require believing things that were hard to believe and a corresponding suspension of the intellect, the latter required both.

At the beginning of this century, as the scientific world-view of the Enlightenment became part of popular culture and no longer just the viewpoint of educated elites, conscious literalism became embodied in a movement known as fundamentalism. Many people are surprised to learn that fundamentalism is neither old nor traditional, but is a twentieth-century reaction to (and rejection of) the effects of Enlightenment knowledge upon the Bible and Christianity. As a literalism become conscious of itself and aware of other possibilities, fundamentalism insists that the Bible literally comes from God and is therefore literally true. The Word of God becomes "the words of God." Only so, from this point of view, does it make sense to treat the Bible as an authority for the Christian life.

Fundamentalism is (and always has been) a minority movement within the church. Yet it is highly visible. It continues to generate a battle over the Bible in entire denominations, most recently in the Southern Baptist Convention and the Lutheran Church–Missouri Synod. Even in mainline denominations and congregations, where the struggle is essentially over with, vocal minorities sometimes advocate a fundamentalist view. Conscious literalism's way of viewing the Bible is responsible for widely publicized conflicts about whether to teach evolution or "creationism" in public schools. It is the basis of appeals to return to "biblical morality," the implication being that there are rules for behavior that come directly from God, namely, those in the Bible.[24] Moreover, this vision of the Bible as a divine authority authored by God is widely assumed by people outside of the church to be what Christians believe, or at least are supposed to believe. Such is the impression created by the most visible and audible forms of Christianity today, namely, televangelists and Christian radio. Yet this understanding is unpersuasive to many, and at least partially responsible for many outside of the church (whether because they left it or were never part of it) choosing to remain outside.

Though the majority of Christians in mainline denominations do not accept the fundamentalist view, many are uncertain about what to do with the Bible. At least fundamentalists have the advantage of being clear and certain. In contrast, in many mainline churches, there is often a polite (but strange) silence about the Bible. An old way of seeing the Bible has vanished. Natural literalism is essentially an impossibility in late twentieth-century Western culture (even fundamentalists are not natural literalists), and conscious literalism is not an option for many. Yet relatively few have found a persuasive alternative. The result: as a culture (and as Christians living in this culture) many of us do not know how to read the Bible.

Beyond Natural and Conscious Literalism

Such an alternative is provided by modern biblical scholarship. This alternative, unfortunately, is not widely known, despite the fact that it is over two hundred years old and is taught in the seminaries of mainline churches (Roman Catholic as well as Protestant). It is one of the best-kept secrets of the church. There is more than one reason for this: we scholars have not often been very adept at writing in accessible language, the teaching of the Bible in seminaries has not consistently enabled seminarians to communicate this different approach, and clergy have often been timid at introducing their congregations to a way of understanding the Bible that initially seems threatening to some.

The Five Gospels is ideally suited as a vehicle for bringing a greater awareness of biblical scholarship to the church and for initiating serious conversation among Christians about what the Bible is. It does this by making the presuppositions and insights of modern biblical scholarship widely available.

The result can be an understanding of the Bible beyond the options of natural and conscious literalism. It is a considerable transformation, affecting our perception of the nature and origin of the Bible. For what *The Five Gospels* makes clear about the nature of the gospels is true about the Bible as a whole: it is the developing tradition of two ancient communities, ancient Israel and the early Christian movement. As such, the Bible is not a divine product that is to be believed no matter how incredible, but a human cultural product that is to be understood. The Old Testament is Israel's story, told by Israel and about Israel. The New Testament is the early church's story, told by them and about them. Together, they tell us how these two ancient communities experienced God, thought about God, and worshiped God, as well as how they thought they should live (communally and individually) in response to God. The Bible's ethical directives and codes of behavior were directly relevant to their lives in their time, not divine laws given by God for all time.

This transformed understanding of the Bible also leads to a quite different perception of its authority. When the Bible is seen as an infallibly true divine product, then it becomes an authority standing over us, telling us what to believe and how to behave, regardless of whether these beliefs or codes of behavior make sense to us. The alternative understanding of the Bible — as ancient Israel's and the early church's witness to their life with God — sees things differently. Within this way of seeing, the significance of the biblical canon is that it affirms that these are the ancient documents with which Christians are to be in a continuing conversation and dialogue. To take the Bible seriously is to seek to understand what our ancestors in the tradition knew of God.

The publication of *The Five Gospels* will put both Jesus and the Bible "in the news." By so doing, it opens a window of opportunity for significant consciousness raising and education within the church, as well as more broadly in our culture. Together with biblical scholarship generally, it can provide a way for people to be both thoughtful and Christian, rather than having to choose between the two. It can help to make the Bible an open book once again.

Notes

1. Robert W. Funk, Roy W. Hoover, and the Jesus Seminar, *The Five Gospels: The Search for the Authentic Words of Jesus* (New York: Macmillan, 1993). The fifth gospel is the gospel of Thomas, discovered in Egypt in 1945, about which I will say more later. In addition to the texts of the five gospels printed in four colors, the over five-hundred-page volume includes an extended introduction and commentary. I wish to thank Charlene Matejovsky, vice president of Polebridge Press and a major coordinator of the seminar's meetings, for providing me with an advance copy of the book.

2. The Jesus Seminar has no formal connection to Pacific School of Religion (PSR) or any other religious or denominational body. Rather, PSR provided the facilities for the meeting, as have several other seminaries or graduate schools of religion, including St. Meinrad's Seminary in Indiana (Catholic), Luther-Northwestern Seminary in Minnesota, and Notre Dame.

3. It is one of several scholarly groups operating under the umbrella of the Westar Institute (also directed by Funk), whose headquarters and publishing house (Polebridge Press) are located in Sonoma, California. Further information about the seminar and its publications (including its journal *Foundations and Facets Forum* and its popular level magazine *The Fourth R*) may be obtained by writing to the Westar Institute, Box 1526, Sonoma, CA 95476.

4. Robert W. Funk, "The Issue of Jesus," *Foundations and Facets Forum* 1, no. 1 (1985): 7.

5. *The Five Gospels* lists the names of seventy-four scholars in its "Roster of Fellows," 533–37. In addition to these, a large number of other scholars took part in one or more meetings.

6. Four women are listed in the roster of seventy-four scholars. At least three more women occasionally took part.

7. It should be noted that Fellows were responsible for paying their own travel, registration, and lodging expenses, either out of personal funds or travel budgets from their own institutions. Thus quite a number could not afford to attend both meetings each year.

8. To qualify this statement slightly, not every saying was discussed and voted on individually. Some blocks of material were affirmed by unanimous consensus to be "black." The procedure involved assigning "likely black" passages to a study group within the seminar and then voting on their recommendations.

9. I believe this language was coined by Leif Vaage, a Fellow of the seminar. It has since become "semi-official" — i.e., widely used within the seminar and seen as a good representation of what the votes mean.

10. A phrase I recall being used by the New Testament scholar Reginald Fuller some thirty years ago. He used it in a different context, namely, to refer to judgments about the historicity of some of the miracles attributed to Jesus.

11. The collection as a whole is known as the Nag Hammadi Library (apparently the library of a Christian monastery in southern Egypt, carefully buried in the second half of the 300s). The standard English edition is James M. Robinson, ed., *The Nag Hammadi Library* (San Francisco: Harper & Row, 1977). On Thomas in particular, see Stephen J. Patterson, *The Gospel of Thomas and Jesus* (Sonoma, Calif.: Polebridge, 1993); Marvin Meyer and Harold Bloom, *The Gospel of Thomas* (San Francisco: Harper, 1992); and an earlier but still valuable work, Stevan L. Davies, *The Gospel of Thomas and Christian Wisdom* (New York: Seabury, 1983).

12. Demuring from this judgment is, for example, John P. Meier, *A Marginal Jew: Rethinking the Historical Jesus* (New York: Doubleday, 1991), 123–39.

13. Mustard seed: Thomas 20, Mark 4:30–32. Wedding banquet: Thomas 64, Luke 14:16–24, Matt. 22:1–13. Wicked vineyard tenants: Thomas 65, Mark 12:1–11.

14. What these parables might mean is not obvious. However, they do have an enigmatic and provocative character typical of what we think we know about the original teaching of Jesus.

15. A closely related saying in Thomas 3 received a gray vote. Here the question is not *when* is the kingdom, but *where;* and the answer is, not somewhere else, but rather the kingdom "is within you *and it is outside you.*" I have italicized the last phrase to emphasize that it extends the notion familiar in some forms of Christian piety that the kingdom is within (a common translation of Luke 17:20–21): it is within you, yes, *and also outside of you.* The implication is that the kingdom is not just within us but all around us — "spread out upon the earth."

16. For description of the earlier eschatological consensus, see especially chapter 3, pp. 48–51.

17. In addition to commentary on the kingdom passages in *The Five Gospels,* see the "cameo essay" on 136–37.

18. A major recent exception is a story in *Newsweek,* April 4, 1994, pp. 53–54. There the Seminar is characterized as "outside the mainstream" of biblical scholarship, and its findings interpreted in a misleadingly negative way. It ignores the fact that both red and pink are very positive votes and implies that the Seminar is unanimous that gray material should be "discarded."

19. The introduction to *The Five Gospels* also uses this example; see xv–xvi.

20. The Scholar's Version is also used in Robert Miller, ed., *The Complete Gospels* (Sonoma, Calif.: Polebridge, 1992). The volume contains not only the canonical gospels, but also other early Christian gospels (including a reconstructed Q gospel), together with commentary. It is not a multi-color edition.

21. For a more extended development of the subversive and alternative wisdom of Jesus, see chapter 7 above, pp. 147–152.

22. On conventional wisdom, see chapter 7 above, esp. pp. 149–150. See also *Jesus: A New Vision* (San Francisco: Harper & Row, 1987), 81–83 and chapter 6; and *Meeting Jesus Again for the First Time,* chapter 4. I want to emphasize that I speak of *religious* conventional wisdom and not specifically of *Jewish* conventional wisdom. True, popular Judaism of Jesus' time commonly

took the form of religious conventional wisdom (a religion of requirements and rewards), but this is characteristic of popular religion in most cultures in most times. Indeed, it is the most common form of Christianity. To equate Judaism with a religion of requirements and reward is no more correct or fair than it would be to say the same about Christianity. The point: religious conventional wisdom is common in both traditions, not a characteristic of Judaism in particular.

23. For natural literalism and the distinction between it and conscious literalism, see Paul Tillich, *Dynamics of Faith* (New York: Harper & Row, 1957), chapter 3, esp. 51–53.

24. Of course, this is done selectively: Jesus' subversive sayings about accepting outcasts, loving enemies, and not grounding one's life in tradition (not even in sacred tradition) are not quoted nearly as often as are biblical passages about the loin issues of fornication, adultery, divorce, lust, and homosexuality (and even birth control and abortion, though the Bible says nothing about either).

Chapter Nine

Does the Historical Jesus Matter?

The historical study of Jesus produces results very different from what Christians are accustomed to hearing and affirming about Jesus. Within Christian devotion, worship, and belief, Jesus is regularly spoken of as divine, indeed as the second person of the Trinity. The Nicene Creed, the great creed of the church formulated in the fourth century, speaks of him in the most exalted language:

> We believe in one Lord, Jesus Christ,
> the only Son of God,
> eternally begotten of the Father,
> God from God, Light from Light,
> true God from true God,
> begotten, not made,
> of one Being with the Father.
> Through him all things were made.
> For us and for our salvation
> he came down from heaven;
> by the power of the Holy Spirit
> he became incarnate from the Virgin Mary,
> and was made man.
> For our sake he was crucified under Pontius Pilate;
> he suffered death and was buried.
> On the third day he rose again
> in accordance with the Scriptures;
> he ascended into heaven
> and is seated at the right hand of the Father.
> He will come again to judge the living and the dead,
> and his kingdom will have no end.[1]

Yet historical scholarship about the pre-Easter Jesus affirms essentially none of this. We are quite certain that Jesus did not think of himself as divine or as "Son of God" in any unique sense, if at all. If one of the disciples had responded to the question reportedly asked by

Jesus in Mark's gospel, "Who do people say that I am?," with words like those used in the Nicene Creed, we can well imagine that Jesus would have said, "What???" Moreover, most Jesus scholars do not think Jesus was born of a virgin, or that he ascended into heaven in a visible way, or that there will be a literal second coming. Indeed, perhaps the only line from the Creed that would be seen as historical is the reference to his death: "he was crucified under Pontius Pilate, suffered death, and was buried."[2]

Thus the quest for the historical Jesus often seems to call into question some of the most common and cherished Christian beliefs. Indeed, its foundational claim — that Jesus of Nazareth was quite different from how he is portrayed in the gospels and creeds of the church — can seem threatening to and destructive of Christian faith. In this concluding chapter, as one who is both a Christian and a Jesus scholar, I want to reflect on the relationship between Jesus scholarship and the Christian life. What is the significance of such scholarship for Christian theology, understanding, and life? Does the historical study of Jesus matter for Christians, and, if so, in what ways?

A Historical Perspective

It is useful to see this issue as a sub-category of a larger question: what significance is to be given to the historical study of the Bible as it has emerged in the last few centuries of biblical scholarship? What happens to the claims of Christian theology, doctrine, dogma, and morals when the Bible is treated not as a divine product whose truth is guaranteed by its divine origin, but as a human product produced by two ancient cultures, namely, ancient Israel and the early Christian movement?

Until about three centuries ago, this was not an issue within the Christian world, any more than it was an issue for Muslims to wonder whether the Koran came directly from Allah through the prophet Mohammed. No effort was required to believe this, for it was part of the taken-for-granted world of shared conviction. The gospels and the Bible as a whole were understood in what I called in the previous chapter the state of "natural literalism" or "pre-critical naiveté." They were seen as divine documents whose truth was guaranteed by God. Therefore, the history that they reported was taken for granted actually to have happened.

This is not to say that every passage was understood literally. Theologians and Scripture scholars could find the "spiritual" or "allegorical" meaning of a text to be more important than the literal meaning, and could deny the literal meaning of some texts.[3] Nevertheless, if the text looked like it described something that happened or was said, it was taken for granted that what it reported was historically true: Adam and Eve in the Garden of Eden, Noah and the flood, God speaking to Moses through a burning bush, the walls of Jericho falling down in the time of Joshua, the miraculous deliverance of Daniel from the lions' den, the virgin birth with shepherds and wisemen in attendance, the stories of Jesus walking on the water, and so forth.

Within this view of Scripture, what Jesus was like could be known simply by combining together all that the Bible said about him.[4] No distinction had yet been made between Jesus as a historical figure and the Jesus who meets us on the surface of the gospels, between the pre-Easter Jesus and the post-Easter Jesus. The Jesus of history and the canonical Christ were seen as identical, and this identification was not even an article of faith. It required neither "belief" nor effort, but was as self-evident to our ancestors as the heliocentric solar system is to us.

It was this understanding of the Bible and the gospels that was initially undermined and ultimately overturned by modern biblical scholarship. Modern biblical scholarship was the child of two parents: the Protestant Reformation of the sixteenth century and the Enlightenment, which began about a century later. The Reformation emphasized the authority of the Bible (in contrast to church tradition), and thus gave to its study an importance that it had not had for over a thousand years. The Reformation also saw the Bible translated into popular languages, thereby making it widely accessible.

The Enlightenment, with its emphasis upon reason and scientific ways of knowing, engendered a revolution in knowledge. No longer could something be accepted as "true" simply on the basis of authority and tradition. Investigation and reason became the new basis for knowledge. Applied initially in the natural world of the sciences, the new way of knowing soon was applied in the human world of history and culture. Within the world-view of the Enlightenment, both sacred authority and supernatural causation were rejected, and instead the effort was made to understand everything within a natural system of cause and effect.

In the sphere of religion and theology, the early bearers of the Enlightenment were the Deists. Like their counterparts in the sciences, they consistently sought "reasonable" and "natural" explanations. Though the Deists still affirmed the existence of God, they rejected the notions of supernatural intervention and special revelation. With these gone, the privileged status of the Bible and of Christian doctrine also vanished. Scripture and doctrine alike were seen as human products, not as the result of special divine revelation.

Accompanying this was the rise of a new historical consciousness. The task of the historian was no longer seen as simply chronicling events reported in authoritative documents. Rather, the historian now became the judge of historical documents, seeking to make discriminating judgments about their origin, character, and ultimately about "what really happened."[5]

Modern biblical scholarship was born in the areas where the Protestant Reformation and the Enlightenment were most influential: Germany, the Netherlands, the British isles, and to a lesser extent France. Most of the early work was done on the Old Testament. In Holland in 1644, Hugo Grotius argued that the Old Testament was to be understood in relation to its original historical circumstances, and not primarily in relationship to the New Testament. A third of a century later, the famous philosopher Benedict Spinoza argued that the author of the Pentateuch was not Moses, but Ezra (who lived about nine hundred years after Moses). In France in 1678, Richard Simon (a Catholic) argued that much of the Old Testament had been compiled by scribal schools rather than written by inspired individuals.

The initial impact of this new approach to the Bible was controversial, to put it mildly, and world-threatening, to put it more accurately. In 1697 an eighteen-year-old Scottish student named Thomas Aikenhead was hanged in Edinburgh for claiming (as Spinoza had some twenty years earlier) that Ezra (and not Moses) was the author of the Pentateuch. Some thirty years later in England, the fate of Thomas Woolston, a professor at Cambridge, was considerably milder: he was sentenced to a year's imprisonment for his claim that the miracles of Jesus did not happen. Near the end of the 1700s, Thomas Paine (of American Revolutionary War fame) in his *Age of Reason* denied the truthfulness of both the Old and New Testaments. His publishers in England were heavily fined and sent to prison.[6]

In that world biblical criticism was seen as a threat to society: it seemed to call into question the truth of Christianity and therefore the underpinnings of Western culture itself. What seemed to be at stake for many was the sacred foundation of a world. Thus it was taken for granted that historical claims regarding the origin of the Bible and of Christianity mattered a great deal.

Early Period: The Historical Jesus Matters

It was in this period that the quest for the historical Jesus began. Like the early forays in biblical criticism, it generated both controversy and conflict. Hermann Samuel Reimarus (1694–1768), a professor of Oriental languages in Hamburg, is usually credited with the honor of being its father.[7] The work for which he is famous — *The Aims of Jesus and His Disciples* (1778) — was published posthumously and anonymously by Gotthold Lessing, who used a ruse to get it past state censorship, which forbad the publication of works injurious to religion. The identity of the author was not disclosed for several decades because of fear of bringing harm to his family. In 1835, a two-volume fourteen-hundred-page *Life of Jesus* by David Friedrich Strauss (remarkably, only twenty-seven years old) was published. Among other things, Strauss argued that the miracle stories were to be understood as myth, not history. He lost his academic position in Tübingen and was in effect banned for life from a university career. One reviewer referred to his book as "the Iscariotism of our day," and another called it the most pestilential volume ever vomited out of the bowels of hell.[8] To say the obvious, many people in this period thought that what one affirmed about the historical Jesus mattered a great deal. Civil authority still sometimes took a hand, and outrage among church officials was common.

Throughout the nineteenth century, there was widespread agreement that the historical Jesus had great significance for Christian faith. About this, hostile debunkers, orthodox defenders, and liberal revisionists agreed. Debunkers delightedly assumed that Christianity could be discredited by showing what the "real" Jesus was like. Orthodox defenders, with their vigorous insistence upon the historical accuracy of the gospel portraits of Jesus, implicitly affirmed that any significant discrepancy would be destructive of the truth of Christianity. Liberal revisionists argued that Christianity could be purified and reformed by rediscovering the Jesus of history behind the doctrinal encrustations of the tradition. But all agreed: the historical Jesus mattered.

The Pendulum Swings

Around the end of the nineteenth century, the claim that the historical Jesus mattered changed. Indeed, it was turned on its head. Throughout much of the twentieth century, the dominant position has been that the historical Jesus (defined more precisely as *the historian's Jesus,* namely, as what the historian can affirm about Jesus) has little or no significance for Christian theology and faith.

The reversal was due largely to the work of two scholars, Martin Kähler (1835–1912) and Albert Schweitzer (1875–1965). In a book published in Germany in 1892 and translated into English as *The So-Called Historical Jesus and the Historic Biblical Christ*, Kähler, a professor of systematic theology, argued that the historical Jesus does not matter for Christian faith and theology; rather, only the biblical Christ does.[9] For Kähler, the historical Jesus was the historically reconstructed Jesus, the result of the historian's activity. The biblical Christ is the Christ of the gospels and the New Testament. The historical Jesus, he argued, cannot be decisively important for Christian faith, in part because the gospels do not provide adequate materials to write a life of Jesus, and in part because all historical reconstructions are relative and can at most be probable, not certain. Christian faith cannot be faith in constantly changing historical reconstructions accessible only through the work of scholars. If it were, it would, among other things, make Christian faith inaccessible to most Christians. Rather, Kähler argued, Christian faith is faith in "the biblical Christ," the Christ of early Christianity's proclamation as found in the New Testament as a whole. It is the Christ of the church's proclamation — the kerygmatic Christ — who matters for faith and theology. The historical Jesus does not.

In different terms, a similar position was articulated by Albert Schweitzer in the epilogue to his epochal *Quest for the Historical Jesus* (1906). In the conclusion of a book in which he (at age thirty) brilliantly systematized the history of the quest to his day and then argued for an eschatological understanding of Jesus that was to dominate scholarship throughout much of the twentieth century, he pronounced the whole enterprise theologically and religiously irrelevant. The Jesus discovered by historical research was, he wrote, "a stranger to our time." He was strange to a large extent because of the eschatological beliefs that, Schweitzer argued, animated his life: Jesus believed that the supernatural kingdom of God was at hand, and that he himself would be transformed into the apocalyptic "Son of man" who would rule that kingdom as God's vice-regent and Messiah. And, of course, he was wrong.[10] But that doesn't matter, Schweitzer continued, for it is *the spiritual Christ,* not the historical Jesus, who matters for us who live in the centuries since. The spiritual Christ is the one who is still known; the historical Jesus is a remote and strange figure from the distant past. To paraphrase the moving paragraph with which Scwheitzer ended his epilogue: the spiritual Christ is a living reality who still comes to us as one unknown, as of old, by the lakeshore, he came to those who knew him not. The spiritual Christ speaks to us the same words: "Follow thou me." And in relationship to *that* Christ (not to the historical Jesus), we come to know him as he is.

The impact of Kähler and Schweitzer extended long into the twentieth century. The claim that the historical Jesus is irrelevant to Christian theology and faith became the dominant position among both theologians and Jesus scholars. In a famous formulation, Rudolf Bultmann (1884–1976) argued that only the "thatness" of Jesus mattered, not the "whatness." That is, only *that* Jesus existed and was crucified matters, not the *what* of his historical life.[11]

For both theologians and Jesus scholars, the position had an attractive feature. It created a "truce" that enabled both to go about their work without needing to pay much attention to each other.

The Current Scene

In broad strokes this was the situation at mid-century. In retrospect, one can see that Jesus scholarship from its beginning up to this period saw a pendulum swing between the poles of two related either/or's. The first either/or was *the historical Jesus or the Christ of faith* (who may also be spoken of as the biblical Christ or kerygmatic Christ). Who is normative for Christian faith and theology? Is it the historical Jesus or the Christ of faith? The second either/or was a common (though not necessary) corollary of the first: *either the historical Jesus is of normative importance, or he is of little or no significance at all.* To speak schematically, scholarship in the nineteenth century generally affirmed the Jesus of history (and thus the theological importance of the historical study of Jesus) and in much of the twentieth century affirmed the Christ of faith (and hence the theological unimportance of historical Jesus scholarship). The present scene is marked both by a continuation of the mid-century position and movement beyond it.

The last few decades have seen an increasing separation between historical Jesus scholarship and systematic theology (including christology) as intellectual disciplines, and a corresponding separation of historical Jesus scholarship from an explicitly Christian theological agenda. The reasons are quite mundane. One is institutional: many Jesus scholars now teach in the increasingly secularized and pluralistic environment of colleges and universities, rather than seminaries. As a result, historical Jesus scholars are not routinely involved in scholarly dialogue with theologians, and the questions they treat are generally not generated by explicitly theological concerns.

A second factor is the increasing specialization of the academy and the proliferation of publication within each discipline. To speak for myself, I simply do not have time to keep up with publications in my own discipline and also to read widely in contemporary theology and christology, especially since my teaching responsibilities (like most of us in small departments) require me to be relatively current in a number of sub-disciplines of religious studies (in my case, as diverse as religion and psychology, environmental ethics, and religion and culture). And for the same reasons, most theologians (including those doing christology) are not involved in sustained dialogue with Jesus scholarship.

There is gain in the separation of Jesus scholarship from a theological agenda. It has generated fresh questions and emphases in historical Jesus scholarship.[12] But it has also contributed to the persistence of the mid-century truce. The basis of the truce — the sharp separation of historical Jesus research and the theological enterprise — continues to be affirmed in many quarters.[13] My impression is that it is still the most common position: historical Jesus scholarship is thought by many scholars (especially by those outside of the discipline itself but in related disciplines such as New Testament and theology) to be not only historically difficult to the point of being problematic, but also without theological relevance. Yet the second half of the century has also seen significant movement away from the sharp "either/or" of earlier scholarship to more of a "both-and" position.

The "New Quest"

That movement began with the "new quest" or "second quest" of the historical Jesus in the 1950s. It accepted the centrality of the kerygmatic Christ for faith and theology, even as it also rejected the sharp separation from the Jesus of history. Initiated in a lecture by Ernst Käsemann in 1953 and crystalized in James Robinson's 1959 book *A New Quest of the Historical Jesus,* the new quest was marked by two central claims regarding the importance of the historical Jesus.[14] Without a connection to Jesus of Nazareth, Christianity risks falling into docetism and/or an ahistorical piety. Moreover, the synoptic gospels themselves provide warrant for taking the historical Jesus seriously: by preserving traditions about Jesus even as they adapt them and create new ones, the evangelists suggest that the *pastness* of Jesus' life was significant for Christian life in their own present time. Thus the new quest affirmed a role for historical knowledge of Jesus, even though its actual focus ended up being quite narrow.[15]

Norman Perrin

In a work published in the late 1960s, Perrin (the most prominent Jesus scholar in North America at the time of his death in 1976) assigned considerable theological importance to the historical study of Jesus.[16] To see this, it is illuminating to begin with Perrin's useful notion of "faith-image" of Jesus. Every Christian has such a "faith-image," which is the product of everything the Christian has assimilated about Jesus, whether from listening to sermons, hearing the gospels, reciting creeds, or singing hymns.[17] Faith-images are ultimately the product of Christian proclamation (in a comprehensive sense), not directly the result of historical research. Thus for Perrin (in continuity with Kähler and Bultmann, both of whom he explicitly cites), the proclaimed Christ is granted primacy.

What then is the relationship between the historical study of Jesus and the proclaimed Christ found in the faith-images of Christians? Here Perrin moves significantly beyond Kähler and Bultmann and assigns two roles to historical Jesus scholarship. First, it can contribute to the formation and revision of the faith-image by providing content. Christian faith, Perrin writes, is: " . . . necessarily faith *in* something, a believer believes *in* something, and in so far as that 'something' is 'Jesus,' historical knowledge can help to provide the content, without thereby becoming the main source of that content."[18]

Second, Perrin affirms that historical knowledge about Jesus can be used as a basis for discriminating among the great variety of proclamations that claim to be Christian. In a situation in which everything from "radical right racism to revolutionary Christian humanism" is proclaimed as Christian kerygma, historical knowledge about Jesus can be "a means of testing the claims of the Christs presented in the competing kerygmata to be Jesus Christ." This leads to a striking statement: "The true kerygmatic Christ, the justifiable faith-image, is that consistent with the historical Jesus." It is a strong statement. The historical study of Jesus is assigned no less a role than the validation or invalidation of a given version of Christian proclamation as really *Christian*.[19]

If we were to emphasize only this part of Perrin, it would seem as if we had gone back to the nineteenth century: the historical Jesus is normative for discerning what is authentically Christian. What makes Perrin's position not simply a return to the nineteenth century is, of course, his strong affirmation of the primacy of the kerygmatic Christ, the Christ of faith. Rather than being a return to one pole of the "either/or" of earlier scholarship, Perrin (like the new quest) represents movement to a "both/and" position.

The "both/and" position affirms that the historical Jesus matters for Christians. Such is also affirmed in two very recent works by major Jesus scholars, John P. Meier and John Dominic Crossan. Though there are central differences between the two, both agree that the historical study of Jesus has significance for Christian theology and life.

John Meier

Meier's position is sketched in a chapter entitled, "Why Bother? The Relevance of the Quest for the Historical Jesus."[20] In continuity with the twentieth century's emphasis on the Christ of faith, Meier affirms that the historical Jesus is not the object of faith. The "proper" and "direct" object of Christian faith is the still living person Jesus Christ, "who now lives, risen and glorified, forever in the Father's presence." The object of faith "cannot be an idea or scholarly reconstruction." Given this, what use does historical scholarship about Jesus have for people of faith? Meier's answer: none — a negation that he immediately qualifies in an important way. Namely, it has no significance "if one is asking solely about the direct object of Christian faith: Jesus Christ, crucified, risen, and presently reigning in his Church." This Jesus — the living lord — "is accessible to all believers, including all those who will never study history or theology for even a single day in their lives," as he was throughout the many centuries before the rise of historical scholarship.[21]

Yet though the historical Jesus is not significant for *faith,* Meier argues that he is significant for *theology* (defined as faith seeking understanding). Contemporary theology, Meier affirms, must appropriate the quest for the historical Jesus. He then lists four ways in which the study of the historical Jesus is significant. The first three include both a negation and affirmation, the fourth only a negation:[22]

1. It rules out reducing Christ to a cipher without content or to a mythic symbol by affirming that Christian faith is "adherence to a particular person who said and did particular things in a particular time and place in human history."

2. It rules out pious and docetic tendencies to ignore Jesus' humanity and to emphasize his divinity by reminding us that Jesus was a fully human first-century Jew living in Palestine.

3. It rules out comfortable Christian domestications of Jesus by disclosing his nonconformist aspects, especially on religious issues.[23]

4. It rules out seeing Jesus as "a this-worldly political revolutionary" and prevents Jesus from being claimed by any ideology.

Meier thus affirms a variation of the "both/and" position: both the Christ of faith and the historical Jesus are significant for theology, even if only the former is significant for faith. Regarding how much of a role is assigned to the historical Jesus, much depends upon whether the negations in his list are emphasized or whether negations and affirmations are given equal weight. If one emphasizes the negations, then the role of the historical Jesus for theology is largely formal: it precludes certain theological positions. It precludes seeing Christianity as an ahistorical myth, precludes docetism, and precludes using Jesus as legitimation for ideology. But if one equally emphasizes the affirmations, then positive content for theology can come from historical Jesus scholarship. The specific content of the message and activity of this "particular person who said and did particular things in a particular time and place" would become theologically important. It is not clear to me how Meier himself would weight the emphases.[24]

John Dominic Crossan

In his recent books, Crossan unambiguously affirms the importance of the historical Jesus. Christian faith, he emphasizes, is "(1) an act of faith (2) in the historical Jesus (3) as the manifestation of God."[25] As such, Christian faith does not even presuppose Easter, but was present even before Easter whenever somebody saw in Jesus "the manifestation of God."[26] Thus Christian faith, as Crossan defines it, preceded the kerygma. Negatively, Christian faith therefore cannot be defined primarily as faith in the kerygmatic Christ. Positively, because the historical

Jesus is seen as the manifestation of God, it follows that what he was like and what he was up to is a disclosure of God.

Crossan grants that it is possible to have Christian faith without any reference to the historical Jesus and then incisively adds, "It is called Gnostic Christianity."[27] But he argues that "Catholic Christianity" is defined by its preservation of the dialectic between "Jesus then" and "Christ now."[28] Within this dialectic, historical reconstruction of Jesus is given a central place. Moreover, it is not to be devalued because it is historical reconstruction; Crossan emphasizes that such reconstruction is our only access to the past. He points out that the text of the Greek New Testament is a historical reconstruction, the product of a committee voting on variant readings. As Crossan puts it, "If you cannot believe in something produced by reconstruction, you may have nothing left to believe in."[29]

Crossan does not spell out the implications for Christian faith and theology of his portrait of Jesus. His treatment of the question occurs as an epilogue to his work. But a few points are clear, it seems. To take the historical Jesus as "a manifestation of God" implies that Jesus' vision of a radically egalitarian society is "of God." So also, at a high level of abstraction, Jesus' practice of free healing and his "commissioning" of others as healers points to unmediated access to the sacred as central to his teaching and activity. Together, they challenge the social, political, and religious hierarchies of his world and every world. Given what Crossan says, taking his reconstruction of Jesus seriously — that is, finding it, in broad outlines, to be plausible — should lead to sharing Jesus' egalitarian vision of an unbrokered kingdom. Moreover, Crossan clearly sees the Constantinian revolution (which was really counter-revolutionary) as a betrayal of the vision of Jesus and hence a betrayal of authentic Christianity. Thus, though Crossan may represent a strong form of the position, he is one with the tendency of post–new quest scholarship to ascribe theological importance to scholarship about the historical Jesus.

My Own Position

Thus the last few decades have seen affirmations that historical Jesus scholarship matters for Christian faith and life. In the last part of this chapter, I wish to describe how I presently see the issues myself. Two central claims seem important.

First, I agree in part with the position of Kähler and Schweitzer, though I think precision in formulating the agreement is very important. Namely, I agree with them that historical knowledge of Jesus is not essential to being a Christian. This seems self-evidently true; if it were not, then we would have to say that the vast majority of Christians throughout the centuries have not had authentic faith, for there was no possibility of historical knowledge of Jesus until the birth of the quest a couple of centuries ago.

Moreover, I do not think the truth of Christianity is at stake in the historical study of Jesus (or the Bible, for that matter). Its truth has at least a relative immunity to historical investigation. By this, I mean that Christianity seems obviously to be a viable religion. That may seem an odd way to talk about it. What I mean is that Christianity seems clearly to "work": it is a means or vehicle by which people experience "the sacred." And I cannot imagine any historical discovery or claim causing it immediately to cease to "work." I say this not simply because religious beliefs tend to persist even in the face of contradictory data, but also because religious traditions can mediate the sacred independently of their historical or literal truth.[30]

Finally, in affirming that historical knowledge of Jesus is not essential for Christian faith, it is important to be precise about what one means by "faith." I am using "faith" in a relatively narrow sense to refer to one's relationship to God, and Christian faith specifically is a trusting relationship to God as mediated by the Christian tradition. Faith in this sense — as one's relationship to God — is not dependent upon historical knowledge of Jesus.

If, however, one uses "faith" in a broad sense so that it refers not only to one's relationship to God but becomes virtually a synonym for the whole of Christianity (as in the phrase "the Christian faith"), then it seems obvious to me that historical knowledge of Jesus is relevant.

This leads to my second main claim: images of Jesus *in fact* very much affect images of the Christian life. Much of the scholarly debate about the significance of historical knowledge about Jesus for Christians has focused on the question of whether it *ought* to be significant. Reasons for and against are then marshaled: to say "yes" risks making authentic Christianity inaccessible to millions of Christians of the past and present; to say "no" risks docetism, gnosticism, and other illnesses. I prefer to begin in another place, namely, with the descriptive statement that images of Jesus do in fact have a strong effect on the lives of Christians. Because of his central place in the Christian tradition, how we as Christians think of Jesus shapes our understanding of the Christian life itself.

Let me illustrate this initially by speaking of the "popular image" of Jesus and how it affects one's image of the Christian life. By the popular image, I mean the widespread image of Jesus that most of us received as children, whether we grew up within the church or only on its fringes. It is an image of Jesus as the divine savior. Its answers to the classic questions of Jesus' identity, mission, and message are clear: Jesus was the divinely begotten Son of God, whose mission was to die for the sins of the world, and whose message was about himself, the saving purpose of his death, and the importance of believing in him. This image of Jesus leads to an understanding of the Christian life as consisting primarily of *believing,* whatever else it may also lead to. It creates what we might call a *fideistic* image of the Christian life, one whose essential quality is believing that Jesus is one's savior. The point: the image of Jesus shapes the image of the Christian life.

A second image of Jesus is not as widespread as the first but still fairly common: not Jesus as savior, but Jesus as teacher. Generally a de-dogmatized image of Jesus, it is what most commonly results when persons are no longer certain about the doctrinal features of the popular image. What remains is Jesus as a teacher of ethics or morals, and it leads to a *moralistic* understanding of the Christian life, often expressed in quite banal terms. The Christian life consists of "being good" or of following "the golden rule."

To illustrate the point with one more comprehensive image of Jesus: the construal of Jesus as an eschatological prophet, which dominated much of this century's scholarship, had two different consequences. For some, it meant that there was no satisfying image of the historical Jesus, and it led to a strange silence about Jesus in parts of the mainstream church. Alternatively, in the hermeneutic that developed out of this image, it led to an existentialist understanding of the Christian life, which in most forms generated a highly individualized and internalized understanding of the message of Jesus.

The same relationship between how Christians think of Jesus and how Christians think of the Christian life is found if we move from global images of Jesus to more particular claims about him. To cite a few examples: if a Christian becomes persuaded that Jesus taught a subversive wisdom, it affects how that person sees the conventional wisdom of his or her own day; if a Christian becomes persuaded that Jesus countered the purity system of his day, it affects how she or he sees purity systems in our day; if a Christian become persuaded that Jesus indicted the ruling elites of his day, it affects how domination systems are seen in the present. Note that I am not saying that these perceptions *ought* to have an effect, but that they do. I have seen this happen again and again: a significant change in a Christian's perception of Jesus in fact affects that person's perception of the Christian life.[31]

My point is the correlation between images of Jesus and images of the Christian life. Given this correlation, the question is not so much *whether* images of Jesus *ought* to have theological significance. Rather, they *do* have theological significance at the very practical immediate level of Christian understanding, devotion, and piety. Our choice is to let that significance be largely unrecognized, unconscious, and unchallenged, or to be conscious and intentional about the relationship. In short, because historical scholarship about Jesus affects our image of Jesus and thus our image of the Christian life, it matters.[32]

Concluding Suggestions

First, I would like to suggest a terminological shift that could affect our thinking and conversation about this subject. Namely, to use terms familiar from the preceding chapter, I would like to replace the phrases "the Jesus of history" and "the Christ of faith" with "the pre-Easter Jesus" and "the post-Easter Jesus." By "the pre-Easter Jesus," I mean of course the historical Jesus; by "the post-Easter Jesus," I mean the Jesus of Christian experience and tradition in the years and centuries after the death of the pre-Easter Jesus.

For two reasons, I have never much cared for the phrase "the Christ of faith." It suggests a rather "iffy" or hypothetical reality that can only be believed in, as contrasted to the "real" Jesus of history. On the other hand, the phrase "the post-Easter Jesus," understood as the Jesus of Christian experience and tradition, makes it clear that "the post-Easter Jesus" is an element of experience and not simply of "faith."

Furthermore, the language "Christ of faith" tends to give "the Christ of faith" a privileged position. That is, because the language itself suggests that "the Christ of faith" is to be believed in rather than subjected to historical inquiry, it suggests that the Christ of faith is immune to the relative and changing character of historical scholarship. But we in fact know "the Christ of faith" of early Christian experience and tradition (the biblical Christ) only through the same processes of historical investigation and reconstruction as are involved in the study of the pre-Easter Jesus. To explain: if one says that the biblical Christ is primary, one still needs to ask, "Whose biblical Christ?" Matthew's, Mark's, Luke's, Paul's, John's? And which scholar's interpretation of Matthew's, Mark's, Luke's, Paul's, John's biblical Christ? Or if a composite, whose version of the composite? The notion that the historical Jesus involves historical reconstruction and the biblical Christ does not is simply wrong.[33]

Second, it seems clear to me that we should not see our question as a sharp either/or between the pre-Easter Jesus and the post-Easter Jesus. Rather, it is more appropriate (though not as simple) to see it as a both/and, as a dialogical and dialectical relationship of the two rather than as a binary choice between opposites. My claim is that theology should deal with both the pre-Easter and post-Easter Jesus. Moreover, it seems inappropriate to talk about *the norm* for christology, as if there were only one. Rather than speaking about *the norm,* it is more helpful to speak about a plurality of data that theology needs to take into account.

Third, historical scholarship about Jesus helps to keep "the dangerous and subversive memory of Jesus" alive.[34] The tendency of dogma and doctrine (and to a lesser extent, of theology itself) is to categorize and domesticate. Historical scholarship about the pre-Easter Jesus — like the historical study of doctrine itself — guards against the tendency of doctrinal formulations to become ideology. Throughout the centuries, it has been easy for Christian doctrine and theology to be co-opted by what Walter Wink calls "the domination system." Historical scholarship about Jesus can help to keep alive the liberating memory of Jesus as one who provocatively and courageously protested against systems of domestication and domination, who pointed beyond himself to the sacred mystery in which we live and move and have our being, and who brought into existence an alternative community with an alternative and egalitarian vision of human life in history.

Finally, it seems to me that the Christian doctrine of incarnation implies that the historical Jesus is important. The claim goes back to the New Testament itself: Jesus was God's Word — God's disclosure — become flesh. I do not presume to know what this might mean comprehensively, and it is important to guard against interpretations that verge on docetism ("Jesus was *really* God") or that restrict God's disclosure exclusively to Jesus, as if he were God's only revelation. But minimally, it seems to mean this: from the point of view of his earliest followers and for Christians in the centuries since, Jesus was an epiphany or manifestation of God. The product of the historical study of Jesus — a historically reconstructed image of Jesus — is, of course, not itself that epiphany. But to the extent that it provides a glimpse of Jesus, it provides a glimpse of the epiphany of God that he was.

Notes

1. From *The Book of Common Prayer* (New York: Oxford University Press, 1979), 358, Rite II. The wording is identical in the *Lutheran Book of Worship* (Minneapolis: Augsburg, 1978), 84.

2. And even the claim that he was buried in a tomb has been questioned. Crossan argues that it was customary for the Romans to prohibit normal burial of victims of crucifixion as a final shaming and humiliation, and that Jesus' body may have been cast into a common grave or even devoured by dogs; Crossan, *Jesus: A Revolutionary Biography* (San Francisco: Harper, 1994), 123–58. To say, as I have suggested, that Jesus' death may be the only historical referent in the creed is not to deny the resurrection. It does, however, imply that the resurrection is not a historical event in the ordinary sense of the word; I do not think you could have "caught" the risen Christ on a videocam,

though I assume that the crucifixion was the kind of event that could have been photographed.

3. Two examples, whose source I do not remember but which are recalled from usually reliable memory: About the part of the temptation narrative in which Satan takes Jesus to a high mountain from which he shows him all the kingdoms of the earth, Origen (early third century) commented: there is no such mountain; obviously, something else must be meant. About the passage in Genesis 3 in which we are told that Adam and Eve heard the sound of God walking in the garden of Eden in the cool of the day, Luther commented: God never walked in any garden; they must have heard something else, perhaps the sound of the wind; nature, which had previously seemed benevolent, had now become a source of fear.

4. See the comment of Craig A. Evans, "Authenticity Criteria in Life of Jesus Research," *Christian Scholar's Review* 19 (1989): 6: "Prior to the critical period of biblical studies, canonicity was the only test for determining the authenticity of the sayings of Jesus. What was in the New Testament was authentic; what was not in the New Testament was suspect."

5. For this change and its effect on theology and Scripture, see especially Van Harvey, *The Historian and the Believer* (New York: Macmillan, 1966).

6. For these episodes and others see W. Neil, "The Criticism and Theological Use of the Bible, 1700–1950," in S. L. Greenslade, ed., *The Cambridge History of the Bible* (Cambridge: University Press, 1963), 3:238–93. For other useful surveys of the history of biblical interpretation, see "Interpretation, History of" in *Anchor Bible Dictionary,* 3:424–33 (J. W. Rogerson), 433–43 (Werner G. Jeanrond). See also R. M. Grant and David Tracy, *A Short History of the Interpretation of the Bible,* 2d ed. (Philadelphia: Fortress, 1984).

7. Ever since Albert Schweitzer's famous *The Quest for the Historical Jesus* (1906), it has been a scholarly convention to date the beginning of the quest to Reimarus's work. He did, however, have predecessors, as N. Thomas Wright ("Jesus, Quest for the Historical" in *Anchor Bible Dictionary* 3:796–802) and Colin Brown (*Jesus in European Protestant Thought* [Grand Rapids: Baker, 1985], 29–55) point out.

8. For the history of this period of Jesus scholarship, see the works by Schweitzer and Brown in the previous note.

9. The English translation by Carl E. Braaten (Philadelphia: Fortress, 1964) is from the 1896 German edition.

10. It should be noted that Schweitzer did not argue (as Kähler and others have done) that we cannot know much about the historical Jesus. That was not the point of Schweitzer's history of the quest; rather, Schweitzer used it as a springboard for creating his own sketch of the historical Jesus, which he himself (and others) found quite persuasive. His point is that the historical Jesus is irrelevant to our time because of his "strangeness," not because he is unknowable.

11. Bultmann as a historian thought we could say quite a bit about the *what* of Jesus' historical life (especially his message); see his *Jesus and the Word* (published in German in 1926, and in English in 1934: New York: Scribner's). Nevertheless, as a theologian he affirmed its irrelevance.

12. See chapter 1 above, pp. 6–7.

13. The separation is not intrinsically an affirmation of theological irrelevance. It is possible to do historical Jesus scholarship without an *explicitly* theological agenda and then to raise the question of theological significance. This is what I have sought to do myself, and Crossan affirms this procedure for his own work. In an essay in Jeffrey Carlson and Robert A. Ludwig, eds., *Jesus and Faith: A Conversation on the Work of John Dominic Crossan* (Maryknoll, N.Y.: Orbis, 1993), 152, Crossan says that though he is "absolutely aware of the theological implications of historical Jesus research," he nevertheless does not think they drive his own process; consistent with this, he treats theological implications at the end of his historical reconstruction. (I thank Prof. Crossan for providing me with page proofs of this book prior to its publication). To deny a theological agenda is not to claim a positivistic objectivity for either myself or Crossan; we are both aware of the subjectivity of the historian, the relativity and particularity of all vantage points, and the fact that unconscious factors (including theological ones) may shape our perception. But it is to say that the generative questions addressed to the texts have not been posed by the doctrinal claims of Christian theology.

14. Ernst Käsemann, "The Problem of the Historical Jesus," English translation in *Essays on New Testament Themes* (London: SCM, 1964), 15–47; James Robinson, *A New Quest of the Historical Jesus* (London: SCM, 1959; reprint, Philadelphia: Fortress, 1983).

15. Its narrowness flowed out of its concentration on the message of Jesus and its use of an existential hermeneutic. It became concerned to show the continuity between the message of Jesus and the kerygma of the early church, and found it in the understanding of existence that they shared: both proclaimed the end of an old world (the world of inauthentic existence) and the coming of a new world (the world of authentic existence lived in relation to God). This is an important insight, but if taken as "the whole" (rather than as a part) of what Jesus was about, it radically internalizes and individualizes his meaning.

16. See the concluding chapter of Norman Perrin, *Rediscovering the Teaching of Jesus* (New York: Harper & Row, 1967), 207–48, still one of the best chapter-length treatments of the subject. Other works from the period that continue to be important include Van A. Harvey, *The Historian and the Believer,* and Leander Keck, *A Future for the Historical Jesus* (Nashville: Abingdon, 1971; reprint, Philadelphia: Fortress, 1981).

17. To quote Perrin, *Rediscovering,* 243–44: "[T]he Jesus of one's faith-image is a mixture of historical reminiscence, at a somewhat distant remove, and myth, legend and idealism." The validity of a faith-image is not directly dependent upon historical knowledge of Jesus, but upon "the fact that it grows out of religious experience and is capable of mediating religious experience."

18. Ibid., 244. The "main source," Perrin continues, "will always be the proclamation of the Church, a proclamation rising out of a Christian experience of the risen Lord."

19. In Perrin's own language: "To this limited extent our historical knowledge of Jesus validates the Christian kerygma; it does not validate it as *kerygma,* but it validates it as Christian." Though Perrin speaks of this as "limited," it

is a broad claim. Why then call it "limited"? I construe his use of it to mean: although the central claims of the kerygma are beyond validation (for example, Jesus lives and is lord), claims about what Christianity means for life are testable by appeal to the historical study of Jesus. Quoted passages all from Perrin, *Rediscovering,* 244.

20. In *A Marginal Jew: Rethinking the Historical Jesus* (New York: Doubleday, 1991), 196–201. The book is volume 1 of what will be a three-volume work on Jesus (in the book itself, Meier speaks of two volumes, but has since decided that a third volume will be needed).

21. Quotations all from ibid., 198.

22. The list is found in ibid., 199.

23. I trust that the last phrase is fair to Meier's position. The examples he cites all have to do with "religious" issues: Jesus' "association with the religious and social 'lowlife,' " his critique of "external religious practices" that "strangle the inner spirit of religion," and "opposition to certain religious authorities" (ibid.).

24. My impression is that Meier emphasizes the negations more than the affirmations, though he could develop his position either way. The ambiguity is seen in the sentence that follows his statement that the historical Jesus can provide content for Christian faith: "While the quest cannot supply *the essential content* of faith, it can help theology give greater concrete *depth and color to that content*" (ibid.; italics added). Given this statement, can the quest provide *new content?* Or does it only add "depth and color" (a deepening and perhaps "toning") to content known on other grounds?

25. The statement is found in Crossan, *Jesus: A Revolutionary Biography,* 200, and in his essay in Carlson and Ludwig, *Jesus and Faith,* 3–4.

26. This is an important point for Crossan. Not only does it give primacy to the historical Jesus (rather than to the kerygma of cross-resurrection), but it fits his perception of early Jesus movements (such as the Q community and Thomas community) for whom Jesus' death and resurrection were not central (if significant at all).

27. Crossan, *Jesus and Faith,* 20.

28. Crossan, ibid., 20–21, 159. See also *The Historical Jesus: The Life of a Mediterranean Jewish Peasant* (Harper: San Francisco, 1991), 423.

29. Crossan, *The Historical Jesus,* 424–26; quoted words from p. 426.

30. Perhaps, over a long period of time, an absolutely outrageous discovery (what could it be?) would weaken Christianity enough so that it would cease to "work" for large numbers of people and cause it effectively to disappear. But my point is that the core validity of Christianity has to do with its ability to mediate the sacred, not with the historical accuracy of any particular claim.

31. I am not claiming that the change in perception leads immediately to a change in how one lives one's life. For most people, the process is gradual and slow. But a change in one's perception of Jesus is most often accompanied by a change in one's vision of the Christian life and what it calls one to.

32. In addition to these remarks, see my comments in the previous chapter (pp. 172–174) about how historical Jesus scholarship can help us to read the gospels more discerningly.

33. A point made forcefully by Leander Keck some twenty years ago in *A Future for the Historical Jesus*, 25: "Historians of Jesus carry no heavier handicap than anyone else. Just as the theologian's God-talk has no fixed Archimedean point but reflects his own historicity without diminishing his intent to talk about God as accurately as possible, so the historian intends his reconstruction to be an accurate comprehension of Jesus, and both the theologian and the historian are open to self-correction by means of the critical method itself. We should no longer be intimidated by the theologian's taunt, 'But whose historical Jesus shall I interpret?' as if that made refusing to deal with any historically recovered Jesus legitimate! This sort of objection has been around long enough; it is time to send it packing."

34. A phrase cited by David Tracy, *The Analogical Imagination* (New York: Crossroad, 1981), 239 and 245 n. 24; I believe that he derived it from Johannes Metz and Hans Küng. Tracy, I should note, does not affirm the position with which I end, which I see as being quite close to Crossan. Tracy gives theological primacy to the apostolic witness to Jesus, and only a subordinate role to the historical study of Jesus.

Index of Ancient Literature

General Index